THE BRITISH ARMY IN ITALY
1917–18

THE BRITISH ARMY IN ITALY
1917–18

by
John and Eileen Wilks

LEO COOPER

First published in Great Britain in 1998 by
LEO COOPER
an imprint of
Pen & Sword Books Ltd
47 Church Street
Barnsley
South Yorkshire
S70 2AS

ISBN 0 85052 608.6

A catalogue record for this book is
available from the British Library

Typeset in 10/11 Amasis by Phoenix Typesetting, Ilkley, West Yorkshire

Printed in England by Redwood Books, Trowbridge, Wiltshire

Contents

Maps

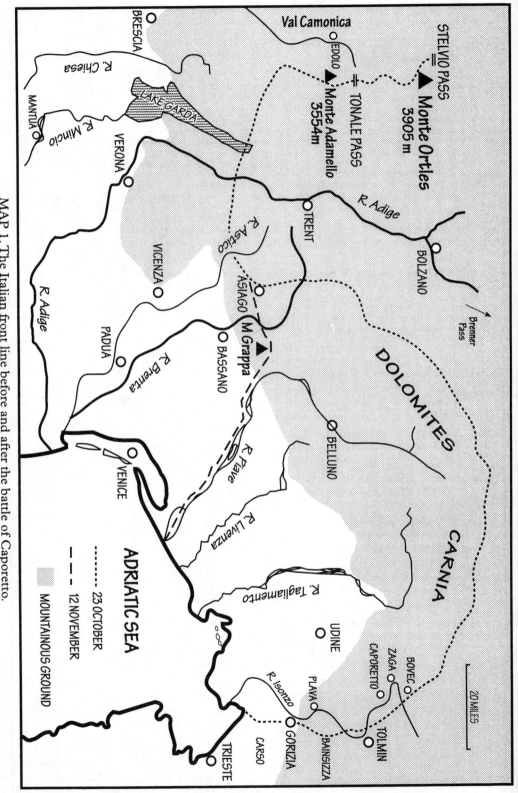

MAP 1. The Italian front line before and after the battle of Caporetto.

Val Camonica

BRESCIA

EDOLO

STELVIO PASS

Monte Ortles
3905 m

TONALE PASS

Monte Adamello
3554m

R. Chiesa

LAKE GARDA

MANTUA

R. Mincio

R. Adige

VERONA

TRENT

R. Astico

BOLZANO

Brenner Pass

DOLOMITES

VICENZA

ASIAGO

M Grappa

PADUA

BASSANO

R. Brenta

R. Piave

BELLUNO

CARNIA

R. Adige

R. Livenza

VENICE

R. Tagliamento

ADRIATIC SEA

UDINE

BOVEC

ZAGA

CAPORETTO

R. Isonzo

PLAVA

BAINSIZZA

TOLMIN

GORIZIA

CARSO

TRIESTE

23 OCTOBER

12 NOVEMBER

MOUNTAINOUS GROUND

20 MILES

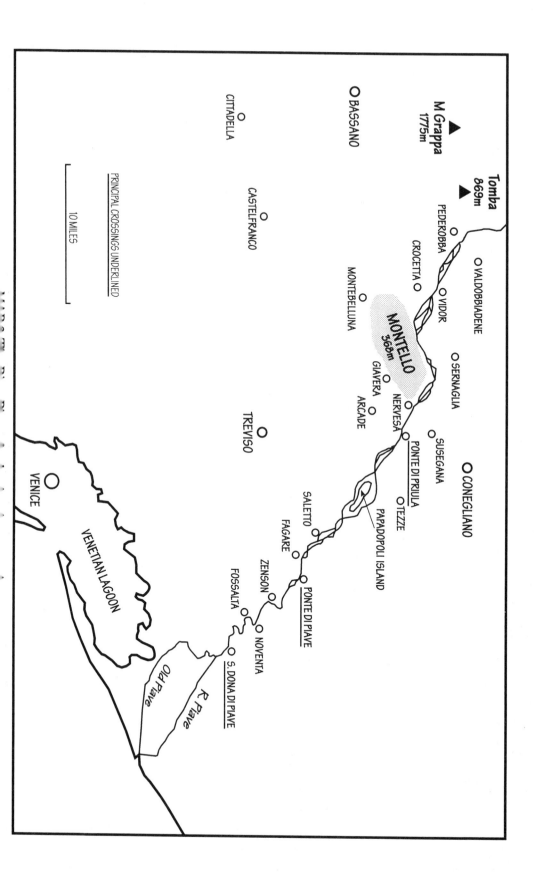

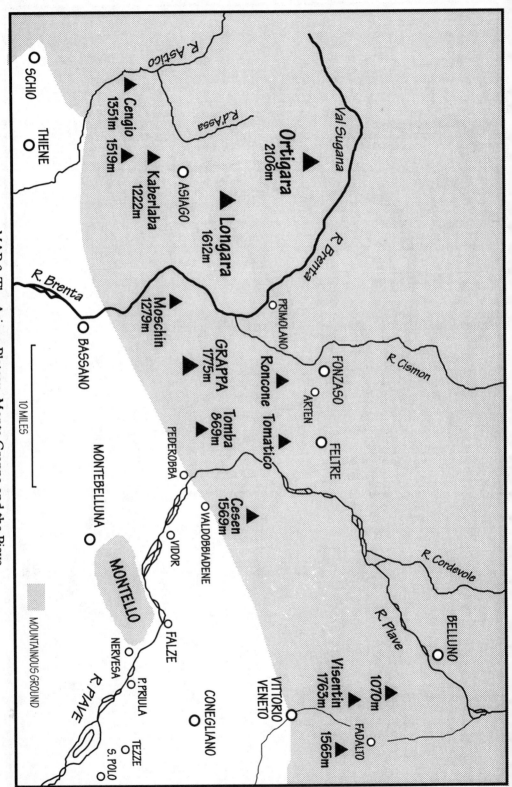

MAP 3. The Asiago Plateau, Monte Grappa and the Piave.

SCHIO

THIENE

R. Astico

R. d'Assa

Cengio
1351m 1519m

Ortigara
2106m

Val Sugana

Kaberlaba
1222m

ASIAGO

Longara
1612m

R. Brenta

R. Brenta

BASSANO

Moschin
1279m

GRAPPA
1775m

PRIMOLANO

Roncone Tomatico

R. Cismon

FONZASO

ARTEN

Tomba
869m

FELTRE

10 MILES

PEDEROBBA

MONTELLO

Cesen
1569m

MONTEBELLUNA

VALDOBBIADENE

VIDOR

R. Cordevole

FALZE

R. Piave

BELLUNO

MOUNTAINOUS GROUND

NERVESA

P. PRIULA

CONEGLIANO

VITTORIO
VENETO

Visentin
1763m

1070m

FADALTO
1565m

TEZZE

S. POLO

R. PIAVE

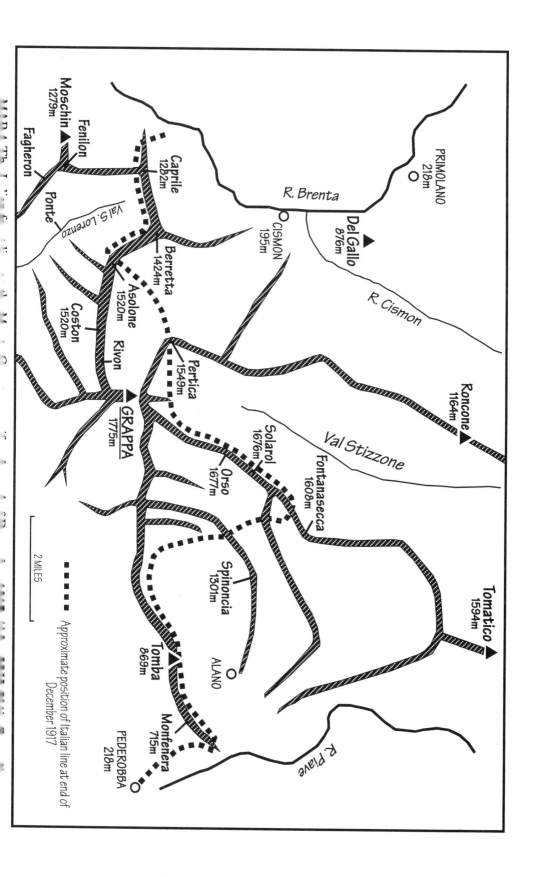

MAP 1. The Massif of Monte Grappa

2 MILES

▪▪▪▪▪ Approximate position of Italian line at end of December 1917

Moschin 1279m

Fenilon

Fagheron

Ponte

Val S. Lorenzo

Caprile 1282m

Coston 1520m

Asolone 1520m

Berretta 1424m

Rivon

GRAPPA 1775m

Pertica 1549m

Solarol 1676m

Orso 1677m

Fontanasecca 1608m

Val Stizzone

Spinoncia 1301m

ALANO

Tomba 869m

Monfenera 715m

PEDEROBBA 218m

R. Piave

Tomatico 1594m

Roncone 1164m

R. Cismon

R. Brenta

CISMON 195m

Del Gallo 876m

PRIMOLANO 218m

Acknowledgements

We are much indebted to the late Professor Alessandro Vaciago, formerly Cultural and Scientific Adviser to the President of Italy, for his encouragement to write this book, and for facilitating our researches in Italy. We also thank Professor John Woodhouse, Fiat Serena Professor of Italian Studies in the University of Oxford, and Sir Frank Cooper, formerly Permanent Secretary at the Ministry of Defence, for their help and encouragement.

We gratefully acknowledge the assistance received from Colonel Ricardo Treppiccione of the Ufficio Storico dell'Esercito in Rome; the help and advice of Aiutante Luigi Diana during visits to the Biblioteca Militare Centrale also in Rome; and the kind hospitality of Senatsrat Mag. Pharm. Rudolf Stutzenstein who introduced us to the National Photographic Collections in Vienna.

We are grateful for the facilities provided by the British Library, the Library of the Imperial War Museum, the House of Lords Library, the Library of the Liddell Hart Centre for Military Archives, and in Oxford the Bodleian Library and the Libraries of Magdalen College, Oriel College and Pembroke College.

We have also much appreciated discussions with Professor Denis Mack Smith concerning the general political background in Italy.

We are indebted to Mr. Paul Wilkinson who has produced the maps from our sketches. For permission to include the photographs from National Collections we thank: the British Library Photographic Collection for Nos. 2, 20; the Kreigsarchiv in Vienna for No.1; the Imperial War Museum Photographic Collection for Nos. 3, 7, 8, 9, 10, 11, 12, 13, 14, 15, 16, 17, 18, 19.

Introduction

During 1917 the Allied Armies fighting Germany and the Austro-Hungarian Empire had endured difficult times. The Nivelle offensive in April had failed, leaving a legacy of mutinies which much reduced the effectiveness of the French armies for the rest of the year. After great exertions and great losses, the Russian war effort had collapsed with the Revolution. The British Army had been battling against the German trench lines on the Western Front, making little progress, and in the latter part of the year was bogged down around Passchendaele in the mud of Flanders.

Italy had been fighting the Austro-Hungarian Empire, or Austria for short, principally by striking across the only approximately flat part of their common frontier, the Carso, a limestone plateau beyond the Isonzo River at the eastern end of the frontier (Map 1). The town of Gorizia had been captured in 1916, but subsequent progress towards the target of Trieste had been slow, with costly attacks on entrenched positions. However, in the 11th Battle of the Isonzo in August and September 1917 the Italians had pushed the Austrians back for a few, but significant, kilometres on the high ground of the Bainsizza Plateau. Then, at the end of October, a combined German and Austrian force attacked Italian positions in the deep and narrow valleys around the upper Isonzo River and inflicted on the Italian Army one of the most striking and unexpected defeats of the war, known as the Battle of Caporetto.

The attack broke through the Italian line, thus forcing the whole of the 2nd, 3rd and 4th Italian Armies to give up all the areas captured during the war and to retreat first to the line of the Tagliamento River and then to the Piave River, a retreat of up to 70 miles, bringing the Austrians to within only 20 miles of Venice. This was a great disaster, so much so that the name of a small village now in Slovenia has passed into the Italian language. When Prime Minister Amado spoke to the nation after the sudden devaluation of the lira in September 1992 he said on television, "This is a very serious matter," and continued, "but not a Caporetto". Today in Britain, a thousand miles away, if the part played by Italy in the First World War is known at all, it is most probably as a recollection of the débâcle of Caporetto.

1

The battle was an upset involving a loss of territory comparable to that lost by the Allies in France and Belgium in 1914, and a loss of men and material on an enormous scale. The whole of the Italian 2nd Army disappeared as a fighting unit. In all, 10,000 Italians died, 30,000 were wounded, 300,000 taken prisoner and another 350,000 troops broken down into dispersed and disordered units. Yet only eight months later a full scale Austrian offensive to knock Italy out of the war was stopped dead in its tracks in a matter of days. Then, after five more months, the Austrian Army finally collapsed during the Allied offensive known as the Battle of Vittorio Veneto.

The part played by the British Army in Italy during the Second World War is well known, but not the role of the French and British troops sent to Italy during the last year of the First World War. Many people are unaware that French and British divisions fought in Italy, and that Italian divisions fought in France. Moreover, comments on Caporetto in works of general reference are sometimes as inaccurate as any to be found regarding the First World War. All this is a matter for regret because the Italian, French and British divisions in Italy made significant contributions to the winning of the First World War I, and the French and British expeditions to Italy were among the most successful Allied expeditions of the War.

The publication of the later volumes of the Italian Official History (IOH) was much delayed by the Second World War. The volume for the last three months of 1917 and the accompanying volume of documents, over 1200 pages in all, appeared in 1967 and the volumes for 1918 only in 1980 and 1988. In consequence the Italian Official History has a rather remarkable background. Most of the official accounts of the First World War were prepared in the inter-war years when official historians were faced with the task of recording events which had caused much pain and grief without adding to that grief by denigrating, or even accurately describing, the actions of famous wartime leaders. However, by the time the final volumes of the Italian history were produced all the principal actors had left the stage and the authors were able to set out a full and balanced account of a very complex subject.

There has been no British account of either Caporetto or of the Allied expeditions subsequent to the publication of the Italian Official History in 1967. Indeed, as far as the part played by the British forces are concerned, the only complete account is that given in the masterly volume of the *Official British History of the War, Military Operations, Italy, 1915–1918*, by Edmonds and Davies, published in 1949. There are, however, several first hand personal accounts of aspects of the campaign, and also various accounts in documents in the Public Record Office, some of which have been opened only

2

comparatively recently. Unfortunately many of these accounts are not too readily available. Hence it appears worthwhile to make use of all the material now available to produce a new account for British readers.

Italy at War 1915–1917

1. The Last Battles of the Risorgimento

The war between Italy and Austria was part of the First World War but was fought for reasons which were specific to Italy and Austria. Geographically Italy has always been a well defined area – the peninsula south of the Alps – but even in the days of the Roman Empire the whole area was never consolidated into a single administrative unit. The decline of Rome was followed by a long succession of invaders whose aims and philosophy have seldom been better expressed than in the young Napoleon's address to the French Army of Italy in 1796. "Soldiers, you are famished and nearly naked. The government owes you much, but can do nothing for you. Your patience, your courage, do you honour, but give you no glory, no advantage. I will lead you into the most fertile plains in the world. There you will find great towns, rich provinces. There you will find honour, glory and riches."[1]

Even in the great days of the rich and powerful city states of the Renaissance, foreign influence was never far away. Spain, France and Austria jostled each other for power and possessions in Italy. However, to understand the background to the war of 1915 it is sufficient to go back no further than the Peace of Utrecht signed in 1713 at the end of the War of the Spanish Succession, the long struggle by England, Holland, Germany and Austria against France and Spain under Louis XIV. So far as Italy was concerned, the Peace replaced a long period of Spanish domination by a long period of Austrian domination.

Under the Peace of Utrecht Austria received Milan, Mantua and Naples, and shortly afterwards Sicily. In 1734 Don Carlos, the son of Philip V of Spain, tried to recover these losses, and by 1738 had retaken Naples and Sicily and established himself as the King of the Two Sicilies until he returned to Spain on the death of Philip V. His young son Ferdinand then became King in Sicily and in 1768 married a daughter of Maria Theresa of Austria, thus reintroducing Austrian influence. Meanwhile Tuscany had also come under Austrian influence after the death of the last Medici Grand Duke in 1737 when the duchy passed to the husband of the young Maria Theresa. Hence the only parts of Italy free of Austria in the latter part of the 18th century were the weak Papal States, the independent but much weakened republic of Venice, and Piedmont under the Counts of Savoy, who had managed to maintain an independent role among more powerful neighbours.

All the above arrangements came to an abrupt end when the French revolutionary army irrupted into Italy. By 1798 the whole of Italy and Switzerland had been reorganized as five republics, except that Savoy had been annexed to France, and Venice, with Venetia and the Dalmatian Coast, transferred to Austria. Ten years later the French Republic had become the Empire of Napoleon, and Piedmont, Tuscany, Rome and the Papal States had been absorbed directly into France. The rest of Italy, apart from Venice and its provinces, was divided into three kingdoms: Italy, Naples and Sardinia. Napoleon himself became King of Italy, which included Lombardy and the Romagna, and gave the crown of Naples first to his brother and then to his brother-in-law. Sicily remained free of French rule under Ferdinand, who had fled there from Naples, protected by Nelson and the British Navy standing off the Straits of Messina.

All was changed again by the fall of Napoleon. The aim of the Congress of Vienna was, roughly speaking, to restore territories to their original owners, or, rather more accurately, to their rulers in 1789. However, Austria was one of the victorious powers and her affairs were guided by one of Europe's most wily statesmen, Prince Metternich. Therefore, besides removing the French invader from Italy, the Congress also endorsed the transfer of Venice and her provinces, Venetia and Venezia Julia, to Austria, even though Venice had formerly been an independent republic.

The victorious powers at the Congress of Vienna were principally concerned with restoring the *status quo* and ensuring future stability. To this end they rearranged frontiers and transferred provinces from one state to another. At no stage in the lengthy discussions did it occur to the debating governments to take serious notice of the views of the peoples inhabiting these lands. Thus the obviously Italian peoples of Lombardy and Venice were brusquely transferred to Austria.

After 1815 the ruling classes sought to return to the world which had passed away in 1789. The old forms of government were restored, apparently with some success, but great changes had come about in the political thinking of Europe. The philosophy and ideals of the early Revolution were to result in a growing demand by the peoples of Europe for a much greater say in the ordering of their affairs, and for an end of rule by foreign powers. Peoples with similar backgrounds and language began to associate to obtain more representative government, and, if need be, to expel foreign governments. These themes had a widespread attraction. The eventual excesses of nationalism were yet to come, and the new movements were wellnigh irresistible.

From 1815 onwards Italy was fertile ground for the new developments. Most of the country was under foreign rule and the years of French occupation had left their mark. The Italians had been shown vistas of better administration with wider social and economic contacts than were to be found in the narrow and restricted courts which came with the restoration of 1815. From then on there was to be continuous political agitation, by propaganda and secret societies, until Italy obtained unity and independence in 1870. The history of this movement, the Risorgimento, is largely the story of a struggle against Austria.

The main concern of Austria throughout the 19th century was to prevent the disintegration of the Hapsburg Empire, a widespread and heterogeneous collection of peoples and races gathered together under Austrian rule. In Italy, as elsewhere, the Austrians relied on a repressive administration and a strong army. Their grip on Italy was strengthened by building up their garrisons particularly in the well sited fortresses of Peschiera and Mantua on the Mincio River, and Verona and Legnano on the Adige River, forming the famous so-called Quadrilateral.

The most independent and powerful Italian state was the Kingdom of Sardinia, ruled by the Dukes of Savoy and based principally in Piedmont, and it was this state which eventually formed the nucleus of a united Italy. However, the Italian states were never able to create sufficient military force to act decisively against Austria, and unification was only possible because of military help provided by France and Germany. In fact the pace of unification was set by the extent to which the other interests of France and Germany permitted their involvement.

Napoleon III had been banished from France in his youth, and while living in Italy had taken an enthusiastic part in the attempted revolution of 1831. As Emperor he seems to have had a romantic vision of a free Italy, and was therefore willing to assist Savoy against Austria. In 1859 the victories of French and Piedmont troops at Magenta and Solferino gained Lombardy from Austria, and caused the flight of the rulers of Florence, Parma, Modena and the Romagna. The following year Garibaldi with his famous 'Thousand Volunteers' gained first Sicily and then Naples.

The liberated states gathered together under Savoy and the first Italian parliament was held in Turin in 1861. However, Venice and her provinces still remained under Austria, and Rome and the Papal States under the Pope. In 1866 Prussia joined Italy in a war against Austria. Despite Italian fiascos at Custoza and Lissa, the Prussian victory at Sadowa in Bohemia resulted in the liberation of Venice. The following year Garibaldi led his march on Rome but was turned back by French troops, for Napoleon was now fearful of offending the clerical party in France. However, three years later France was forced by the outbreak of the Franco-Prussian war to withdraw those troops back to France.

Then, on 20 September 1870, Italian troops under General Raffaele Cadorna occupied Rome, and in the following year Rome became the capital of a united Italy.

After 1870 almost all Italians were united in the State of Italy but there were still areas where a largely Italian population was governed by Austria, principally in the Trentino and in the town of Trieste at the head of the Adriatic. The Trentino coincided with the present province of Trent, situated on either side of the Adige River and the road to the Brenner Pass, and forming part of a large salient projecting into Italy (Map 1). Its population was overwhelmingly Italian in thought and outlook.

As the Brenner is one of the easiest routes through the main chain of the Alps, the salient had originally been settled from both the north and the south, with a quite well defined language frontier a few miles south of Bolzano. Hence, although the Trentino was Italian speaking, the majority of the people of Bolzano province spoke German and regarded themselves as part of the Austrian homeland. In the 14th century all the salient was held by the Counts of Tyrol with their main residence at Tyrol about twenty miles from Bolzano. About 1420 the Counts built a new castle at Innsbruck and this became their main residence. Later, during the reign of the Hapsburg Emperor Maximilian (1493–1519) the whole of the Tyrol was firmly incorporated into the Austrian Empire, so that even after 1870 the entirely Italian province of the Trentino was still part of Austria.

There were also considerable numbers of Italians in the towns which had been colonized by the energy of the Venetian republic, such as Trieste and Fiume on the Adriatic, and Gorizia on the lower Isonzo. The native peoples generally spoke Slovene as most of their descendants still do in the countryside, but the main commercial activity, trade with the East, was conducted by Italians in Italian. Thus the towns became increasingly Italian in their views and culture, so that even after the decline of Venice they remained as Italian enclaves in a hinterland of Slav peoples all under Austrian administration.

After 1870 the Nationalists viewed these Italian enclaves in the Austrian Empire as *Italia Irredenta*, the unfinished business of the Risorgimento. The argument for the Trentino was overwhelming, but for the other areas somewhat debatable. The rallying cry for the Nationalists was the Trentino and Trieste, the latter having the strongest claim after the Trentino. The presence of *Italia Irredenta* after 1870 was a permanent reminder to the new state that the aim of the Risorgimento was not yet completely fulfilled. The war when it came in 1915 was about frontiers and can certainly be viewed as the last stage of the Risorgimento. Yet the reasons for Italy's entry into the war were varied and more complex.

The new Italy was formed by an association of states differing greatly in form and outlook, stretching from the liberal conservative Piedmont to the radical disorganized south. It was to be a long time before these disparate parts would weld together and produce a coherent government with a clear programme of policies. However, in the field of foreign affairs the first objective was quite clear, to ensure the security of the state against interference by more powerful neighbours.

Austria still regretted the loss of Lombardy and Venetia and would have been all too willing to take control again should opportunity present. Moreover, the Trentino salient gave the Austrians an ideal starting point for an attack on the Italian plain, as well as strong defensive positions against any Italian attack. Relations between the two countries would have been greatly improved by the transfer of the Trentino to Italy, thus removing a genuine cause of political instability and providing a military frontier more equal to both sides. However, Austria was determined to resist any further reductions in her empire, and attitudes were allowed to harden.

France had played a large part in the unification of Italy and might have appeared the obvious ally to support the new state. Yet French troops had protected Rome against Garibaldi's march in 1867 and were only recalled to meet the Prussian attack on France in 1870. Moreover, by 1880 a serious dispute had developed between France and Italy, as the French in Algeria wished to expand their interests into Tunisia where the Italians were already the most numerous group of European colonists. Hence in 1882 Bismarck, seeking to protect Germany against France, persuaded Italy to join with Germany and Austria in the Triple Alliance which guaranteed Italy support against attack from either France or Austria, in return for her support if Germany or Austria were to be attacked.

With the signing of the Triple Alliance the Italian government formally renounced any claims to *Italia Irredenta*. In fact the Trentino did enjoy a certain degree of autonomy. Italian was the official language of the schools, the courts, and the administration, though not of the police or the army. Yet there remained sufficient discrimination to stimulate the activity of the mainly middle-class intellectuals. The provision of German speaking schools in the Trentino for the children of Austrian officials was much resented. Attempts to establish Italian speaking universities at Trent and Trieste were blocked by Vienna. In 1891 Austria deprived Trieste of the long established trading privileges of an imperial free port, and the authorities encouraged Austrian and Slav immigration to offset the Italian population.

During the years before the war relations between Italy and Austria slowly deteriorated. Beyond the particular details of the Irredentist claims lay the suspicion that the ageing Empire still looked backward resentfully to its lost powers. The Commander in Chief of the Austrian Army was the old Emperor Franz Joseph, but the effective commander was the Chief of Staff. For most of the time since 1906 the post had been held by General Conrad von Hotzendorf who believed that war with Italy was inevitable and argued that Austria should strike first in a 'preventive' war against her partner in the Triple Alliance.[2] Thus, in an atmosphere of suspicion, both sides set about building up their forces and defensive positions, particularly in the Trentino where their impressive array of roads and fortresses remain to this day.

Under the terms of the Triple Alliance Italy agreed to support Austria and Germany if they were attacked. However, if either Austria or Germany themselves took the initiative Italy was committed only to a benevolent neutrality, and this was the position when Austria initiated the fighting in the First World War by attacking Serbia. There was also a clause in the treaty which laid down that any extension of Austrian territory in the Balkans should be accompanied by equivalent territorial compensation for Italy. Austria neither informed nor consulted Italy prior to her declaration of war, and refused to discuss the question of compensation, which Italy held to refer to the Trentino. Thus the bonds tying Italy to the Triple Alliance, both formal and moral, were now minimal, and Italy declared her neutrality on 2 August 1914.

It seems probable that the silent majority in Italy in 1914 had had enough of war after the events of the colonial campaign in Libya from 1911 onwards and wanted peace and quiet, although sympathetic to France and Britain. There were, moreover, many divisions and currents in Italian opinion. Many industrialists had close links with Germany. The Catholic Church still resented the loss of its temporal powers and estates in 1870 and looked for support towards the Catholic Emperor of Austria. Some socialists were against the war because they feared it might strengthen the authority of the Imperial Russian Government. More importantly the veteran politician Giolitti, who had immense personal influence, also opposed intervention. In favour of intervention, besides the Irredentists and friends of France, there were also Nationalists and enthusiasts for war like the poet Gabriele D'Annunzio. However, whatever their views, all agreed that Italy could not enter the war immediately as the army was not yet ready.

During the later months of 1914 Italy had the opportunity to reflect on the German occupation of Belgium and a large part of France, on the German defeat of the Russians at Tannenburg, and the Austrian invasion of Serbia. It was difficult to avoid asking what would be the position of Italy after a German-Austrian victory, and urgent steps were taken to bring the army up to strength. The government tried to negotiate with her partners in the Triple Alliance to obtain the transfer of the Trentino but the attempt failed after drawn out discussions.

Finally, on 26 April 1915 Italy signed the secret Treaty of London which committed her to join Britain, France and Russia in the war against the Central Powers, and promised in return the transfer to Italy of the whole of the Trentino salient as far north as the Brenner, of Trieste and the adjacent region of Istria, and of parts of the Dalmatian coast, as well as rights in Albania and the Dodecanese.

There remained only one difficulty to be overcome. The negotiations on the Italian side had been conducted in secret by Prime Minister Salandra and Foreign Minister Sonnino, consulting only with the King, Victor Emmanuel III. It was now necessary to obtain parliamentary approval for a declaration of war, but it seemed that some 300 out of the 500 deputies were against intervention. On 4 May 1915 Italy withdrew publicly from the Triple Alliance, and the government set to work to obtain the necessary consent of parliament for war.[3]

The poet-agitator D'Annunzio was brought back from France to make rabble rousing speeches on the beauty of war and the glory of Italy. According to the American Ambassador his first speech at Genoa had the effect of a firebrand struck into a charged magazine.[4] Similar assistance was provided by the journalist Benito Mussolini, observing at first hand how to subvert a parliamentary majority. The Austrian Ambassador reported demonstrations by "the hired mob" in "all the larger cities". Deputies in Rome were roughly handled and a cavalry guard had to be placed on the home of Giolitti, the leader of the parliamentary opposition.[5] Giolitti had been somewhat out of touch with events and had only recently been informed of the Treaty of London. He now realized that, after breaking with Austria, the King's position would become impossible if Italy then failed to honour its obligations towards the Allies, and he therefore left Rome. The demonstrations had the desired effect, and parliament declared war on 24 May by 407 votes to 74, after three weeks' uproar and debate which gave Austria time to alert her defences.

2. The War to October, 1917

The nominal Commander in Chief of the Italian Army was the King, but the effective Commander was General Cadorna, the Chief of Staff and head of the Comando Supremo, the Italian High Command. Indeed Cadorna had accepted this appointment on 27 July 1914, on the death of his predecessor General Pollio, only on condition that the King played no executive role. Cadorna was then faced with the task of strengthening and replenishing the army which was in rather a poor state following its campaign in Libya during the previous two years. He was a capable organizer and set about building up an army for any eventuality. (The term Comando Supremo is commonly

11

used to refer both to the Chief of Staff and to the Italian High Command.)

The course of the war was greatly conditioned by the mountainous nature of the border regions between Italy and Austria. The front line was about 300 miles long and, except for about 20 miles, was either mountainous or very mountainous (Map 1). Moreover, this frontier had been drawn many years previously to give considerable military advantage to Austria, because being near to the edge of the mountains, a short advance by the Austrians would take them into the Italian plain. On the other hand, if the Italians were to advance, they would find themselves going deeper and deeper into increasingly difficult mountain country.

The only obvious place to deploy large bodies of troops was on the relatively flat ground on either side of the last twenty miles or so of the Isonzo River below Gorizia. Therefore the Italian plan in 1915 was to attack across the lower reaches of the Isonzo, thrusting towards Trieste and perhaps eventually to Ljubljana and Vienna. As Italy had entered the war at a time of her own choosing it might seem that her army had the opportunity of striking an overwhelming blow against Austria whose army was heavily engaged with the Russians.

In fact, as described in the previous section, the timing of Italy's entry into the war on 24 May was governed by the exigencies of political considerations rather than by a well prepared military programme. As a result of these circumstances the Austrians were able to obtain at least three weeks warning of Italy's move. In addition the Italian army was not yet completely ready for a major action. Hence the first stage of the war was not an Italian onslaught on the Austrians but rather a re-adjustment of positions on both sides, mainly along the Isonzo and in the Trentino salient.

The pre-war frontier followed the watershed to the west of the Isonzo River for about 100 miles from the mountains to the sea, but did not give the Austrians a good line of defence. Hence, as the Austrians were already heavily engaged on their Eastern Front, their first move was to draw back from the frontier and take up previously prepared positions on either side of the river. The Italians then carried out a series of inter-mittent attacks during 1915 known as the 1st, 2nd, 3rd and 4th Battles of the Isonzo.

On the upper Isonzo the Italians made a considerable advance across the river between Tolmin and Bovec (Map 1), where they even gained positions on the summit of Monte Nero (2346m, now called Krn). This was a fine effort by the alpini, the Italian mountain troops,but did not offer much prospect of any subsequent advance in force. Below Tolmin, the river was forced at Plava and a small bridgehead established on the east side of the Isonzo. However, beyond the river the ground rose steeply to the plateau of the Bainsizza some 600 or so metres above, and the bridge itself was open to enemy artillery fire. Further south, strong Italian forces had come up to the considerable defences of the town of Gorizia on the west side of the river, including the surrounding hills of Sabotino (609m), Podgora (240m) and San Michele (275m).

Along the lower Isonzo the Italians were across the river in force and on the edge of the Carso, a green but infertile limestone plateau which extends from below Gorizia almost to the coast. Its general level is from 100 to 200 metres above the river and its undulations have gentle slopes, save on the western edge where the plateau drops down to the plain. In fact the Carso, though in no way mountainous, formed the type of defensive barrier so eagerly sought by the warring armies on the plains of France, particularly as the hard limestone rock, barely covered by the soil, had permitted the Austrians to construct bunkers and gun positions well protected from attack. The British historian Cyril Falls comments that the Italian infantry "showed splendid courage in hopeless tasks".[6] By the end of the year the Italians had suffered losses and casualties amounting in all to about 180,000, but had made little significant progress.

The next year, in May 1916, General Conrad, the Austrian Chief of Staff and virtual Commander in Chief, launched a full scale offensive with the aim of breaking out of the mountainous Trentino Salient into the Italian plain, behind the main Italian armies on the Isonzo. He gathered together fourteen divisions with 180 battalions in the south-eastern corner of the Trentino salient together with a superior force of artillery, and on 15 May launched the so-called Strafexpedition (*Straf*: punishment) designed to punish Austria's former ally. Despite strong resistance, the Italians were forced to give ground. At the end of the month, after heavy fighting all along the line, the Italians had been pushed to the very edge of the mountains overlooking the Venetian plain.

The Italian Commander, General Cadorna, believed that this line would hold, but at the same time decided to transfer the reserves of the armies of the Isonzo to create a new 5th Army ready in the plain to deal with any Austrian forces which might break through. Between 21 May and 2 June a complete army of 179,000 men was gathered and assembled in the region of Vicenza, Padua and Cittadella (Maps 1,2). In the end, however, the Austrians failed to break out from the mountains due to epic Italian resistance at many points along the line. On and near Monte Cengio (1351m, Map 3) a brigade of Granatieri delayed the advance during crucial days between 22 May and 3 June; of the original strength of 6217 men, 951 were killed and 2004 wounded. Such heroic efforts had their effect and on 16 June Conrad decided to break off the attack, and by 26 June the Austrians had drawn back considerably to new prepared positions.

Cadorna now made use of units of the 5th Army to counter-attack from 27 June to 24 July, but in spite of desperate attempts and very heavy losses only limited progress was made in dislodging the Austrians from their new positions. The battle for the salient had now worn itself out. The losses in dead, wounded and missing had been considerable, perhaps 70.000 on each side. Nevertheless by the end of July Cadorna was already returning troops ready for the 6th Battle of the Isonzo which opened a few days later on 4 August. The river was crossed, Gorizia captured, and the Italian front pushed forward into the Carso. But three subsequent battles in September, October and November made little more progress except for some small advances on the northern half of the Carso.

The battles were renewed on much the same lines in 1917. In the 10th Battle of the Isonzo during May and June the Italians extended their bridgehead at Plava down the river to Gorizia, while below Gorizia the line was pushed forward another two or three miles into the Carso. Also in June, an attack in the Trentino salient to capture the region of Monte Ortigara (Map 3) produced little result, but over 23,000 casualties (dead, wounded and missing), of which 13,000 came from only twenty two alpini battalions.[7] However, the 11th Battle in August and September made a relatively sizeable advance of up to four miles across the Bainsizza plateau and also some further advance on the Carso.

At first sight the results of over two years' fighting on the Isonzo appear rather modest. The great hopes of sweeping on to Trieste and even to Ljubljana and Vienna had not been fulfilled. The Italian army had lost about 200,000 men dead, and very many more wounded, but was virtually no nearer to Trieste. Even so, the results of the 11th Battle of the Isonzo, with its casualties totalling about 26,000 dead and 96,000 wounded, compared not unfavourably with those obtained by the British army struggling in the mud of Passchendaele at about the same time.

Italy, like all the other belligerents, had found herself involved in a war of attrition, which had not been foreseen. Her losses had been grievous and her advances small. Yet Italy had played a considerable role in this war of attrition, so that by September 1917 the Austrian High Command feared that they could not face another Italian attack on the scale of the 11th Battle. Therefore Austria appealed to Germany for help and the German High Command decided that urgent steps were necessary to prevent the defeat of Austria on the Italian front.[8] Thus began the story of Caporetto.

3.   The Breakthrough at Caporetto

Having decided to aid Austria by a joint offensive on the Isonzo the German High Command sent a very able staff officer, General Krafft von

Dellmensingen, to reconnoitre the ground. He had climbed in the Dolomites before the war, and had commanded the German Alpenkorps in the Dolomites in 1915 before Germany was officially in the war. Following his reconnaisance, arrangements were made for a surprise attack against the Italian 2nd Army holding the line in the upper part of the Isonzo valley where at first sight the ground is too mountainous to permit any hope of success.

The Germans planned to attack all along the mountain line from Bovec to the region south of Tolmin with the object of driving across the Isonzo, through the further defences on the far bank, and then perhaps into the Venetian plain. To make a success of this ambitious programme the Germans relied on sound planning, surprise, and the use of first class troops. Sixteen divisions, nine Austrian and seven German including the Austrian Edelweiss Mountain Division and the German Alpenkorps, were grouped together to form the XIVth Army under the German general Otto von Below and assembled secretly behind the front.

An army at war may succeed in spite of mistakes and ill fortune, provided these hazards come in moderation, but before and during the opening stages of the Battle of Caporetto everything went wrong for the Italians. The region of the Upper Isonzo is so mountainous that it seems to have been regarded as a relatively safe sector. The English historian G.M. Trevelyan, who directed an ambulance unit working with the 2nd Army, wrote that the region was regarded as a rest area.[9] It is also said that disaffected factory workers who had been called up had been sent, rather unfortunately, to this quiet sector.[10] Thus the troops on the ground were not the best units in the Italian Army and during the past two years had had little or no experience of either defence or attack.

The Italian Army was further handicapped by divided councils in the High Commands. As early as 18 September Cadorna had decided against a further offensive in 1917, and had ordered that all the troops on the Isonzo should adopt a defensive posture ready to deal with any Austrian attack.[11] Action was taken immediately by the 3rd Army on the lower Isonzo between Gorizia and the sea, commanded by the Duke of Aosta,[12] but not by the 2nd Army on the upper Isonzo, commanded by General Capello.[13] Relations between Capello and Cadorna were not good and Capello preferred offensive to defensive operations.

Few preparations were made by the 2nd Army until evidence began to arrive on 9 October suggesting that German and Austrian troops were considering an offensive in the region of Tolmin. In fact effective preparations began only in the last week or so when more troops were hurriedly brought up to the front in movements which the Italian Official History describes as "tumultuous in the final two days".[14] Moreover, between 5 and 19 October Cadorna was away from his headquarters at

15

Udine taking what appears to have been a working holiday in the Trentino, while Capello was becoming increasingly unwell with a kidney complaint which confined him to his bed for some days.

The Austrian and German troops began their attack at 02.00 hrs on 24 October with a heavy concentration of gas shells which did considerable damage, for the Italian gas masks seem to have been of limited value. Then from 06.30 the artillery switched to a massive concentration of high explosive which damaged gun positions and broke communications. The weather was foul, the whole area covered with dark cold mist, and snow fell intermittently. Finally, to complete the misery of the Italian troops, there was almost no artillery support from their own side when the attack began, for reasons never completely explained.

The main defence line from Bovec to just north of Tolmin (Map 1) lay on the high ground east of the river, often in the unfavourable positions which marked the limit of the advance in 1915. This sector was held by the 50th, 43rd and 46th Divisions of IV Corps and faced a frontal attack by the 55th and 50th Austrian Divisions. At the same time the 12th German Division, starting from Tolmin, moved up the valley towards the Italian line which crossed the river about two miles above Tolmin. To the north of the crossing the front was held by the 46th Division of IV Corps and to the south by the 19th Division of XXVII Corps, and neither corps had given sufficient attention to the defence of this part of the line.

Opposite Tolmin the 19th Division had been reinforced above its normal complement but was required to cover a wide stretch of critical ground. Then, on 22 October, orders were received that some of its front line battalions near the river were to relocate elsewhere, but the moves were not carried out with adequate liaison with the neighbouring IV Corps. Hence, the 12th German Division was able to move up either side of the river without encountering any real opposition, and by the early afternoon had arrived at Caporetto (today Kobarid in Slovenia).

Meanwhile the Austrian Edelweiss and the 22nd German Division, aided by a heavy gas attack, had crossed the river near Bovec and moved down the valley to Zaga. Hence, by the end of the first day the Germans and Austrians were all along the valley floor from Tolmin to Caporetto and Bovec, thus isolating most of IV Corps from the rear. In addition the Alpenkorps and the 12th German Division had broken up the 19th Italian Division on the left of XXVII Corps, and reached the line of the summits about 800m above the west bank of the river (with two young officers, the future Field Marshals Schoerner and Rommel, playing a prominent role).

On the second day, 25 October, the weather cleared and gave good visibility for the Austro-German XIVth Army which concentrated on gaining the second and third lines of defences on the high ground west of the river held by the recently created VII Corps. But this Corps had arrived only at the start of the battle, without time to prepare proper defensive positions. The Germans and Austrians saw that matters were going well for them and pursued the action with great vigour.

A failure of morale in some Italian troops was already apparent to the Germans on 24 October, but many continued to fight back as best they could. However, the isolation of IV Corps, the failure of VII Corps, and the breakdown of communications meant that a great part of the 2nd Army was largely in chaos. This in itself encouraged a further break-down of morale so that many of the troops of the 2nd Army decided that the war was now over and set off for home in what appears to have been a spirit of good nature rather than revolution. See, for example, the vivid and sympathetic description given by Trevelyan.[15]

Italy now faced complete disaster as the Austrians and the Germans pushed hard through the mountains to reach the Italian plain. General Cadorna had no alternative but to order a complete withdrawal from the Isonzo to either the Tagliamento or the Piave, the two principal rivers running behind the Isonzo from the mountains to the sea. In their middle course both these large rivers flow in channels through a very open and stony bed up to a kilometre or so wide, flanked by high artificial embankments, and thus form strong barriers to an invad-ing army. In fact the speed of the enemy advance left no time to organize a stand on the Tagliamento, so there was little choice but to retire to the Piave.

For armies which had been on the offensive for over two years the retreat was an immensely difficult operation, yet it was carried out successfully by the whole of the 3rd Army from the Carso and lower Isonzo, as well as by parts of the 2nd. Good accounts of the retreat have been given by Trevelyan,[16] by Freya Stark[17] who was a nurse at the time, by Hugh Dalton with the British Heavy Artillery,[18] and by Ernest Hemingway,[19] who arrived in Italy the following year.At the same time the 4th Army had to give up all its positions in the mountains of Carnia and the Dolomites and move down to the summits of the Monte Grappa massif on the edge of the plain between the Brenta and Piave rivers. This redeployment was much facilitated by a good new road from Bassano to the summit of Grappa (1775m) which had been built on Cadorna's orders after the Strafexpedition in 1916 in order to safeguard this vital strongpoint dominating the plain.

By 8 November most of the 4th Army had reached their new line, and by 10 November all the 3rd Army and parts of the 4th Army were in position behind the Piave. The Italian losses had been enormous, mostly from the 2nd Army. The actual battle casualties were about 10,000 dead and 30,000 wounded, but about 300,000 had been lost as prisoners, and about 350,000 as stragglers and deserters, still to be regrouped and organized.[20] However, in spite of these losses, the situation was saved by the steadfastness of the remaining troops, and the fact that the new line was much shorter than the old one.

The French and British Response

1. The Rome Conference

It was fortunate that some preparations had already been made for sending French and British expeditionary forces to Italy should the occasion arise. When Lloyd George became Prime Minister on 7 December 1916 he immediately began to look for alternative strategies to win the war, particularly in Italy. By 12 December General Robertson, the Chief of the Imperial General Staff (CIGS), was writing to General Haig in France that "he [Lloyd George] is after lending some of your big guns to Italy during the winter ... I've no doubt we can keep him straight.[1] On 26 December an Anglo-French Conference in London accepted Lloyd George's proposal for a meeting of representatives of the governments and high commands of Britain, France and Italy for "frank discussions on the whole military and political situation".[2] On 28 December Robertson wrote to Brigadier Delmé-Radcliffe, the Head of the British Military Mission in Italy, to stress the shortage of guns in the British Army, and also the time taken to move guns to and from Italy.[3] This letter was followed one day later by a second with the order "Don't discuss guns with him [Cadorna] at all".[4]

When the projected meeting was held in Rome on 5 to 7 January 1917, Lloyd George presented a memorandum which gave a critical summary of the progress of the war and concluded by asking the conference to consider (1) sending aid to Russia, (2) sending more Allied troops to Salonica, and (3) the development of defensive and offensive schemes of cooperation on the Italian front.[5] (General Wilson later described this memorandum as an amazing document written without Robertson's knowledge or consent.[6])

The conference discussed the various issues, but without making much progress. Lloyd George felt strongly that Austria was the weak link in the Central Powers, and that increased pressure on the Italian front could lead to an advance into Austria itself. He urged the conference to consider plans for an assault on Austria involving either the provision of Allied heavy artillery or by the provision of both guns and infantry.

On the Italian side Cadorna stated his willingness to undertake a substantial offensive, but to do so would require the assistance of an extra 300 heavy guns and eight French and British divisions.[7] However, it was soon apparent that both the French Government and the French and British High Commands were unwilling to divert any of their divisions to Italy. Nevertheless, the French and British offered the loan of some heavy guns to assist an Italian offensive. Yet this offer was qualified by the French insisting that their guns be returned by the end of April, and as Cadorna pointed out, the weather would only be suitable for large scale operations after that date. Thus the conference ended with Cadorna feeling that the Allies, although anxious for an offensive against Austria, were not willing to provide much assistance. While Lloyd George was left disappointed that Cadorna had not responded more positively to the offer of guns.[8]

Despite Lloyd George's disappointment, the Rome Conference set in motion various developments concerning the Italian front. At the beginning of February the new French C.in C., General Nivelle, visited Italy to discuss Cadorna's concerns over possible German attacks through Switzerland or the Trentino.[9] At the end of March Robertson and the French General Weygand visited the Italian front and were concerned that the Italian defences were of pre-war pattern, lacked depth, lacked good cooperation between infantry and artillery, and had only elementary communications. Indeed they "came to the conclusion that an occasion might easily arise when the Italians even in defence would require help in infantry as well as in heavy guns".[10]

On Robertson's return to London Brigadier Crowe was sent to Italy on 5 April to make a preliminary study of the arrangements that would be necessary to transfer six British divisions (120,000 men and 26,000 animals) by rail from France to Italy.[11] Heavy artillery units with forty howitzers were sent to the Carso on 7 April.[12] On 8 April General Foch, the French Chief of Staff (Chef d'État d'Armée), visited Italy to discuss with Cadorna how French and British units might best intervene in Italy "in case of a very heavy attack by the enemy".[13] On 20 April Robertson was in Paris to confer with Painlevé, the newly appointed French War Minister, in order to settle "the basis of the initial organization of a relief force".[14] On 7 May Brigadier Crowe signed an Anglo-Italian convention concerning a possible concentration of six British divisions in Italy.[15] The French authorities had already promised to provide trains from France either by the Modane or Riviera routes, and the convention dealt with the provision of the necessary facilities (transport, billetting, lines of communication, hospital accommodation, interpreters, etc.)that would be needed once the troops arrived in Italy.

On 18 August the Italians launched the 11th battle of the Isonzo which pushed the Austrians up to 4 miles back from their defences on the

Bainsizza. By 29 August the Italians had outrun the range of their guns on the right bank of the Isonzo, so the offensive was temporarily suspended in order to move the guns across the Isonzo and up to the plateau of the Bainsizza. On 11 September the British Secretary of State for War attended a conference in Udine and discussed the possibility of supplying an extra forty batteries of heavy guns. Cadorna was pleased to hear of this offer, but then asked for field guns so he could prepare a defence against a possible attack by the seventy or eighty Austrian divisions which, he said, could now become available from the Russian front.[16]

This latest request from Cadorna was a surprise and a disappointment to the Allies who were looking forward to their guns being used in offensive actions rather than in waiting to be attacked. Then on 18 September Cadorna ordered his Armies on the Isonzo to move to the defensive, and informed the French and British of this change two days later saying, *inter alia*, that it was necessary to economize in ammunition.[17] This was unwelcome news to the British bogged down in Passchendaele and to the French preparing for the Battle of Malmaison. Both decided on 25 September to recall most of their heavy batteries which had been sent to Italy solely in order to assist offensive operations.[18]

As matters now stood it seemed that Lloyd George had made little, if any, progress in obtaining some new action and a greater coordination of the Allied war effort. The most concrete achievement was no more than some administrative arrangements to ensure the rapid transfer of troops between France and Italy should this be necessary at some time in the future. Yet these arrangements would play a significant part in the Allied response to the German breakthrough at Caporetto.

2. Appeal and Response

It was only on 28 October that the full scale of the disaster at Caporetto became clear in London and Paris. The French Government immediately offered reinforcements and General Foch telegraphed to the Comando Supremo in Italy "*Le Gouvernement Français vous fait savoir que, si vous avez besoin de nos troupes, nous sommes prêtes à marcher*".[19] In London, Lloyd George, without calling a meeting of the War Cabinet, directed General Robertson to send two British divisons from France to Italy as a precautionary measure.[20] Instructions were then telegraphed to General Haig, the C.in C. in France, adding the information that the French were sending four divisions.

Robertson was not happy with this decision and the next day, 27 October, complained to Lloyd George that Italy had "stacks of men of her own", and that there was no <u>military</u> necessity to send troops provided the Italians fought reasonably well themselves. Robertson was in favour of waiting unless as he wrote to Lloyd George, "you think that for political reasons we ought not to be outdone by the French".[21] Robertson also argued that, as the divisions involved would be coming from Flanders and Passchendaele, "it is really very hard on our men after what they have recently gone through to send them to Italy". In fact the troops who went from Passchendaele found Italy a considerable improvement.

Lloyd George replied that it was necessary to help extricate our Allies in trouble, in the same way as the Germans did, adding "We cannot do so merely by lecturing them at conferences".[22] Robertson also grumbled to Foch, who replied that it was incontestable that Cadorna had all the men and resources to stop the enemy if he made use of them, but "*les événements dominent les raisonnements*".[23] Finally at 23.15 instructions were sent to Haig to select a "good man" as corps commander, and a later telegram emphasized the need for two good divisions.[24]

During 27 October preparations continued for the despatch of four French divisions with heavy artillery. The first two French divisions began to entrain on 28 October, and to arrive in Italy on the 31st. The seven groups of French heavy artillery already in Italy, which were due to return to France after Cadorna had decided against any further action, were now assigned to cover the bridges over the Tagliamento, and orders were given for six more groups to be sent out to join them.[25] Likewise the withdrawal of the one British Group of heavy artillery still in Italy, the XCIVth with the 3rd Army, was cancelled.

The news of the Allied aid was of "great comfort" to General Cadorna, but he was still much concerned that the Austrians might launch further offensives on other parts of the front.[26] On 28 October intelligence reports suggested (incorrectly) that 50,000 or so troops from Alsace had arrived in the region west of Bolzano. Therefore Cadorna proposed, via the French Military Mission in Italy, that the French divisions should go to the region of Bassano and the British divisions to the region of Brescia (Map 1), so as to be ready to meet attacks either across the Piave, on the Asiago plateau, down the valley of the Adige, or down the valley of the Chiesa.[27] The same day, apparently before receiving any response to his proposal, Cadorna ordered the Italian 1st Army and III Corps to prepare to receive these French and British divisions in the proposed concentration zones.[28] However, the next day 29 October, Cadorna changed his mind and suggested that the French should concentrate in the region of Montebelluna, Castelfranco and Treviso, in order to oppose any move by the XIVth Army across the Piave between Vidor and Ponte di Priula (Map 2).[29]

Meanwhile the French and British Governments, anxious to obtain more information, decided that Foch and Robertson should go to Italy and consult with the Government and the Comando Supremo. (In fact, since 21 October there had been a political crisis in Rome not directly related to the military situation. Signor Bosselli's Government had resigned on 26 October, but was carrying on until a new government was formed by Signor Orlando on 30 October.)

On 30 October Foch met Cadorna for a general discussion at his Headquarters at Treviso and were joined by Robertson for further talks the next day. The discussions between Foch and Cadorna appear to have got off to a poor start. Foch's manner, perhaps intentionally brusque to inspire confidence, was not well received.[30] According to Cadorna, after hearing a summary of the present position, Foch studied the map for a few minutes and made several remarks in a very peremptory manner of the type "One must do this" or "One must do that". To each of which Cadorna replied calmly that it had already been done or ordered.[31]

Discussions continued during the next two days (30,31 October) and Foch and Cadorna agreed that the French troops should detrain in areas near Cittadella and Vicenza, ready to defend the line of the Piave.[32] However, Foch was firmly opposed to these troops entering the line immediately, taking the view that they would be more properly employed forming a coherent striking force to deal with any new break-through on the Piave or elsewhere.[33] (Unfortunately on 30 October Cadorna had already issued directives to the Italian and French Army Commanders which assumed the presence of four French divisions on the middle Piave.[34])

This divergence of view between Foch and Cadorna was underlined when, soon after agreeing the above concentration areas, Cadorna received further information suggesting that an enemy offensive was imminent north of Lake Garda. He therefore requested that first one and then two divisions be put at his disposal near Brescia to deal with such an attack. However, it was never the intention of either the French or British governments that their forces should be used piecemeal in larger Italian units. Their immediate aim was to provide new reserve forces strong enough to oppose any further enemy incursions, just as Cadorna had created the 5th Army in 1916 to deal with a possible break-out from the Asiago plateau during the Strafexpedition (Section 1.2).

After further discussions it was eventually agreed, in order to meet Cadorna's concern for an attack west of Lake Garda, that the first four French divisions, under General Duchêne, should concentrate between Brescia and Verona. Unfortunately Cadorna seems not to have appreciated the responsibility that France and Britain felt towards their own troops, or that they would be unwilling to relinquish all control to him or anyone else. Hence, although agreement was reached on the location of the French forces, the Italians were somewhat disappointed, as shown by a comment in the IOH referring to "the intransigence of General Foch" in not agreeing to put the French troops immediately at Cadorna's disposal.[35]

At the end of the two days of talks a memorandum on the meeting was written by Foch and signed by him and Robertson setting out their considered view of the military position. Their main conclusion was that most of the Italian army remained undefeated, that by taking efficient measures it would be able to deal with the enemy, and that not all the twenty divisions requested by Cadorna would be necessary.[36] The memorandum was essentially a vote of confidence in the Italian army, but it was somewhat harsh in tone, and must have seemed so to the Italians who at that time were still in the midst of their difficult retreat.

Meanwhile the British advance parties of the GHQ, XIV Corps, and the 23rd and 41st Divisions had left Paris on the night train of 30 October with orders to report to the British Military Mission already in Italy. Previous to Caporetto the Mission had considered that the most likely direction of attack would be from the Trentino towards Verona, Vicenza or Brescia, and studies had been made of three possible areas for concentration: (a) Padua – Rovigo; (b) Vicenza – Verona; (c) Milan – Lodi. It appears that, in view of the uncertainties of the situation, the War Office decided on 2 November to fix on option (c) and informed the Italians that they intended to concentrate on the line Milan – Lodi. On the same day the recently appointed British Commander, Lieut.-General Lord Cavan, was asked for his views on where to concentrate and, after ten minutes' discussion, selected Mantua on the Mincio River.[37] However, this later decision was apparently not passed on to the Italians.

Cavan left London the same day with a small staff, including the Prince of Wales as an ADC and Brigadier H.L.Alexander (later Field Marshal Earl Alexander). They arrived at Pavia at 10.00 on 5 November and then motored to Padua where they met King Victor Emmanuel, General Piccione, the head of the Italian operations branch, and Brigadier Delmé-Radcliffe of the British Military Mission. The next day Cavan talked with Cadorna at Treviso, and Cadorna expressed disappointment on having learnt that the concentration area had been chosen so far back as the line Milan – Lodi. Cavan agreed and next day, 7 November, received the War Office's consent to concentrate on the west bank of the Mincio near Mantua (covered on the north by the French concentration near Lake Garda). Cadorna appeared pleased and satisfied with these arrangements.[38]

3.   The Move of the Allied Troops

The Allies now faced the formidable task of moving up to 200,000 men, their equipment and their supply lines, from the Western Front to

Northern Italy at very short notice. It was fortunate that, following the Rome Conference in January 1917, the British Mission of five officers had been sent to Italy to make preliminary arrangements for the arrival, concentration and maintenance of a force of perhaps six divisions with all due despatch should occasion arise.

The speed of any transfer was set by the capacity of the only two railway links between France and Italy, one via Nice and Genoa, and the other by the Modane tunnel and Turin. According to Lieut-Colonel Beadon of the RASC the capacity of the Genoa route was sixteen trains per day and of the Modane route twelve. On average moving one division required sixty-one trains, plus perhaps another nine for its associated artillery, in all seventy trains. The total capacity of both lines was twenty-eight trains per day, assuming that all other commitments on the lines could be dropped.[39]

It was clear to the planners that more trains would be desirable and various expedients were considered. The capacity of the southern route was limited by the first 60 miles beyond the frontier at Ventimiglia being only single track, so if the troops detrained and marched over this section the overall capacity might be increased by six trains per day. There was also the possibility of marching from Nice over the Col di Tenda to another section of the Italian rail system. Similar expedients would also be possible on the northern route to avoid the bottleneck of the Modane tunnel, but only in the summer when the road passes were not blocked by snow.

Concentration areas large enough to deal with six divisions were selected: one between Milan and Pavia, one in the plain south of Verona and Vicenza, and one further east near Padua and Rovigo. A main base was also required with communications by sea and rail. Genoa was an obvious possibility, but had already been chosen by the French. In fact a suitable site of sufficient size was available only at the small town of Aquarta on the Genoa to Turin railway, about 40k m from Genoa.

Three months after these plans had been drawn up they were put to the test. As mentioned above, the French Government moved very rapidly and two French divisions began entraining on 28 October and detraining in Italy on 31 October. By 5 November two French divisions had completely detrained, followed by a further two by 10 November, travelling by both the Ventimiglia and the Modane routes. Trains then became available for the British forces, and the 23rd and 41st Divisions left France between 6 and 13 November followed, by the 7th and 48th Divisions between 17 and 24 November.[40]

The journey via Nice and Genoa was a memorable experience for the British troops.[41] Most of them had never been out of Britain except with the army. Then, shortly after leaving the dreary fields of Flanders and Northern France, they found themselves travelling down the Rhone valley into Provence, past Avignon to Marseilles and the green hills sloping down to the intense blue of the Mediteranean Sea. The weather was warm and sunny, and the local inhabitants friendly. Then along the glorious coast of the Riviera. For most of them it was a revelation of another and very splendid world, even if they were travelling twenty-six men to a cattle truck in normal military fashion.

Crossing into Italy at Ventimiglia, their route continued by the sea as far as Genoa where they turned away from the sunny coast to pass through the Apennines to the flat Lombardy plain, at this time of the year cold, frosty and misty. The first division to arrive began detraining at Mantua on 12 November and marched to billets in nearby villages. Here they paused for almost a week, because although it had been agreed on 11 November that the British would concentrate in the region of Vicenza, their move was delayed until the Italian staff were able to arrange the necessary billeting facilities. Therefore the next few days were spent near Mantua marching and resting.

During this time Private Norman Gladden, in the 11th Battalion of the Northumberland Fusiliers with the 23rd Division, was keeping a diary which was eventually published by the Imperial War Museum under the title *Across the Piave*. This book provides an excellent and very readable account of the Italian campaign as seen from the lowest level by a stalwart 20-year-old fusilier, with first hand accounts of actions with the enemy and details of life in the line and in reserve. Gladden describes how his division eventually marched out of Mantua on 19 November towards Vicenza. On 22 November they reached Montagnano about half-way to Vicenza where they received yet another large civic welcome. By this time it had been decided that they would take over part of the front line on the Piave so the Division marched on to Castelfranco (Map 2) where they halted on 29 November before entering the line on 2 December.

There are also good accounts of the 48th Division in Italy by Barnett (48th Division), and of several of the infantry battalions by Carrington (5th Battalion, Warwickshire Regiment), Cruttwell (4th Battalion, Royal Berkshires), Pickford (4th Battalion, Oxfordshire and Buckinghamshire L.I.), Stacke (Worcestershire Regiment), Wright (1st Battalion, Buckinghamshire Regiment), and Wyrall (Gloucestershire Regiment). These accounts show that the 48th Division's journey to Italy was not unlike that of the 23rd, but in addition at Bologna station Captain Wright observed "the pitiful sight of strings of deserters chained together".[42]

The Italian railway system was having to deal with vast numbers of Italian troop movements and was very overloaded, so timetables were much disorganized. All the divisions experienced difficulties in detraining and probably none more than the 48th. Wright refers to "hopeless confusion" and Barnett tells of trains sent to any vacant sidings with or without facilities for unloading the guns, the transports and the animals. Elderly station masters wearing impressive hats, and naturally speaking only Italian, were at a loss to deal with situations for which they had not been prepared (such as "several trains standing head to tail on a single track for several hours").[43]

Under such conditions it was not surprising that different units of the division and indeed different halves of a battalion found themselves spread over an area stretching 15 or 25 miles east to west and over 20 miles north to south. It was a nightmare scenario, only redeemed by the fact that the weather, though cold, was fine, and that because of the glamour of the journey and the friendliness of their reception, everyone had arrived in a good humour. To use the words of Edmonds "The utmost goodwill prevailed", and problems were eventually sorted out despite the language difficulties.[44]

Although nearly all units travelled by rail, the vehicles of some Divisional Supply Columns were sent by road from France to Italy because of the shortage of rail capacity. Each column consisted primarily of five officers and 250 men, and the sixty or so 3-ton lorries required to transport a day's supply of rations, forage and ammunition from the railhead to the divisional distribution points. In order to operate and maintain their vehicles each column also included two mobile work-shops, a car and a motor cyclist.

Today a similar journey is hardly worthy of comment, but conditions were much more arduous in 1917, as described in an excellent account of the move of the 17th Divisional Supply Column (DSC), *With the Mad 17th in Italy*, by its commander Major Hody. He received orders at St. Omer in northern France to stock up with 24,000 gallons of petrol and rations for 250 men for three weeks, and set out on 30 October with a schedule of overnight halts, via Lyons and Marseilles, which programmed them to arrive at Ventimiglia on the frontier on 9 November where they were to await further orders.

This was not fast travelling – 750 miles in ten days at an average speed of 10 mph, but lorry speeds were low and the column had to push on with much determination to keep to their schedule. Their lorries were not as reliable as those of another make issued to the supply column for the 41st Division and needed constant nursing. The two mobile work-shops travelled at the rear of the column and were kept busy with a variety of problems including broken valves and pistons, and cracked cylinders. During November sixty-four tyres became unserviceable or came off on the road and the only tyre presses which enabled tyres to be changed quickly were at Paris, Lyons and Marseilles.

Everyone having worked hard to arrive at Ventimiglia on schedule, Major Hody was surprised to find no further orders awaiting them. Despite enquiries, orders to proceed only arrived after almost a week, which was spent enjoying the sunshine. Then the column set off again along the coast to Genoa stopping for the night in a village near the coast where they were warmly received and the officers photographed at an official reception each holding a bunch of flowers. After passing through the Apennines, with no sun and no welcome, and another night on the road, they reached Mantua in the evening just in time to begin the supply of the 23rd Division.

The next day the Division began to march eastwards, by which time a day's supply should have arrived by train from France. However, after waiting all day for news of these supplies, the DSC was obliged to collect emergency stores at Mantua, to scrounge 35 tons (sic) of oats, and then set out at 02.00 on a cold dark night with heavy fog to deliver to the division. Then, as soon as the column had returned to camp and eaten breakfast, it was time to begin the next delivery. Again there was no sign of any packs of supplies, but after waiting all day the column was told they could pick up Italian rations in Mantua. To draw British packs took just over an hour, but picking up the Italian rations took longer. Hay, oats, groceries, bread, and meat were located in different stores each in some obscure part of the town. It was necessary to bag the oats by hand in 550 hundred-pound sacks, which then had to be weighed and carried down three flights of narrow steps. At the meat store bullocks were slaughtered on the spot and half an hour later their "dripping quarters" thrown on the lorries. It was only at 06.00 that the column could set out to deliver its loads. This was probably the worst night, but difficulties of the same nature continued for about a week until eventually the supply system became more organized.

4.   The Deployment of the Allied Troops

By 9 November the Italian Armies were on their new defence line Asiago – Grappa – Piave (Map 1). French forces had begun to arrive at the beginning of November. Two divisions were fully detrained by 5 November and two more by 12 November. The first two British divisions arrived by 18 November, two more French by 22 November, two more British by 1 December, and a fifth British Division (the 5th) by 17 December.[45] As already outlined, the Italians were very anxious for these units to relieve their tired troops in the front line, whereas the British and French saw the overriding priority as the need to deploy their divisions as an efficient striking force which would be capable of dealing with any further breakthrough.

Meanwhile, on 5 November the Allied leaders had met at Rapallo in order to coordinate their military effort and to discuss LLoyd George's proposal of setting up a permanent staff of military officers to study the war as a whole. The Allied Prime Ministers, Orlando, Painlevé and Lloyd

28

George, were accompanied by Sonnino and Alfieri,the Italian Foreign Secretary and War Minister, and by Foch, Robertson and General Sir Henry Wilson, an officer of wide experience well known to Lloyd George. Cadorna failed to attend, saying that it was more important for him to remain at his headquarters as the retreat still continued, and was therefore represented by his deputy, General Porro. Edmonds states that the latter gave the meeting a general description of the serious military situation, and according to Lloyd George "made the poorest impression on every mind at that conference".[46]

The Conference had to deal with at least three dominant issues: how many French and British troops were required, how they should be deployed, and the question of the Italian Command. Edmonds states that General Porro asked for at least fifteen Allied divisions, stating that nine German divisions were engaged in the attack, and that twelve or fifteen more had left the Western Front for Italy. Foch and Robertson said that this was unlikely to be correct as there were only six German divisions in action at present (having overlooked the Jäger Division). Therefore they considered that a total of eight French and British divisions would be sufficient, but Lloyd George and Painlevé promised to send more divisions if necessary, and by mid-December six French and five British divisions had arrived in Italy. (Cadorna had instructed Porro on 5 November to present an estimate of thirty-five German divisions but amended this figure to at least twenty-one divisions on 6 November.[47])

On 5 November Porro also asked that, besides the French 64th and 65th Divisions which had now arrived near Brescia, another French division should be sent to Val Camonica below the Tonale Pass (Map 1), as a matter of urgency because of a suspected Austrian attack. Therefore Foch ordered General Duchêne, then in command of the French troops in Italy, to direct the next two French divisions to Val Camonica and Brescia, so that all four French divisions would take up positions west of Lake Garda ready to resist the attack foreseen by Cadorna.

Cadorna also requested that the French divisions be placed under the orders of the local Italian commanders, but Foch made the counter-proposal that all the forces from the shores of Lake Garda to the Swiss frontier at the Stelvio Pass be placed under Duchêne. The following day 6 November Duchêne ordered the 47th French Division to move by lorry to Val Camonica, and the 65th Division to move to Val Chiesa ready to reinforce the 6th Italian division in the mountains north east of Brescia. The other French divisions due to arrive were to concentrate between Brescia and the west bank of Lake Garda.[48]

One other weighty matter was discussed at Rapallo. Although the King was nominally the C.in C., the Italian military effort had been directed by Cadorna, acting effectively (in British terms) as C.in C. and CIGS. Since he had been appointed in July 1914 he had been responsible for raising and training a huge army and then for the conduct of the war. Cadorna was a respected soldier with considerable ability and much strength of character, and during the war the Italian Army had obtained moderate successes such as the taking of Gorizia in 1916 and the advance on the Bainsizza in 1917, together with heavy casualties comparable to those of the French and British on the Western Front.

During the Strafexpedition, Cadorna had kept his head under pressure, and made good preparation with his reserves to deal with any Austrian incursion into the plain. Then he had foreseen the need for a supply road to the summit of Monte Grappa. Yet as Colonel Gatti, the military historian at the Comando Supremo, noted in his diary on 27 June 1917, the headquarters staff was very small. The command was run by Cadorna, General Porro the sub-chief of the general staff, and Cadorna's secretary Colonel Bencivenga, or rather by Cadorna and Bencivenga. This, comments Gatti, was an impossible task even if Cadorna had had a mind like Napoleon.[49] Nowhere was there a part for other able generals.

After the loss of so many troops and of so much Italian territory and material there was clearly a *prima facie* case for a change in command. To quote Villari, "the mere fact of Cadorna's defeat was enough to destroy the confidence of the army and the nation in him, and that this lack of confidence, even if not wholly justified, would be fatal for future success".[50] Quite apart from the above considerations, Cadorna almost certainly sealed his fate by his communiqué of 28 October which sought to explain the defeat solely as the result of sections of the 2nd Army either retreating without fighting, or ignominiously surrendering to the enemy.

When Cadorna's communiqué arrived in Rome the Government immediately realized the disastrous effect it could have on morale. Hence Orlando (still the Minister of the Interior) changed the opening words to "the violence of the attack and the deficient resistance of some parts of the 2nd Army . . .", but this was done too late to prevent the initial version becoming common knowledge. As might have been expected, by throwing all the blame on the troops the communiqué aroused much ill feeling in the country. Colonel Gatti wrote in his diary, "This morning's communiqué has made an evil impression".[51] Thus it was not surprising that when Orlando announced his new Government on 30 October, the War Minister General Giardino was replaced by General Alfieri, known to be critical of Cadorna.

On 1 November Foch talked with the Duke of Aosta, the King and the new Prime Minister, Orlando. Foch says in his Memoirs that

Orlando took an intelligent and calm view of the situation. He was ready to fight to the bitter end, even to retreat to Sicily. "There is no question of retreating to Sicily," replied General Foch, "It is on the Piave that we must resist.". Then, in further talks on 2 and 3 November with members of the Government, Foch emphasized "the necessity of reorganizing the Comando Supremo with a view to making it more vigorous".[52]

On 3 November Cadorna decided on the retreat to the Piave and sent a report to Orlando which is printed in full by Seth.[53] This necessarily somewhat gloomy report ended with a short but opaque paragraph which called on the Government to take some action which only the Government could take. It may be that this action was to urge the French and British governments to provide more assistance, but critics of Cadorna[54] have read his words to suggest that he was convinced of disaster and was thinking in terms of seeking an armistice. On the other hand, there appears to be no positive evidence to support this suggestion, and Cadorna's written orders do not always show the clarity of, for example, the 3rd Army orders from the Duke of Aosta reproduced in the IOH.

As a result of their visits, both Foch and Robertson, officers of considerable experience, had serious reservations on the quality of the Italian High Command, Robertson in a report to London referring to "great confusion and lack of grip of the situation at GHQ".[55] Foch judged that the Italians should easily be able to hold their line, provided the Comando Supremo showed determination and supervised the execution of its orders. Lloyd George, advised by Foch and Robertson, expressed concern about the staff of the Comando Supremo, and stated on behalf of the French and British Governments that they were not prepared to send their divisions, amounting in all to about 200,000 men, unless they were assured of a new and more rigorous command. In fact the matter had already been discussed in the Italian Parliament on 4 November,[56] and Orlando replied that a change of command was already under consideration.

At the final meeting on 7 November the Rapallo Conference took the decision to establish a Supreme War Council at Versailles. The next morning most of the Allied representatives were at Peschiera, near Verona, for a meeting presided over by the King. During this meeting the King announced that it had already been decided to replace Cadorna by General Diaz, then in command of XXIII Corps in the 3rd Army, and that Cadorna would go to Versailles as the Italian representative on a Supreme War Council. (The French and British representatives were to be General Weygand and General Wilson.) The French and British Prime Ministers then returned home, leaving Foch and Robertson with complete discretion on the use of the Allied Divisions.

(Seth[57] makes the rather remarkable claim that the dismissal of Cadorna was due to the hatred of Lloyd George, arising because Cadorna had not supported him at the earlier Rome Conference. This suggestion may have arisen in conversations between Seth and Cadorna's son, General Raffaelle Cadorna, but overlooks the fact that on this issue Lloyd George had the full support of both Foch and Robertson.)

5. A Difficult Meeting

General Diaz learnt of his appointment as Comando Supremo during the afternoon of 8 November and early next day was confronted by Foch, Wilson and Weygand, "all in an extremely inquisitive frame of mind".[58] He declared his intention to hold the line of the Piave and referred to the danger of attacks at Asiago and between the Stelvio and Lake Garda. Foch confirmed that one French division had already been directed to Val Camonica and an additional one to Brescia, and Diaz agreed with Foch's earlier suggestion that Duchêne should take command of all the troops between the Stelvio and Lake Garda from midday on 12 November.[59] It was also agreed that when the British and the other French divisions arrived they should concentrate in the region of Vicenza where they would be behind both the Asiago and the Piave fronts. After this meeting Robertson, who together with Foch had been in Italy since 31 October, decided that it was now possible for him to return to London, while Foch continued to provide support until 23 November.

Meanwhile Lord Cavan was occupied in drawing up plans for the British troops now beginning to arrive. On 10 November he sent a report to London setting out his assessment of the current situation, together with contingency plans for the employment of the British divisions on their arrival. He first considered a worst case scenario in which the Piave line was broken before the further French and British divisions had arrived and concentrated. He judged that the Italians would hold the Piave line at least until the enemy was able to bring up a really big concentration of guns and that this would take at least ten days, and possibly three weeks. Hence the worst possible case would be for the Piave line to be breached in the next few days, say by 17 November, that is about the same time as when the two British divisions would be detraining near Mantua behind the Mincio River.

Cavan also estimated that the enemy, once having broken through, would need at least fourteen days to cover the 140 km to the Mincio. This would give just enough time for the two British divisions to prepare for a stiff defence of a ten kilometre length of the river, located sufficiently far to the north to be in touch with a French force with its left flank on Lake Garda. This was his preferred policy and he explicitly rejected any attempt to move forward. Cavan had already seen the roads west of Padua choked with refugees and he concluded that "<u>any forward move to the east under the conditions imagined must be hopelessly involved by streams of refugees and retiring troops, and the force would lose its cohesion and much of its fighting value.</u>" (Cavan's underlining).[60]

Cavan's report then went on to consider the position if the Piave line was held for a month or appeared reasonably likely to hold for that time, and if the fall of snow obstructed the passes in the Trentino. In this case the British divisions should move gradually forward to positions of readiness on the line Montebelluna – Treviso (Map 2) with the French on their left, more closely behind the front line as Diaz desired. Then, at the first sign of any break in the line, these forces would be ready to deliver a strong blow at the enemy and drive him back across the Piave. Meanwhile defence works on the line Vicenza – Monselice (south west of Padua), and behind the Mincio, should be vigorously prepared by all available labour, civilian and military.

After his meeting with Foch, Wilson and Weygand early on 9 November Diaz presumably spent the next two days taking over his new post and being briefed on the general situation. Then, on 11 November, he held what turned out to be a difficult meeting with Foch and Wilson.[61] During this meeting Diaz expressed concern that the French troops were so distant from the front and insisted most strongly that these divisions, the only Allied troops yet available, should take over the line between Nervesa and Crocetta. Foch was unwilling to agree to this proposal immediately because it would involve the French troops moving into an area with roads already crowded with Italian troops, where they ran the risk of being involved in a retreat, and where they could do little to help. Diaz then read a telegram from the Prime Minister, Orlando, urging that the Allied troops be moved up, and stating that public opinion in Italy was becoming unfavourably impressed by the Allied armies being kept so far from danger.[62] There followed a long and heated discussion.

The two French divisions then in Val Camonica and near Brescia were certainly a considerable distance from the Piave, but Orlando appears to have been unaware that the French dispositions had been made at the request of Cadorna. Eventually it was decided to place the main body of the French forces between Vicenza and Valdagno (in the foothills of the mountains north of Vicenza), with the British forces on their right, south of Vicenza. The next day Cavan was informed of these decisions in a letter from Wilson which stated that the south end of the French line was to rest on Vicenza (inclusive), that the British XIV Corps should take up positions on its right behind the Bacchiglione River south

33

of Vicenza (Map 6), and that the British should detrain as close to the Bacchiglione river as the military situation permitted.

6. Other Support

France and Britain were also able to assist by providing guns, rifles and ammunition. During the retreat the Italian Army had lost about 3000 of its 7000 guns.[63] Although no very precise figures are available, it appears that by 15 April 1918 about 1900 of these guns had been replaced by modern up to date equipment.[64] This had been achieved both by the prodigious efforts of the Italian factories, and by the foresight of the Ansaldo company which had in stock "hundreds" of guns made over and above those ordered by the government.[65] In addition, during December and January 225 French and 260 British guns were loaned to support the Italian artillery.[66]

Various other material supplied by the Allies included 2000 French machine guns with 20 million rounds, and 2000 British Lewis guns. Italy had requested 300,000 rifles and it appears that at least 150,000 were provided by the French. Requests were also made for 800,000 gas masks as the Italian type was not proof against all gases, and 300,000 were received by 13 January 1918.[67]

In addition Italy was experiencing acute shortages of coal and grain, and the impact of Caporetto induced the Allies to provide more help. Italy had virtually no coalfields and before the war all coal supplies were obtained from abroad. Hence since the outbreak of war the supply of coal had presented a continuing problem. Pre-war imports had come from France, Britain and Germany and had amounted to about 1 million tonnes a month. But now France had lost most of its coalfields and Britain was short of shipping for transport. Hence all through the war there were severe shortages of coal, with little or none available for domestic heating. In the period July – October 1917 the average imports of coal amounted to 508,000 tonnes per month (in return for which Italy had lent 100,000 men for labour in France), "but the total for December was expected to be no more than 300,000 tonnes, with 350,000 tonnes in prospect for January". On 23 December Orlando wrote privately to Lloyd George setting out Italy's minimum requirements in tonnes per month as: munition factories, 200,000; light and power 70,000; Navy 60,000; railways 240,000; ships,food supply,etc 120,000. In all 690,000 tonnes per month. France was unable to help, but Britain agreed to comply to this request.[68]

In 1913 Italy grew about 5.8m tonnes of wheat and 2.7m tonnes of maize, which were supplemented by imports of about 1.2m tonnes The war saw a fall in production as men were called up from the farms and imports were increased to reduce the shortfall. Conditions were particularly difficult in 1917; the total production of wheat and maize had fallen to 5.9m tonnes,[69] leaving a shortfall of about 2.6m tonnes per year. Hence, in his letter of 23 December Orlando also stressed that Italy had needed to import 750,000 tonnes of cereal for the quarter September – November, but had only received 370,000 tonnes, and food riots were threatening. As with coal the principal bottleneck was the supply of shipping for bringing grain to Italy. Therefore Orlando asked for the available tonnage of shipping to be increased from 110,000 to 220,000 tons. Edmonds states that this was agreed to, "although it interfered with the transport of U.S.A.troops to Europe".[70]

Finally, under the Treaty of London, Britain agreed to facilitate a loan to Italy of at least 50 million lire. In fact this sum turned out to be a gross underestimate of Italy's needs, and between 1915 and 1918 about £800 million was loaned to Italy, of which less than half was eventually repaid.[71]

3

The Arrestamento

1. Recovery and the New Command

By 12 November the 3rd and 4th Armies had taken up positions along the right bank of the Piave and across the summits of Monte Grappa to link up with the 1st Army on the Asiago plateau (Maps 1,3). The Italians now had to deny the enemy any further progress, and to reorganize the 300,000 stragglers mainly from the 2nd Army. When Lord Cavan arrived at Padua on 5 November he saw many thousands of men marching westwards, on the whole of fine physique, who did not appear to be unduly demoralized.[1] On the other hand the war reporter Warner Allen arrived at Mantua from Paris on 17 November to see stragglers moving back as "a disorderly rabble of tattered, panic-stricken soldiers".[2] Lieut.-Colonel Barnett of the 48th Division describes a column of infantry "straggling along in a rough column; there was no march discipline; the men looked dispirited, apathetic, sullen, and, above all, dog tired. They seem to have hardly any arms and little food".[3]

Carta 25 of the IOH shows that by 12 November many of the former divisions of the 2nd Army were being collected together in reception areas about 70 miles or so behind the front line. A few units were ready to return to the front quite soon, but the majority of the troops were moved still further back to vast camps between Mantua and Modena, and near Ferrara. Eventually, by the end of February these men had been formed into two new Armies, the 2nd and the 5th, each with six divisions grouped into three corps.[4] Meanwhile, as early as 24 November the strength of the army in the war zone had grown by the arrival of 170,000 young troops of the class of 1889, by 50,000 troops recovered from illness and wounds, and by 80,000 men returning from leave.[5]

For all Italians the disaster at Caporetto marked a turning point in the war. The debatable aim of acquiring Trieste and the Trentino was now replaced by a much greater and clearer objective. All Friuli, Venezia Giulia and part of the Veneto had been occupied and the Austrians were no more than 20 miles from Venice. Press reports in the *Cologne Gazette* on 5 November foretold retribution against Italy,[6] and an article in the

Vienna Reichpost on 9 November called for the dismemberment of Italy.[7] A report to the Foreign Office in London from the Netherlands Embassy referred to a press report in *Der Tag* of 27 November saying that early vegetables and fruit would be imported into Germany.[8] The issues were now very stark. Was the invader to remain? Was his advance to be halted? On these issues the country was united. The Catholic church, hitherto somewhat equivocal in its attitude to the war against Catholic Austria, now continued "to do all in their power to rally the people in the face of the enemy", while Cardinal Maffi made "a noble appeal for union and sacrifice".[9]

The doubts of the previous summer were now largely set aside. For the first time the country was united in its efforts to resist and defeat the enemy. During this time the great majority of the stragglers returned to their units or were regrouped in new units without much difficulty. Yet there remained some underlying air of disquiet. Warner Allen, soon after his arrival at Mantua, commented that "the military authorities had been dealing severely with the officers and men responsible for the disaster, and in every town one might see lists of traitors or mutineers condemned to be shot in the back. There was fear in the Italian ranks".[10] In fact the Government and Comando Supremo remained concerned that perhaps several thousand stragglers and deserters might make trouble with their pacifist and anti-militarist views, aided perhaps by enemy propaganda, see for example Melograni.[11] However, no serious trouble arose, although the authorities continued to watch the situation.

The new Comando Supremo, General Diaz, had fought with distinction in Libya, and had subsequently served on the staff of General Cadorna. He had been a successful divisional commander and then a corps commander on the Carso. In June 1917, during discussions prior to the appointment of General Giardino as Minister of War, Diaz had been mentioned as a possible candidate.[12] Hence his appointment as Comando Supremo was not as surprising as is suggested by Gatti's contemporary comment in his diary "Diaz? . . . Who knows him?"[13] He had, however, a very different personality from Cadorna.

Diaz took up his duties on 9 November and was soon given some light on the quality of the staff work available at the Comando Supremo. One of his first actions was to send Fonogramma N.5468 to the 1st and 4th Armies suggesting that they should continue to hold the line on Monte Caldiera, to the east of Monte Ortigara (Map 3). The command of the 1st Army replied that this was not possible as the previous order to withdraw had already been carried out.[14]

Cadorna had worked with a very small staff and General Caviglia has described a lack of trust between the command and the troops arising principally because of "operational orders which produced grave losses without tangible results". In addition, "almost all the staff officers had never commanded units on the Carso or the Isonzo and had no first hand experience of the war", and when their orders did not produce success they blamed the failings on the troops.[15] However, the Government had already taken measures to strengthen the staff of the Comando Supremo. The sub-chief, General Porro, who had made a very bad impression at the Rapallo Conference (Section 2.4) was subsequently replaced by two sub-chiefs, General Badoglio and General Giardino, previously the War Minister.

Badoglio had played a distinguished part in the capture of Monte Sabotino near Gorizia in 1916, and by 1917 was the youngest corps commander in the Italian Army. Nevertheless, he was fortunate to obtain his new appointment, as his XXVII Corps had performed disastrously on 24 October. However, this was not revealed until the subsequent Commission of Enquiry into the defeat of Caporetto. But by the time the Commission's report was published the war had been won, Badoglio was a national hero, and thirteen pages of the report were excised before publication.[16] Badoglio was thus set on his military career which, though not entirely successful, was to dominate the Italian Army for almost the next twenty-five years.

The arrival of the new team of Diaz, Badoglio and Giardino soon produced a considerable effect. Colonel Gatti had been much concerned at the dismissal of Cadorna, but the entry in his diary on 20 November reads, "Things are now much changed. There is something freer in the working of the command. The work done by General Giardino is enormous. Badoglio is reorganizing and visiting the troops. General Diaz takes decisions tranquilly and unperturbed. Calm and confidence has returned."[17]

Besides the immediate task of holding the new line, the new command also turned its attention to various deficiencies of the Italian Army hitherto unaddressed. For example, an order on 11 December to all army commanders stressed the importance of defending positions in depth, and not siting most of the troops in a single front line with insufficient troops to man rear defence points and to mount counter-attacks.[18] The same order continued by stressing the need for the infantry defences to be closely coordinated with the artillery support. Later in December the Comando Supremo sent all divisions copies of a memorandum by General Fayolle, now commanding the French troops in Italy, setting out the latest views from the Western Front on the holding and manning of a trench line.[19]

Diaz was also concerned that not only were troops too concentrated in the front line, but were left there for too long. At the end of December he stressed the need for periodic reliefs of troops before they became worn out, and the need to desist from using the best and the specialist troops for longer and excessive spells in the front line. Emphasizing this point the order continued that "The tendency to leave in the line certain units such as batteries, machine-gun companies, and technical detachments, on the specious pretext that they are indispensable, must be eliminated . . . [such action] may appear to be the easier course, but it is nevertheless a dereliction of duty, and defeats our one and only object – the maintenance, at any cost, in its entirety of the material and morale of the Army."[20]

Before and during the Battle of Caporetto brigades and battalions had been passed feverishly from one division to another to meet various crises as they arose, moves which had too often proved ineffective. Therefore Diaz had now to stress the importance of the division as the basic tactical unit, which could only be successful if all its component units were trained to work together with each other as a coherent whole. Moreover, for the same reason, reliefs should be organized by withdrawing complete divisions and should be carried out as swiftly as possible.[21]

Diaz also turned his attention to two other matters vital for the welfare of the troops and the *esprit de corps* of units, food and leave. During the war difficulties on the farms and in the importation of food had led to a noticeable reduction in the soldiers' rations. However, a decree of 18 December stated that the level of rations was to be restored to rather more than the level at the start of the war.[22] In addition, stores were to be set up near the front where troops could buy food, drinks and other necessities. Eventually the entitlement to leave was increased above the annual fifteen-day winter leave by an additional ten-day leave.[23] Also, and perhaps more importantly, it was laid down that all troops were to receive their entitlement of leave regularly and without any suspension except in quite exceptional circumstances.[24]

As in all the warring armies, it had been difficult to find suitable officers to command the hundreds of thousands called up for service. On 27 June 1917, Gatti had confided to his diary that some corps commanders had only been lieutenant-colonels at the start of the war and still had the minds of lieutenant-colonels.[25] Inevitably, as in other armies, senior Italian officers from lieutenant-colonels to generals, 669 in all, including four army commanders, had been judged inadequate and removed from their commands. However, because of lack of time and understanding, many of those dismissed were judged very hardly and went away bitter against Cadorna. Indeed the number of dismissals was sufficient to create a feeling of "What I do does not matter much. It's always wrong. We are fired whatever we do." As one General later told the Commission of Enquiry, "It was a well known principle. Enemy trenches not taken or trenches lost, dismiss a commander of a brigade or a division."[26]

Diaz adopted a different and more pragmatic approach. In a memorandum written twelve days after his appointment he said, "severe measures should not be too hastily taken against a man who goes wrong either through inexperience or because an initially sound idea does not meet with success, or for some other reason which well-disposed examination may show not to be too culpable".[27] Also, he noted that "frequently the substituted man is worth no more than the man who has been dismissed", and stressed that he would only support dismissals after other means of correction had failed. Then in January 1918 he established a commission to review previous dismissals. In 206 cases involving brigadiers, major-generals and lieutenant-generals the commission exonerated ninety-five, and in 669 cases involving all ranks down to lieutenant-colonel, 262 were exonerated.[28]

2. On the Piave

From 11 November onwards the enemy armies renewed their attacks between Asiago and the sea. We now outline the form of these attacks and their outcome in each of the three main sectors, beginning with the attempts to cross the Piave. More detailed accounts are given in the IOH and by Pieropan.

Below Pederobba the valley of the Piave opens out into the Venetian plain, and the waters of the river meander in several channels across a wide bed of stony gravel, which between Pederobba and Vidor is sometimes over a thousand yards wide. At Vidor the river narrows as it cuts through low foothills on either side, but soon spreads out again in several channels on a gravel bed up to two miles wide. Below Vidor the right bank of the river comes hard against the side of a prominent and isolated hill known as the Montello (368m) which forces the Piave to flow in an easterly direction until the foothills finally end at Nervesa (Map 2).

All the way for the 30 miles or so between Vidor and Ponte di Piave the river meanders in several relatively narrow channels along its shingle bed which varies in width from 1000 to as much as 4000 yards. Rough tracks down to the shingle bed are used by lorries carting away stones and gravel, and much of this bed is covered by low scrub. Seen from the hills on the edge of the plain on a fine day, the Piave like the Tagliamento is a most characteristic sight quite unlike any British river. The river also responds very rapidly to the heavy storms of rain which come in from the Adriatic and its waters then spread all across the shingle bed.

Below Nervesa the Piave emerges into an almost totally flat plain and is confined between artificial embankments up to five or six metres high to contain the flood waters. In dry seasons these embankments may appear remote from the river, but at any time they form a good foundation for a system of defence, particularly with machine gun posts near the crest and in tunnels cut through the base. On either side of the river the ground is traversed by minor streams and canals, often with containing dykes which made any enemy advance very difficult, particularly as it was possible to flood certain areas without flooding adjacent areas. On the other hand the land was heavily cultivated with crops of high corn and numerous orchards. The roads were hidden by the bushes and trees at their side, and the fields divided by high hedges and rows of trees, making it difficult for the defenders to obtain adequate views and adequate fields of fire.

The enemy made various attempts to cross the Piave between 10 and 16 November. The 12th German Division of the XIVth Army tried to cross at Vidor and near San Vito, west of Valdobbiadene, and the 13th Austrian Division near Mina south of Valdobbiadene, but all failed as their artillery was still insufficient to deal with the Italian machine guns and artillery.

Lower down the river the Austrian IInd Isonzo Army captured the island of Papadopoli in the widest part of the Piave, but failed to reach the far bank. Further downstream, a dawn crossing surrounded an Italian garrison of 400 men and two field batteries near Fagare, but three counter-attacks forced the Austrians to retreat, leaving 500 prisoners.[29] However, four miles further downstream the Austrians gained a foothold across the river near Zenson and held out against Italian counter-attacks which were beaten back by machine-gun and artillery fire from the opposite bank.[30]

Below Ponte di Piave, the Piave flows in a single channel perhaps one or two hundred yards wide. Below San Dona di Piave it passes through very flat ground intersected by many drainage channels making movement difficult, and the ten miles or so of front from San Dona to the sea were held by only one division on either side.[31] Yet on 13 November Austrian attacks forced the Italians back about three miles from the Piave to its former course the Old Piave. The Austrians were now close to the edge of the Venetian Lagoon, but this whole area of waters, islands and marshes was organized as the Piazza Marittima di Venezia, a marine fortress with guns of all calibres, on mobile barges and on shore, together with defence lines, trenches and barricades.[32] Hence the Italians were able to maintain their position on the line of the Old Piave for the rest of the year.

During December the general situation all along the Piave front remained unchanged, despite considerable patrol and artillery activity and attempts to effect local improvements in the line, particularly against the enemy bridgehead at Zenson which was finally retaken on 1 January.[33] Hence, at the end of the year the Italians still held the whole

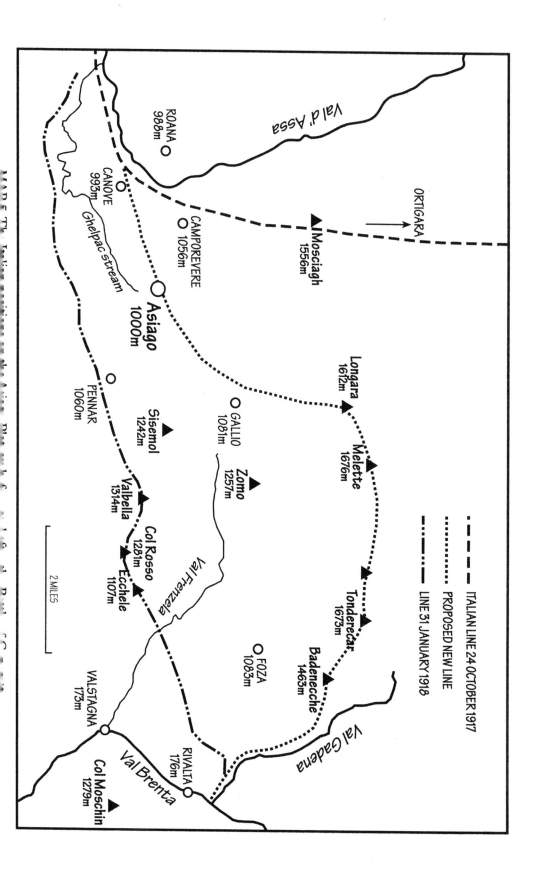

MAP 5. The Italian position on the Asiago Plateau before Conrad's offensive of 15 June 1918.

Legend:
- – – – ITALIAN LINE 24 OCTOBER 1917
- ·········· PROPOSED NEW LINE
- –··–··– LINE 31 JANUARY 1918

ROANA 988m
CANOVE 993m
Ghelpac stream
CAMPOREVERE 1056m
Asiago 1000m
PENNAR 1060m
Sisemol 1242m
GALLIO 1081m
Zomo 1257m
Valbella 1314m
Col Rosso 1281m
Ecchele 1107m
Val Frenzela
FOZA 1083m
VALSTAGNA 173m
RIVALTA 176m
Col Moschin 1279m
Val Brenta
Val Gadena
Badenecche 1463m
Tonderecar 1673m
Melette 1676m
Longara 1612m
Mosciagh 1556m
ORTIGARA
Val d'Assa

2 MILES

line of the Piave, except that they had been forced back from the Piave to the Old Piave, and here they were in strong positions, even if uncomfortably near to Venice.

3. At Asiago

The small town of Asiago (Map 3) stands near the centre of a plateau which extends from east to west for about six miles, and from north to south for about three miles, at an altitude of about 1000 metres. The plateau is fairly level or gently undulating, and cultivated and interspersed with several small villages. To the north and south the ground rises and is rough and rocky underfoot and given over to forestry.

The plateau is bounded to the west and to the east by the deeply cut valleys of Val d'Astico and Val Brenta, the ground falling steeply to both these valleys. From the northern edge of the plateau wooded hills rise steadily first to altitudes of up to 1500 metres about three miles from the town, and then after a further six miles of mainly wooded terrain to the bare summits around Monte Ortigara (2106m). Here the relatively accessible mountain ground extending back towards Asiago ends abruptly above the northern cliffs of Ortigara and its neighbours which plunge steeply down into Val Sugana, the upper part of Val Brenta, some 1500 metres below.

South of the town of Asiago, the ground is fairly level for a mile or so, and then rises over rough terrain mainly covered with pine woods to summits at altitudes of up to 1500 metres, standing four or five miles south of the town and about 500 metres above the plateau. To the south of these summits, the ground falls steeply to the plain but in no way as precipitously as the drop from Ortigara to Val Sugana. One must also remember that before the war the whole region was much more isolated than today, many of the present roads being litle more than mule tracks.

The withdrawal of the 4th Army involved the right of the 1st Army on the Asiago plateau moving back a considerable distance, not much troubled by the Austrians, to a line running from Asiago across the summit of Monte Melette (1676m) to the south side of Val Gadena (Map 5). The line then ran down this deeply incised valley to cross the Brenta river near Rivalta and join up with the 4th Army line on Col Moschin in the Monte Grappa massif (Map 4).

The Commander of the XXII Italian Corps thought that these positions could be firmly held, but General Peccori-Giraldi in command of the Italian 1st Army was not so sure, and on 8 November asked the Comando Supremo for reinforcements of men and guns.[34] Diaz replied the next day stating that four brigades would be sent, that they would be of young men of the Class of 1899, and that maximum care should be taken over their food, quarters and health. No extra guns were available.[35] The following day the Austrians began a series of attacks on the new Italian positions which led to fighting on a considerable scale for the next two months.

The Austrians began their offensive on 10 November along the front between the town of Asiago and Val Brenta, with the initial aim of wiping out the Italian salient jutting out to Monte Melette. In the first stage of the battle, from 10 to 14 November, the Austrians forced the Italians back somewhat on the west side of the salient, and on 22 November launched a substantial attack on Monte Melette which was repulsed with such heavy losses that the offensive was temporarily suspended.[36]

A further heavy Austrian attack on 4 and 5 December inflicted very severe losses on the Italian 29th Division, and the Italians were forced to withdraw to new positions on the lower hills along the foot of the salient. Then from 23 to 25 December the Austrians attacked again and took Monte Valbella, Col Rosso and Col d'Ecchele, but this action marked the end of the Austrian offensive at Asiago. The three hills were retaken by the Italians between 27 and 31 January and the line then remained unchanged for the rest of the winter.

The losses on both sides had been considerable During November the Austrians had suffered 23,000 casualties (dead, wounded, missing and ill). On 4 and 5 December, during the Austrian attack on Melette, the 29th Italian Division lost 539 officers and 14,236 men (including perhaps 11,000 taken prisoner). The overall figures for the losses are less certain but were probably of the order of 30,000 on each side.[37]

4.   On Monte Grappa

The principal summits of the Grappa massif (Map 4) stand only two or three miles beyond the edge of the plain, which here runs along a line from Bassano to Pederobba, a distance of about 12 miles (Map 3). The heights of these summits range from about 1000 to 1775 metres. The lower slopes of the hills are wooded, but higher up they become open and grassy. They formed a lonely area giving summer pasture for sheep, goats and cows, traversed by some few mule tracks and paths. The long high ridges between the summits are generally broad and grassy, but occasionally interrupted by rock cliffs. On its west side the massif is separated from the Asiago Plateau by the steep sided valley of the Brenta; to the east it is cut off from the steep and mountainous group of Monte Cesen by the valley of the Piave River, which hereabouts is generally confined in a single channel.

The view from the summit of Monte Grappa (1775m) on a clear day is extensive and splendid. The ground drops steeply to the plain which lies all before one, scarred by the great stony bed of the Piave, and stretching away to Venice, the Adriatic and the Apennines. Turning one's back on the plain the view is totally different. Long ridges run out northwards from the summit ridge, dropping slowly over a distance of seven miles or so to end at Monte Roncone (1164m) and Monte Tomatico (1594m), which overlook the road from Fonzaso to Feltre. To the north-west the mountain is bounded by the dark cleft of the Brenta valley, while to the north stands a backdrop of innumerable Dolomite peaks.

Monte Grappa and its outliers formed a strategic bastion. Besides linking the Piave and Asiago fronts, the high ridges provided gun positions which could dominate the surrounding country in all directions. Therefore after the Austrian offensive in 1916, Cadorna had commissioned the construction of a good military road from Bassano to the summit up the southern slopes of the mountain. This was now complete and the principal route of access, and two major cableways had been installed for the transport of supplies. Quite extensive defence positions had been prepared high up,[38] but most faced north-west rather than north-east, and further defence works had been ordered by Cadorna on 27 October.[39]

On 12 November the Austro-German XIVth Army had reached the line of the Feltre – Fonzaso road but had still to occupy the key points on the summmit ridge of the Grappa range by advancing along the spurs and valleys sloping up from the road. Progress was soon held up by the Italian forward defences including those on Monte Roncone and Monte Tomatico, and it was not until 18 November that an attack was launched on the main defence line near the summmits. The fighting continued all day against sustained and effective resistance. By nightfall it was clear that all the attacks had failed with heavy casualties. Von Below noted in his diary that "the enemy is defending himself with extreme determination despite the excellent action of our artillery"[40]. Krafft makes various suggestions to explain the lack of success. There was no surprise, the enemy knew we were coming. The Austrians had difficulty in bringing forward their artillery, as well as their food, water and ammunition. The Italians were deploying their best troops. The Italians were encouraged by the presence of the French and British in Italy, and were now confident that they could hold the line of the Piave and Grappa.[41]

After regrouping, the XIVth Army launched another general attack on 22 November all along the Grappa front, and for the next four or five days some of the best troops in the Austrian and German armies sought to fight their way up the steep slopes and high spurs leading to the summit ridges. At the end of 26 November the XIVth Army had little to show for its efforts. The only gain was a foothold along a length of the summit ridge of Monte Tomba, but the troops there were contained by the Italian line somewhat below the ridge, and subject to artillery fire from higher positions.

There was now a prolonged pause while preparations were made for a further assault by the 4th Austrian Division, the 200th Jäger and 5th German Divisions. Meanwhile the conditions for both sides, living and fighting at altitudes up to 1500m and more, were harsh and became steadily worse with the approach of winter. The troops found themselves occupying bare summits with only light tents as protection against the weather. Moreover, hard rock often only inches below the surface made it very difficult to improvise even minimal trenches at short notice, and on occasion "individual machine gun and rifle nests were small depressions on the steep, bare slopes and offered little cover".[42]

The XIVth Army renewed its attack from 11 to 17 December but the Italian 4th Army resisted strenuously. Some ground was gained at the cost of heavy casualties, but the enemy had not much improved his tactical positions. Moreover, on 7 and 9 December the temperature in the mountains had fallen to minus 20 and minus 27 degrees, and eventually on 17 December von Below ordered all operations to cease. The fighting on Grappa was now almost over for the year with the Italians still holding positions along or near the summit ridges, but one successful counter-attack was yet to come.

At the beginning of December French mountain troops, the 46th Division Chasseurs Alpins, took over the Italian line below the ridge of Monte Tomba. Then on 30 December three battalions of the Chasseurs launched an attack to regain possession of the 2500 metres or so of the ridge of Tomba lost on 22 November. The French were holding inferior positions on the south facing slope of Tomba somewhat below the summit ridge, while the Austrians were in good positions above. But this disadvantage was offset by careful planning and the deployment of some 500 guns of various calibres (including some Italian units) which had been brought up very discreetly.

After five hours of artillery preparation the three battalions launched their assault at 14.05. According to the French Official History the 51st Battalion on the right reached its objectives in a few minutes; the 115th battalion in the centre made equally good progress; the 70th battalion on the left obtained its objective despite having to traverse an artillery barrage. By 14.30 complete success had been obtained, for the Austrians made no attempt to retake the ground. Their losses had been severe: 500 dead in the abandoned positions, 1546 prisoners, eight guns, six mortars, and sixty-three machine guns. The French losses were given as fifty-four dead, 205 wounded.[43]

The cemeteries on Grappa, at Bassano and Feltre record the burial of about 19,000 Italian soldiers, and the casualty figures for 1918 suggest that about half these soldiers died in 1917. With this number of dead one might expect perhaps 20,000 wounded, and Krafft and von Below refer to the capture of about 12,000 prisoners. Hence the losses of the seven

Italian divisions principally involved were probably of the order of 40,000. The enemy losses are less clear but the Austrian Official History refers to Austrian losses in the XIVth Army of about 16,000 (dead, wounded and missing), and to probably similar German losses, in all about 30,000 most of which would have been on Grappa.[44]

5.   The Offensive Abandoned

Throughout November several factors weighed on the command of the Austro-German XIVth Army. The Army's supply lines had been greatly extended and much effort was needed to maintain roads and bridges, and to avoid delay in bringing up supplies and ammunition. The troops had now been fighting for four weeks and were becoming tired. The onset of winter would soon make conditions impossibly severe on the high ground of Asiago and on Grappa. Both von Below's diary and Krafft's account show a growing preoccupation with the presence of French and British troops in Italy. On 11 November von Below noted that the far bank of the Piave was now strongly defended and was supported by good French guns.[45] On 15 November it was thought that the Allied presence would amount to three British and twelve or fifteen French divisions, constituted from some of the best assault troops in both armies.[46] On 18 November artillery fire falling on a XIVth Army attack on Monte Tomba was apparently sufficiently troublesome that it was thought (incorrectly) to be either French or British.[47]

On 21 November von Below wrote in his diary that the XIVth Army offensive had come to a dead end, in that any further advances beyond the Piave would now be slow with heavy losses.[48] He laments that the Austrians had not known of the Italian defence preparations on Grappa, and fears that left to themselves the Austrians would "melt as summer snow" before an Allied attack. However, he thought it still very necessary to stabilize the present positions by obtaining complete control of the Grappa massif.

On 22 November the Emperor Karl, who had succeeded the old Franz Joseph in November 1916, temporarily suspended the Austrian offensive at Asiago to avoid further loss of life. Then on 24 November he sought to persuade von Below to end all the fighting immediately, including that on Grappa, but without success.[49] However, von Below was becoming increasingly concerned at the slow progress of the Austrians, particularly on Grappa and at Asiago. Both he and Krafft were increasingly disenchanted with the performance of their Austrian allies, both in the XIVth Army and in the Austrian Armies on either side of the XIVth, and on 26 November von Below sent one of his staff officers to talk with the Bavarian Minister of War.

On 27 November von Below's diary recorded increasing concern

47

over the slow build up of his ammunition supplies, due he suspected to their being diverted to the Austrian forces attacking at Asiago.[50] Progress everywhere was now very slow, and on 28 November von Below was informed by the German High Command that sixteen Franco-British divisions had arrived in Italy.[51] Hence he was forced to conclude that the situation had now changed to his disadvantage and on 29 November suggested to the Austrian High Command that the XIVth Army offensive be temporarily halted.[52]

On the same day (29 November) the German High Command sent a telegram to the Austrian High Command expressing views similar to von Below's, and on the evening of 2 December von Below received orders that the offensive be suspended.[53] However, at the insistence of von Below, it was stated that the XIVth Army should continue to improve its positions in the mountains, and to give the impression that the offensive was still continuing.[54] Hence the final run down of the offensive was marked by considerable renewed activity during the second part of December both at Asiago and on Grappa.

Meanwhile the Germans prepared to leave and on 3 December their 5th, 12th and 26th Divisions were withdrawn from the front.[55] Then on 14 December the German High Command decided that all their forces would be withdrawn from Italy.[56] By the end of the year it was clear that the Italian army had held fast and that the line of the Piave remained secure.

6.   The French and British Forces

The meeting between Foch, Wilson and Diaz on 11 November had agreed that the French and British forces should concentrate in an area around Vicenza and we now describe the subsequent movements of these troops. After the conference at Rapallo (5 to 7 November) orders had been sent to General Haig in France that General Plumer, then commanding the 2nd Army on the Western front was to take command of all the British forces in Italy. Plumer left the 2nd Army on 9 November and next day attended a conference with Haig and Robertson, where the CIGS laid down that his task was to make every effort to save Italy from further invasion. He was to regard himself as an independent commander but was to cooperate with and conform to the wishes of the Italian Commander in Chief in respect to the disposition and employment of his troops and to give all assistance in his power. On the other hand if he were asked to carry out an operation which he thought might unduly endanger the safety of his troops, he was to make representations first to the Italian Command and then if necessary to the War Office in London.[57]

Plumer decided to take his principal staff officers with him and left for

Paris, where on 11 November he saw Lloyd George and the French Prime Minister, Painlevé. He then went on to Mantua where he arrived on 13 November and took over command from Cavan. The next day he had a meeting with Generals Diaz, Foch, Weygand and Wilson, and confirmed the previous decision of 11 November that the 23rd and 41st Divisions would move to the Vicenza area as soon as the Comando Supremo could give road and billeting facilities (not it was thought until 19 November at the earliest). Also on 14 November Plumer sent his first report home, giving an assessment of the situation, and recommending that two more divisions and a cavalry brigade be sent out to give further support[58] (a recommendation reluctantly accepted by Robertson because Plumer had already made his views known to the Italians[59]).

Foch, reporting to Paris the following day 15 November, stated that the situation on the Italian front was apparently improving and that morale seemed to be getting generally better. He was also considering how best to use the French and British forces, and the next day produced a memorandum[60] suggesting that the French should take over the sector west of Asiago town and the British the adjoining sector from Asiago to Val Brenta. Besides the French and British troops, the suggested commands would include a rather greater number of Italian troops who would be used in the higher positions in the mountains for which the French and British were not sufficiently equipped. An advantage of having a majority of Italian troops in the two commands would be that "the will to hold fast might be spread through the largest possible number". This scheme was put forward by Plumer to Diaz who politely declined, saying that the difficulties of supplying the French and British troops in the hills in winter, albeit in the foothills, would be very great.[61]

There were by now clear signs that the enemy was being held, and on 19 November the head of the British Military Mission, Delme-Radcliffe, gave encouraging reports on the state of the 3rd and 4th Armies.[62] However, Diaz was still worried and on 18 November the Italian General Staff sent Foch a series of documents setting out possible arrangements for the eventuality of a retreat either to the Adige or to the Mincio. Foch refused to contemplate any such eventuality, and notes that two or three days later during heavy fighting in the region of Asiago, Grappa and Monte Tomba "the Italian soldiers put up a splendid resistance everywhere".[63]

Meanwhile on 22 November, a conference between Diaz, Foch and Plumer had agreed that the French and British troops were now in sufficient strength to relieve the Italians in the right hand sector of the 4th Army front between Monte Tomba and Nervesa. Although fighting was still continuing at Asiago and on Grappa, there was a general agreement that the most critical period of the battle was now over, and on 23 November Foch felt able to return to France.

On 23 November Cavan issued the British Expeditionary Force Operational Order No.1 for the occupation of a British sector on the Montello and Piave between Crocetta and Nervesa. The 23rd and 41st Divisions, which had detrained in Italy between 11 and 23 November,relieved the 30th and 1st Italian Divisions between 30 November and 4 December, and on 4 December Cavan took over the command of the sector. The British 7th Division came up behind to act as a reserve a few days later. The British 48th and 5th Divisions were completely detrained by 1 December and 17 December respectively, and took up reserve positions behind the Italian 1st and 4th Armies. On 3 December the French 47th and 65th Divisions began to relieve the Italian Divisions on the left of the British, the 47th Division from Monte Tomba to the Piave at Pederroba, and the 65th Division on the Piave from Pederroba to Crocetta (Map 6).

Although at the end of November the general situation had appeared much improved, on 4 December the Austrians delivered a heavy attack on the Monte Melette area on the Asiago plateau which resulted in the near annihilation of the Italian 29th Division. On 6 December General Fayolle, now the senior French officer in Italy, wrote to the War Minister and French GHQ saying that he thought that attacks on the Piave and in Val d'Astico were imminent. He was doubtful whether the Italian forces could hold because they had few reserves, were now fatigued, *"et manque de confiance de haut commandement qui envisage toujours retrait"* (and lack the confidence of the high command which always thinks in terms of retreat). Therefore Fayolle recommended the sending of two more French divisions in addition to the six already in Italy, and that the British should hasten the despatch of the last of their promised six divisions.[64]

The next day, 7 December, the French and British commanders, Fayolle and Plumer, conferred on how best to make use of their forces to prevent any further enemy incursions, either from Asiago, from Grappa, or across the Piave. Their plan proposed that, while maintaining the positions on the Piave, a strong reserve force should be created to block the exits of the Astico and Brenta valleys from the mountains, and to protect the flanks of the French and British communications to the Piave. To this end it was suggested that in the event of any break-through, the French and British forces should be used in two Groups under the commands of General Plumer and General Duchêne.[65]

The right hand Group under Plumer would consist of the XXXIst French corps (47th and 65th Divisions) and the XIVth British corps (23rd and 41st Divisions) already in line on the Piave between the Italian 4th and Italian 3rd Armies, together with a reserve consisting of the 7th British Division and an Italian corps. The left-hand Group under Duchêne would consist of the XIIth French corps (23rd, 24th and 46th

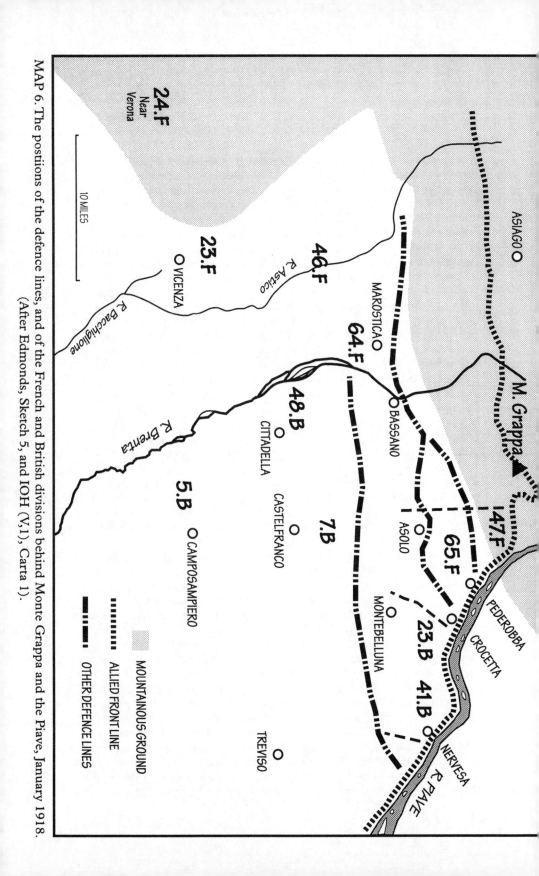

MAP 6. The positions of the defence lines, and of the French and British divisions behind Monte Grappa and the Piave, January 1918. (After Edmonds, Sketch 5, and IOH (V,1), Carta 1).

24.F Near Verona

10 MILES

23.F
○ VICENZA

R. Astico

46.F

R. Bacchiglione

MAROSTICA ○

64.F

R. Brenta

48.B
CITTADELLA ○

5.B
○ CAMPOSAMPIERO

CASTELFRANCO ○

7.B

BASSANO ○

ASOLO ○

65.F

23.B

MONTEBELLUNA ○

TREVISO ○

ASIAGO ○

M. Grappa

47.F

PEDEROBBA

CROCETTA

41.B

NERVESA

R. PIAVE

MOUNTAINOUS GROUND

········· ALLIED FRONT LINE

▬·▬·▬ OTHER DEFENCE LINES

Divisions) and the XIth British corps (48th British and 64th French Divisions), with the newly arrived British 5th Division and one Italian corps as reserves. These latter French and British units were currently further back on the plain behind the Italian 1st and 4th Armies: the four French divisions near Verona, Vicenza, Thiene and Marostica, and the two British divisions near Bassano and Vicenza. Thus the two Groups would form a strong reserve force behind the troops at Asiago, Grappa and the Piave, and a guard to cover Verona and the Adige valley.

Fayolle and Plumer presented their plan to Diaz on 8 December. He accepted their plan, noting that it was only tactical and not administrative, and that it was only to take effect at a time decided by the Comando Supremo. Diaz also asked if the French and British units could operate in the mountains and was told that this was impractical without special clothing and equipment which could not be provided in time.

Plumer saw Diaz again the next day, 9 December and found him in a somewhat gloomy mood. He was concerned that the line on Grappa might not hold, but assured Plumer that the Italian Army would continue to fight even if it had to retreat to Sicily. There was talk also of retiring towards Rome and taking up positions on a narrow front across the peninsula. Plumer responded by saying that he was placing his divisions in the angle between the Piave and the mountains and that so long as they could hold these positions there could be no reason why the troops on either side should retreat further.[66] According to a subsequent account by Cavan,[67] Diaz then said, "If I retire from the Piave you cannot stay on the Montello". And Plumer had replied, "If I stay on the Montello you cannot retire". Nothing further seems to have been heard of this particular proposal of retirement.

At the beginning of December there were six French and five British divisions in Italy, and a final British division still to arrive. However, following the German counter-attack at the Battle of Cambrai, the despatch of the last British division (the 21st) to Italy was cancelled. Moreover, on 10 December Foch replied to Fayolle's request sent on 8 December by saying that no further French divisions were available. In fact in a few days the situation improved and these extra troops were not needed.

During December, while the Austro-German attacks continued on the Asiago and Grappa fronts, French and British commanders with the collaboration of the Comando Supremo were drawing up a system of defensive lines on the edge of the plain[68] ready to meet any enemy irruption. Map 6 shows the principal line, later known as the *linea inglese*, running from Val d'Astico via Bassano to Pederobba, backed by a second line about four miles to the rear from Bassano to the Piave. Responsibility for the general layout of the line was assigned to Major-General Glubb, Plumer's chief engineer, and the construction work was carried out by working parties from the French and British reserve divisions and from some Italian units. Finally, in addition to this work, Diaz ordered the construction of a third line running west from the Piave about four miles from Nervesa. By the end of December good progress had been made on these lines. It was then decided that, should the 4th Army be forced to retreat from Grappa, the sector of the new line from Bassano to Pederobba would be commanded by Plumer, with the left of the front held by some of the retiring troops, and the right by the 65th French and the 7th British Divisions who would be ready to launch a counter-attack as soon as possible.

When the French and British troops took up positions on the Piave and the Montello at the beginning of December it had been expected that they would soon be attacked from across the river. Not only did this section of the Piave offer various possibilities for such attacks, as were made by the Austrians in their offensive in June 1918, but the opposite bank of the river was held by the German and Austrian troops of the formidable XIVth Army. In fact, no enemy assault was made in this sector, so the French and British troops were mainly engaged in no more than sporadic patrol and artillery actions. The only occasion in 1917 when the French and British were engaged in any substantial combat was on 30 December when the French made their small-scale but brilliant attack to retake Monte Tomba. In addition, the arrival of some French and British fighter squadrons behind the Piave had helped to regain air superiority which had been lost during the retreat because of the loss of Italian airfields and the presence of German fighter aircraft.

Although few of the British and French forces had been engaged in active combat, the Allied expeditions had played a not insignificant part in the Arrestamento. After their heavy losses at Caporetto the Italians were at full stretch to man their front line and had virtually no efficient troops in reserve to deal with any further breakthrough. This situation contrasted starkly with that in 1916 when the Austrian offensive in the Trentino reached the south edge of the Asiago plateau and threatened to debouch on to the Italian plain. At that time General Cadorna had been able to assemble a reserve army of 179,000 men on the plain ready to meet any incursion (Section 1.2). The position at the beginning of November had been very different. The 4th and 3rd Armies were efficient and were holding the line, but they were very tired and knew that behind them there was virtually no reserve force. However, by 5 November the 64th and 65th French Divisions had both completely detrained in Italy, and two more divisions, the French 47th and 46th, were about to commence detraining, to be followed by the British.

As early as 27 October the British Military Mission in Italy had reported to London that the Italian General Staff were "very anxious that there should be announced even small contingents of French and British troops on their way in order to encourage country and army".[69] In fact there are several references in the various accounts to the strikingly smart and cheerful appearance of the British troops as they marched from the trains through the towns and villages of northern Italy.[70] Their appearance no doubt made all the more striking in contrast with the often dejected picture presented by columns of the retreating Italians. The very presence of these troops was a direct boost to morale both civil and military and a direct assurance of military support. It was an assurance whose significance was not lost on General von Below and General Krafft, and had been one of the principal factors determining their decision to suspend the Austro-German offensive.

The British Forces in Italy

1. On the Piave

As described in the previous chapter, the French and British troops were
first deployed in the front line along the Piave between Pederobba and
Nervesa. The first British divisions, the 23rd and the 41st, took over the
section of the line between Crocetta and Nervesa, mostly near the foot
of the Montello. This hill, about 6 miles long and 3 miles wide, dominates
the level plain in every direction. The moderately steep sides rise to an
undulating plateau standing about 150 metres above the plain, the
whole area being a typical form of karst landscape. The ground is everywhere extremely broken and covered with trees, undergrowth and
heather. The surface area of the plateau is broken by the so-called *dolini*,
irregular depressions originally produced by water erosion, which may
be up to 10 metres deep or even more.

At the Crocetta end of the sector the ground by the Piave is quite flat,
but about a mile downstream the hill of the Montello drops down to the
river. At this point the road from Crocetta to Nervesa rises and runs
through woods at a height of about 40 metres above the river, dropping
back to the level of the river just before Nervesa. Today much of the
area of the front line is neither readily accessible nor readily visible.
The line ran low down close to the river with a good view over the
shingle bed, between 300 to 2000 yards wide, towards the enemy on
the other side. The river itself flows in comparatively narrow channels
except in flood conditions when it spreads out over its bed.

There are several British accounts of the units occupying sites on
the Montello.[1] Private Gladden describes the front line as a deep
trench dug out of the river bank, well made with fire steps and bays,
but with shelters roofed over only with light branches.[2] About a
hundred yards or so behind was a row of support posts, often consisting of houses on the river bank in full view of the enemy a mile or so
away, a strange sight for the troops from the Western Front, the only
obvious precaution being boards across the windows to prevent showing a light at night. Captain Pickford states that his battalion of the
Oxfordshire and Buckinghamshire Light Infantry "were holding a cliff

250ft high by a line of defence posts pushed out on the foreshore of the river".[3]

Most of the first few weeks was spent in improving the line of defences left by the Italian divisions who themselves had only been on the ground from the beginning of November. The front line was strengthened by improving and wiring the existing trenches and particularly by the construction of shellproof strongpoints and emplacements for machine guns and trench mortars as used in France. In addition, to give as much depth as possible to the positions, two reserve lines were dug by the infantry, one along the edge of the Montello plateau overlooking the river and the other parallel to it along the middle of the plateau.

The artillery soon found that there were no obvious sites for gun positions. Both the banks of the river and the forward slope of the Montello provided few possibilities for either concealment or for protection from enemy fire. The best positions for the 18-pounders were found in the numerous dolini on the summit plateau where they might be concealed by screens of branches. There was also the difficulty that because the river was some 150 metres below, care had to be taken that the trajectories of the guns cleared the edge of the summit plateau.[4]

When the first British divisions took over at the beginning of December it was expected that the enemy would soon make an attempt to cross the Piave. However, for most of the time the front was fairly quiet, with only two episodes worthy of mention by Edmonds. On 8 December there was fierce shelling as the 12th German Division fired off all its surplus ammunition across the river before returning to Germany, and on 11 December strong enemy artillery fire on the flanks of the Montello suggested that an attack was imminent. The British artillery then searched the locality where the Austrians were reported to be massing, and no attack materialized.[5]

The troops found their new posting a welcome change from the battlefields of Flanders and Passchendaele where most of them had been engaged only a month or so earlier. In fact the casualties (killed and wounded) for the two divisions in the front line up to 31 December were no more than 121 in the 23rd Division and 158 in the 41st Division. The weather was often fine and sunny and Gladden writes of the magnificent view from the front line trenches of mountain and river, and of the clear days after rain when the mountains capped with snow stood out against the deep blue sky, "a sight that took my breath away". Even so the nights were very cold and fuel everywhere was very short.

Heavy snow in the mountains by the middle of January ruled out the possibility of any enemy offensive operations, so on 14 January Plumer and Fayolle suggested changes in the deployment of their forces. In consultation with Diaz it was agreed that the British 5th and 48th Divisions should also take up positions on the Piave, subject to the proviso that the Fayolle-Plumer plan could be revived at short notice if necessary. Therefore on 22 January the 5th Division, which had completely detrained by 17 December and was now billeted near Cittadella, marched to the Arcade sector on the right of the Montello sector, and by 27 January had completed the relief of the Italian 48th and 58th Divisions. At the same time the 48th Division moved from near the Brenta to an area west of Treviso to act as a reserve for the other divisions.[6]

Although the period from January to mid March was a dormant time for both sides the British continued to indicate their presence by periodic shelling, by patrols to the islands in the bed of the river, and by building some twenty footbridges to some of the islands of shingle between the channels. Edmonds quotes the Austrian Official History as saying that these activities prevented the Austrians from refurbishing their defences and giving their troops a much-needed rest. As a result some of the German divisions about to leave Italy for the Western Front were detained as reserves on the Tagliamento, and were not gone completely until mid-March.[7]

The work of the patrols was particularly arduous. Their task was to make their way under cover of darkness across the bed of the river in order to locate any enemy outposts and perhaps to bring back prisoners. Much depended on the state of the Piave. Gladden describes how he took part in a fifteen-man patrol on the night of 8 January when the river was flowing strongly. Setting off across shingle covered with snow, the patrol came to the first small stream and waded through a torrent of icy water no more than a foot deep, but enough to take away all feeling from Gladden's legs. Moving on through the scrub, they crossed some smaller streams, surrounded all the time by the roar of unseen waters. Then came a bigger stream, perhaps thirty yards wide, and they began to wade across. Towards the middle the water was nearly waist deep. They pressed on to find the water moving faster under the far bank, and several including Gladden were swept off their feet, fortunately towards the bank.

They continued to advance under a starlit sky, hoping that the noise of their boots on the shingle would not alert any enemy sentry, and hearing all the time the steadily increaing roar of the water in the main stream ahead. Here the water was running at such a rate that it was quite impassable. Retracing their steps, the patrol paused for thought at the thirty yard stream and moved across by linking hands to form a continuous chain, and thus were able to hold together and get across safely. With their clothes soaked with icy water, numbed and exhausted, they stumbled back to their lines to find hot baths, helpers, clean clothes, warm blankets and tots of rum. "With the morning we awoke refreshed and none the worse for our adventure."[8] On later occasions, with less flow on the river, other patrols succeeded in forcing their way across the main stream, but sometimes found themselves so cold that they would hardly have been able to use their weapons had they encountered an enemy. Edmonds describes a perhaps more practical method where the patrol was hauled across in boats by men stripped and well rubbed with oil.[9]

All depended on the mood of the Piave. Gladden describes how a spell of fine weather was broken by a fierce storm, typical of north-east Italy, which raged from 1 to 4 March, drenching the troops and swamping the shelters. The dirty, turbulent, ugly waters of the river rushed and broke over the shingle beds carrying a detritus of trees and branches and all sorts of broken material, accompanied by the noise and roar of the force of the water on the shingle. Next day the water was still rising and the river bed becoming a vast, growing expanse of water. On the far side the Austrians could be seen hurriedly vacating positions on the shore too low down to maintain now that the river had come into its own.

The same flood affected a projected operation involving the 5th Division. At the beginning of February the Italian 3rd Army was planning an attack near the coast from their line on the Old Piave to regain the line of the main Piave lost during the Battle of the Arrestamento. To aid this operation the British had agreed to send a force across the Piave in their sector in order to seize and hold a bridgehead for 48 hours before returning, so as to divert attention and attract the enemy's reserves. A plan was drawn up for one brigade of the 5th Division to force the river in two places, across the wrecked railway bridge at Ponte di Priula, and at a point below Nervesa, using both boats and bridge-building. At the same time another brigade was to make a dummy attack on the right, perhaps sending across a battalion-strength raid. However, the state of the Piave left the Italians no choice but to abandon the whole operation.[10]

2.　Allied Plans for 1918

At the start of 1918 General Fayolle was considering plans for later in the year when the weather improved and the snow melted in the mountains. On 1 February he sent a memorandum to Foch[11] in Paris suggesting an offensive which would strike northwards from the Asiago plateau in the general direction of Trent, with the initial objective of cutting the important strategic railway which ran from Trent through Val Sugana and Val Brenta to Primolano (Map 3). This operation would be carried out by three groups: on the right, five British and two Italian divisions commanded by General Plumer making for Primolano by Val Brenta; in the centre four French and six Italian divisions under the French General Maistre (soon to succeed Fayolle) making for

Caldonazzo by Val d'Astico (Map 1); and on the left, two French and six Italian divisions under an Italian general moving up the Adige valley towards Rovereto south of Trent, twenty-five divisions in all.

Fayolle's memorandum said surprisingly little about how the proposed advances were to be made, other than to move up the valleys mentioned (which were served by railways and good roads). Nowhere was there any comment that these valleys were dominated by substantial forts and by the surrounding mountains. However, the Italians had always been concerned that the Austrians were dangerously near the southern edge of the Asiago plateau, and were eager to force them back. On receiving Fayolle's plan, Diaz accepted the proposed area for an attack in the spring, but decided that the offensive should be entrusted to a newly formed Italian 6th Army under General Montuori composed of two Italian corps reinforced by a French corps and a British corps.[12]

On 21 February Plumer's Chief of Staff, General Harington, conferred with Diaz's senior deputy, General Badoglio who set out the necessary rearrangements preparatory to the offensive.[13] The new 6th Army would take over the whole of the front between Val d'Astico at the western edge of the Asiago plateau, and Col Moschin on the western edge of the Grappa massif overlooking Val Brenta on the left of the 4th Army. The attack would be delivered across the whole width of this 6th Army front, and it was suggested that the French and British divisions on the Piave should move to Asiago during the second half of March, and build up stores and ammunition for the offensive at the beginning of May. On 28 February General Diaz met General Plumer and General Maistre and they decided that the French and British should go to Asiago as soon as possible. However, these plans were soon to be modified by events remote from Italy.

Since the end of October information reaching Paris and London from various sources indicated that the Germans were transferring forces to the Western Front following the collapse of Russia. It appeared that "10 and probably 15 divisions" had already been transferred from the east to the west, as well as selected drafts totalling about 80,000 officers and men. On 4 January information reached London from "a high neutral source" that Germany intended to play her last card, a formidable offensive in France. On 7 January the British Intelligence Summary reported the impression that the whole Austro-German offensive on the Italian Front had been suspended and that all the German troops were being withdrawn, apparently to the Western Front. On 19 January the General Staff in London asked GHQ in France how quickly the divisions in Italy could be brought back to France if need be, and for calculations on the times of the rail journeys which would be involved.[14]

Since the end of 1917 the British Government had been seriously concerned with the mounting manpower losses suffered by the Allies. The enormous French losses during the first two years of the war and the British losses on the Somme and at Passchendaele had drawn heavily on allied reserves. The United States, with its immense resources, had entered the war in April 1917, but at the start of 1918 its total strength in France was no more than 175,000.[15] Therefore both Robertson and Haig, always committed to the overriding importance of the Western Front, were increasingly anxious to maintain the strength of those armies and looked very critically at the number of British and French troops tied up in Italy.

As early as 10 November 1917 Lord Cavan, in a report to the War Office, had referred to motoring many hundreds of miles through Lombardy and Venetia, and seeing "enormous numbers of men of military age in civilian clothes with apparently no particular business".[16] Robertson, also, believed that Italy had plenty of men, and in a letter to Plumer dated 26 November mentioned a British proposal that 100,000 to 150,000 Italian men should be sent to our Armies in France for labour purposes.[17] This suggestion eventually bore fruit and by the end of March some 70,000 Italian soldiers no longer subject to service in the fighting line were in France as pioneers working on the defence lines,[18] thus setting free other Allied troops.

During a discussion of the manpower situation at a meeting of the War Cabinet on 15 February, Robertson read reports from Foch saying that the Germans were gaining numerical superiority in France, while the Allied forces still had superiority in Italy. Foch therefore suggested the return of two British and then two French divisions and announced that General Fayolle had already been recalled to France. Robertson himself recommended that two divisions should return, but that it should be arranged via the Allied Executive War Board which had the responsibility for the general reserves. This recommendation was then considered.[19]

The War Minister, Lord Derby, agreed that the divisions should return, but also added that the British and French Governments were quite entitled to bring them back irrespective of the views of the Allied Executive War Board and should do so. However, as was soon pointed out, this approach would hardly encourage current discussions in the War Board to persuade Italy to send Italian divisions to the Western Front. Hence, after further consideration, it was suggested that Italy should be informed that, unless four Italian divisions were sent to France, Britain would be compelled to withdraw two British divisions from Italy. However, the point was then made that Haig might prefer two British to four Italian divisions.

The War Cabinet decided to consult Haig and then, either forgetting or ignoring the role of the Allied Executive War Board, decided that, should Haig prefer two British divisions, the CIGS should send orders to Plumer, and inform the Foreign Office who would at once notify the Italian Government. Haig replied on 15 February saying that he preferred two British divisions. Therefore on 18 February Plumer was ordered to send two divisions to France and the next day he received orders to arrange to hand over his command to Cavan and return to France. However, the matter was not so quickly settled, for when Plumer informed Diaz of these changes Diaz said that he had heard nothing about them from his own government and that until he did he was unable to take any action or provide any transport facilities.[20]

On 21 February the War Cabinet discussed a communication from Prime Minister Orlando pointing out that the coming peace with Rumania would release more Austrian troops for the Italian Front, and expressing surprise that the decision to recall the British divisions had not followed the procedure laid down by the Supreme War Council, namely that such decisions were to be taken via the Allied Executive War Board. On 22 February General Wilson, who had now replaced Robertson as CIGS, told the War Cabinet that a message from Plumer dated 21 February said that Diaz was rather perturbed. Wilson explained that he (Wilson) had sent a telegram of apology to the Italian War Minister, Alfieri, saying that the two divisions would form part of the Allied general reserve in France. Wilson had thought that this information would satisfy Diaz and therefore had sent no letter to him.[21]

On 1 March General Smuts gave the War Cabinet an account of his recent meeting with Sonnino, the Italian Foreign Minister, in Rome. Sonnino was "strongly dissatisfied" and took the line that if Italy was to be kept in the war the removal of British divisions was not the best way to achieve this purpose.[22] The Cabinet was also told that Foch admitted that the transfer of the troops had been decided by him personally because the Executive War Board was not yet in action, and that the Italians had not been consulted. As the return of the 41st Division was due to start that day the Cabinet allowed the move to go ahead, but the question of the second British division and of the Italian divisions for France was passed to the War Board at Versailles and the Italian Government was so informed. Finally on 10 March, at Haig's insistence, Plumer returned to the 2nd Army and handed over his command of the British forces to General Cavan.

Meanwhile in Italy on 28 February Diaz, Plumer and General Maistre meeting to prepare the Asiago offensive, had accepted a request from Foch that the decision to launch the attack would depend on the scale of the expected German offensive in France.[23] During March it became increasingly likely that further French and British divisions would be required in France, but nothing had been decided before the Germans launched their Michael Offensive, the great attack on the Western Front. Then on 21 March the German Army overwhelmed the British 5th Army in France and after a week had penetrated to depths of up to 40 miles.

At a meeting of the War Cabinet on 22 March General Wilson reported a telegram from General Rawlinson, the British Military Representative at the Supreme War Council. This said that he, Foch and Bliss, the American Military Representative, had come to the conclusion that the time had come to transfer two French, a further British, and two Italian divisions to France. General Giardino, the Italian Military Representative, thought that the two Italian divisions should go immediately but that the position of the others should be considered later. However, Clemenceau, who had now replaced Painlevé as the Prime Minister of France, advised the despatch of all five divisions and the War Cabinet agreed.[24] The French 46th and 64th Divisions began entraining on 25 March, another French Division, the 65th, on 26 March, and the British 5th Division on 5 April.

The preparations for the offensive at Asiago continued but on a somewhat reduced scale. The objective was still the line of the railway from Trent to Primolano via Val Sugana, but two intermediate objectives were given. The operation was now to be conducted by three corps of the 6th Army under General Montuori: on the left, the British XIV Corps with three British and two Italian divisions; in the centre, the French XII Corps with two French and three Italian divisions; on the right, the Italian XX Corps with six Italian divisions; in all sixteen divisions as against the twenty-five proposed in the earlier plan.[25]

To put these arrangements into effect the French XII Corps began to take over part of the line at Asiago on 24 March, and the British 23rd Division (Major-General Sir James Babington) and the 7th Division (Major-General T.H. Shoubridge) took over from Italian units between 26 and 31 March. Finally on 2 April the British 48th Division (Major-General Sir Robert Fanshawe) which was to act as the reserve for the British Corps moved to an area west of Vicenza. Here they were joined by the British heavy artillery in Italy which had moved up from the Piave.[26]

To complete these rearrangements the Italian II Corps under the command of General Albrici and consisting of the 3rd and 8th Italian Divisions arrived in France between 18 and 27 April.[27] Here the Corps played a full part in defeating the German drive to the Marne in July 1918 at a cost of about 11,000 dead and wounded. Then, after incorporating fresh drafts from the pioneers already in France, the Corps took part in the crossing of the Aisne and the occupation of the Chemin des Dames in September and October 1918. Over 4000 of its troops remain buried in France mainly in the military cemeteries at Bligny and Soupir.[28]

3. Cooperation between Allies

Relationships between allies are often influenced by old friendships and rivalries. Britain, with no common frontier with Italy, had been entirely supportive of the movements which had achieved the unification of Italy in the previous century. On the other hand Italians still remembered that as early as 1849 French troops had put down Garibaldi's Roman Republic, and then remained in Rome for the next twenty years. Since the time of Napoleon there was always some apprehension that French visitors might return home with some form of treasure, land or otherwise, and as recently as 1870 France had taken Nice from Savoy. However, despite old memories and recent rivalries in North Africa, Cadorna's appeal for help in October 1917 received a rapid response from France, followed shortly after by a similar response from Britain. Yet decisions on how the French and British troops were to be employed soon produced differences of opinion which called for negotiation and understanding in a position not made easier by Italian embarrassment at having to ask for help.

Difficulties became apparent during Foch's first meeting with Cadorna at Treviso on 30 October (Section 2.2) which began with a private conversation between the two generals alone. The only account of this initial talk is that given by Cadorna, according to which Cadorna stung by Foch's attitude was forced to some very plain speaking, but "from that moment he ceased to give me his unsolicited advice".[29] The next day the conversations continued, together with General Robertson who had just arrived. Some progress was made but Gatti's entries in his diary recording the impressions gained at mealtimes showed little sign of much rapport. (The diary describes Robertson as "a sort of English peasant"[30] at a time when Robertson was writing to Haig in France that "A more disgraceful sight than the returning Italians, without arms & equipment, was never seen".[31])

A further potential difficulty arose because during 1917 both Foch and Pétain (the French Commander in Chief) had come to feel the need for a unified allied command on the Western Front, each no doubt seeing himself as the ideal C.in C. In addition, by the beginning of October the French Government and High Command were increasingly concerned with the course of the war, and with the possibility that German troops released from the Russian front might mount new attacks, perhaps in Lorraine, in Alsace, or even through Switzerland. Hence the French High Command was greatly concerned at the first news of the breakthrough at Caporetto.

Some light on French preoccupations is given by the entry for 26 October in the diary of Colonel Herbillon, a staff officer at French GHQ who acted as the liaison officer to the Government. This recommended urgent action to counter any German thrust towards France's eastern frontier. It stated that up to thirty divisions might be needed in Italy to contain a German thrust, and that the essential point for successful operations would be one unified command of all French, British and Italian forces, and that the overall commander should be a French general who would be "free of any territorial prejudices".[32]

In fact General Foch had gone to Italy in a purely advisory capacity as the senior allied general (Section 2.2), and there was no further mention of sending thirty divisions, nor of a French general in charge of the Italian Army. (General Pershing, the American C.in C. then in Paris, heard of the latter proposal and later commented in his memoirs "that no such change was necessary or even remotely possible".[33]) However, when Foch returned to France on 23 November his place as C.in C. of all the French forces in Italy was taken by General Fayolle, an Army Group commander on the Western Front. Then on 27 November Fayolle wrote to the French Government suggesting that the British forces should come under his command.[34] This suggestion did not find favour with Robertson who stated that it had already been decided that General Plumer should command the British forces, that Plumer had already been given orde establishing an independent command, and in any case he was too brilliant a commander to serve in a subordinate capacity.[35]

General Plumer was soon to find himself involved in continuing French efforts to obtain a unified command. Colonel Herbillon quotes a letter of 24 November, obviously from someone close to Fayolle, which argued for a single Franco-British command under Fayolle, as a first step to persuade the Italians to follow the British example in accepting a French general.[36] However, according to Faldella,[37] after Plumer had agreed with Foch on 22 November that British troops should take up positions on the Montello, he asked Diaz on 24 November that two available British divisions be sent to the Montello, but did not receive a reply. This, again according to Faldella, was because essential questions regarding the chain of command were still unclear. Therefore on 26 November Plumer asked to be given "orders" for the British divisions to enter the line, and "orders" were then issued by Diaz. Faldella comments that Fayolle could not do less than follow Plumer's example, "albeit with gritted teeth", and in fact Diaz issued orders to Fayolle on 29 November[38].

At the time of his appointment to Italy General Sir Herbert Plumer was commanding the British 2nd Army on the Western Front. This notable officer, later Field Marshal Lord Plumer, engaged in no controversy, wrote no books, and left no papers. The only biography written between the wars, by his Chief of Staff, Major-General Harington, is so laudatory as to create a suspicion of undue bias. Indeed Harington states in his preface that he aims to avoid "one unkind word of either the living or the dead". For a more complete and critical account see the biography by Powell.

Plumer was painted by Sargent[39] and Orpen[40]. In Sargent's huge picture of General Staff Officers of the First World War, Plumer stands out as the striking central figure immediately on Haig's right, with puffy rosy red cheeks, slightly protuberant eyes, and a great white walrus moustache. Even an admirer of Plumer, such as Cruttwell, comments on his "comic music hall appearance",[41] and it seems likely that Plumer was the inspiration for one of David Low's most famous cartoon characters, Colonel Blimp, the prototype of a vacuous British officer.[42] Yet nothing could have been further from the reality.

Plumer had a wide experience as a corps and army commander on the Western Front. His Second Army was renowned for the quality of its staff work with its attention to completeness and detail. The capture of the Messines Ridges on 7 June 1917 was "one of the most complete local victories of the war",[43] and a siege-war masterpiece.[44] General Harington has emphazised how Plumer impressed on his staff "that we were nothing but servants of the troops", and that no order was to be issued "without considering how it would be received by the regimental officer and soldier".[45] Harington also describes how "every Corps and Divisional Headquarters and most Brigade Headquarters were visited almost daily by either the Chief himself or by one of his team and always with the object of ascertaining if there was anything we could do to help".[46] A young liaison officer was attached to each corps to know every battalion and to spend at least two nights a week in the front line trenches.

By his methods and personality Plumer gained the confidence of his troops to a quite unusual extent. Lieut.-Colonel Barnett of the 48th Division wrote that Plumer "had the rare and wonderful gift of inspiring confidence and devotion in the troops under his command".[47] Private Gladden wrote that Plumer's "great popularity with the troops was rooted in their feeling that this strict old aristocrat had a genuine sympathy for the men in the ranks, on whom people in his position had so often to call to perform the impossible".[48]

Plumer had not welcomed his posting to Italy. He regretted leaving the Second Army, and had thought that "from a military point of view only it was a mistake to send British troops to Italy".[49] However, after arriving in Italy and seeing the situation for himself, his first report home on 14 November had recommended that the four British divisions due to arrive during the second half of November should be augmented by a further two divisions and a cavalry brigade (Section 3.6).

When Plumer made his recommendation the Italians were holding the line of the Piave, but he feared that any further enemy pressure might force another withdrawal. The troops in the front line were very tired, and had been led to expect that they would be relieved by the Allies in a few days. Enemy aircraft were dropping leaflets over the front line saying that the Allied troops had come to Italy to live off the land but not to do any fighting.[50] Hence it was evident to Plumer "that if the Piave line was to be held, the British troops must go into the front line as soon as possible".[51] Nevertheless, he was also aware of the need to maintain a strong reserve force to counter any enemy penetrations. Hence his request for enough troops to give effective relief at the front while maintaining a sufficient reserve to deal with an enemy incursion.

When the British divisions took over from the Italians on the Montello they found only one defensive line, close to the river, and set about digging two more lines higher up on the plateau, as well as improving the construction of the defence posts on the front line. Plumer was well aware, in the words of one of his staff officers, that the tactics of both the Austrian and Italian armies "were years behind those of the German, French and British armies",[52] but he was equally aware that advice must be offered with consideration.

When opportunity arose, Plumer invited Diaz to inspect the British troops saying, "what would really please [the troops] . . . and give them confidence would be a visit of inspection from the Allied Commander in Chief, General Diaz". Diaz naturally agreed and the 23rd and 41st Divisions were told to "work night and day to prepare the very best defences the world had ever seen". Thus when Diaz arrived he was extremely impressed as Plumer took him round apologizing for his inability to do better in the time available. Soon after, the British divisions observed adjacent Italian units digging in places hitherto undisturbed.[53]

At the end of the year the positions at the front had been largely stabilized, as described by Fayolle on 26 December[54] and Plumer on 20 January[55] in their assessments of the military situation to their military superiors. Both the French and British Commands were much concerned by the low standards of training in the Italian Army and by the handling of the troops by the higher commands. According to Plumer, "By far the greater proportion of the rank and file of the infantry is excellent material, and the spirit and morale of the majority of the battalions is good, notwithstanding the very trying and strenuous time many have experienced." But they lacked training and "as in the other branches of the Army the Brigades and Battalions are very much behindhand in higher tactical training". Of the Italian artillery he wrote, "Individual batteries can shoot, and with proper organization they could be made into an effective force. As it is their organization is defective and their application of fire poor, while counter-battery work is hardly carried out at all." Hence both Plumer and Fayolle took the view that until improvements were effected a French and British presence in Italy would be necessary to avoid any danger of a further collapse.

During the first months of 1918 both the French and British units established numerous training schools similar to those behind the Western Front. (Some details of these are given in Edmonds and the French Official Account.[56] Hardie and Allen describe a visit to a British school giving instruction in the use of the efficient British gas masks in conditions of a simulated attack.[57]) At all these courses places were made available for Italian officers as well as for French or British allies. Then in February Fayolle and Foch arranged with the Comando Supremo for some twenty-four French staff officers to serve on the staffs of major Italian units, and in April the Comando Supremo sent twelve Italian majors to work with French staffs.

Useful as these measures were, there was a limit to what could be done. As Fayolle observed,[58] any advice had to be given most tactfully as the Italians were all too ready to take offence. Even when Italian officers attended the French and British schools the results only reached their own units at second hand. In fact most impact was probably made by example, as in the striking French attack on Monte Tomba using coordinated artillery fire, and the details of the defence works set up by the British on the Montello and along the line of the plain from Bassano to the Piave (Section 3.6).

Finally we note that when General Plumer returned to France on 10 March, the Italian Government was sorry to see him go. They had, correctly, seen him as a very supportive ally and indeed had approached the British Government to see whether he could stay longer, fearing also perhaps that his departure might be followed by the withdrawal of some of the British troops. However, the helpful relations established by Plumer were maintained by Lord Cavan who was already on good terms both with General Badoglio,[59] and with General Caviglia commanding the Xth Italian Corps at Asiago, who was a friend from the days before the war when they were both military attachés in Japan.[60]

4. The Asiago Sector

At the end of March the 7th and 23rd Divisions received orders to move from the Piave to the Asiago plateau, where the Allied front line ran from west to east at the foot of the rising ground about a mile south of the town, looking out towards the Austrian positions on and below the hills to the north. This move took them into country very different from that of the Piave and the Montello. The routes from the plain to the plateau climbed up the steep southern escarpment by zigzag roads or tracks of a kind that few of the British troops had seen before. Yet when they reached the rim of the plateau and began to descend the less steep north-facing slopes towards the front line they came to a landscape not greatly different from that in some parts of Britain.

Quite extensive accounts of the Asiago sector and the work of the British divisions are given by Edmonds and by the divisional, regimental and battalion accounts listed in the bibliography. In addition Private Norman Gladden has described his battalion's move to Asiago,[61] particularly the final stages which began with a twenty-mile march through the plain from near Vicenza to the small town of Thiene at the foothills of the mountains. The troops marched down wide dusty roads with the sun shining down and in the distance the snow capped summits of the mountains ahead. Next morning at 06.00 they were off again, loaded with two blankets and a jerkin on top of their normal pack, to a car park about a mile outside the town. From here small but powerful Fiat vans took them up a thousand metres or so to the outer rim of the plateau. At first the road ran through green fields and little hamlets but then began to climb the hillside with innumerable hairpin bends giving an ever-increasing view of the plain spread splendidly below like a map. It was their first experience of a mountain road, carved in the hillside, with formidable drops on one side of the road and little or nothing in the way of protective barriers. Probably all would have agreed whole-heartedly with Gladden that it was "a thrilling ride" and "an unforgettable experience".

As the vans made their way upwards, the mist drifting about the mountain tops came down as if to greet them. Soon a cold dampness blotted out the sun. The mountains, so fine from afar, suddenly lost their appeal. Gladden and his battalion saw patches of snow on the hillside, felt the freezing wind, and realized that charming sunny Italy was now left way behind. They stopped for the night at a desolate clearing in the woods, in huts buried deep in snow. The next morning, with their backs to the great drop to the plain, they marched or slithered along an icy road, threading their way down the undulating wooded terrain to arrive at their positions in the reserve line. It was freezing cold and Gladden remarks that "it was an unfortunate introduction to a new front which was later to prove not quite as unattractive as at the outset".

A somewhat similar journey was experienced by a battalion of the Oxfordshire and Buckinghamshire Light Infantry of the 48th Division when they went up from the plain in mid-April.[62] The road was busy with traffic, so packs were placed in lorries and the battalion marched up one of the mule tracks in single file, at a rate of twenty minutes' climb followed by ten minutes' halt, for the next four and a half hours. All the way to within a few hundred feet of the top they were in bright sunshine. Then abruptly the sun clouded over, cold air arrived as if from nowhere, and a slight drizzle began to fall. They spent the night at Granezza, a level clearing in the forest between masses of rock piled up on either side, perhaps 600 yards long and 300 yards wide. Here was a camp of huts for two battalions of infantry, canteens, a cinema, dumps and all the other paraphernalia of a division in the field.

In the wet atmosphere the huts and trees dripped with water, while a motley collection of muddy soldiers, English, French and Italian, flowed backwards and forwards along the grey sticky road. Captain Wright later commented that a more depressing sight could hardly be imagined. The next day rain in the morning was followed by a full-dress snowstorm with thunder and lightning, a prelude to two or three more days of snow, during which all time and energy were directed to clearing road and tracks. But then the weather improved, at first bright sunshine alternating with violent thunderstorms, and finally the "glorious weather of August and September and October".

The section of the front taken over by the British and French divisions (Map 7, p.94) lay between the Italian X Corps on the left and the Italian XIII Corps on the right. The French XII Corps next to the Italian XIII Corps had a front of about 3000 yards held by two divisions, while the British Corps, further to the left, had a front of about 7500 yards held by three divisions, two in line and one in reserve. In the British sector the main defence line, a deep narrow trench with a high firing step, was sited a little way up the rising ground at the edge of the plateau, and where possible either in or near the edge of the woods. The trench itself was well built, either dug out of the earth or cut out of solid rock, but the associated shelters or dugouts were found to be of poor construction, insufficient in number, and except in a few cases provided little protection against shellfire.

Map 7 also shows various support lines lying up to about 1000 yards behind the front line, sited somewhat higher up the slopes of the hills, and often totally in the woods and cut in the rock. However, these support lines were neither as continuous or so well laid out as the figure suggests. A more complete picture is given by the trench map reproduced by Barnett which shows both trenches and wire, and indicates the variable and sometimes intermittent nature of the support lines (see also Sandilands). There were no communication trenches as they were thought to be unnecessary in wooded ground and of little use on the exposed slopes in front of the woods. In addition Map 7 shows the so-called reserve line about four miles behind the front line on the crest of the hills overlooking the Venetian Plain: (Monte Pau or Gallo (1420m) – Cima di Fonte (1519m) – Monte Corno (1384m).

The British sector was divided into two divisional sectors each with its own road system, the Granezza sector on the right and the Carriola sector on the left. The Granezza sector had a front of about 3500 yards and was served by a good road from the plain to Granezza, which then ran through the woods to the front line, with a lateral road about two miles behind the front leading to Handley Cross in the Carriola sector. Another lateral road lay near the reserve line at the rear.

The front line of the Granezza sector ran from the junction with the French corps on the right along the foot of a subsidiary lateral ridge known as the San Sisto ridge. This section of the line ran just inside the edge of a wood for rather more than a thousand yards and was said to have a rather poor field of fire because of the trees and the broken ground. Emerging from the wood the line continued for a somewhat similar distance across the bare slopes of Monte Kaberlaba (1222m) where it had a good field of fire and good defensive posts. As in the Carriola sector on the left, one of the most striking features of the scene to troops arriving from the Western Front was the distance between the two front lines, with a no-man's-land generally between 1000 and 2000 yards wide.

The Carriola sector, also with a front of about 3500 yards, had a more complicated topography and trench system, and not such a good road to the plain. Unfortunately the available maps of roads and trench systems are not always complete or fully consistent. Starting from the right at the junction with the Granezza sector the front line ran through thick woods for 1500 yards or so. Then, leaving the woods, it crossed open country, facing out across the small Ghelpac stream towards the Austrian line 2000 yards or so away. Finally, in the last 1000 yards of the sector where the Ghelpac stream drops into a deep gorge, the front line was again in trees, close to the ravine and within about 200 yards of the enemy line on its far side.

The left end of the British line was in a strong position behind the Ghelpac gorge, but the front line in the next section, between the gorge and the wood on the right, followed a series of zigzags imposed by the contours reflecting the sharp meanderings of the Ghelpac stream. As a result, some adjacent sections of the line were out of sight of each other, making it difficult or impossible to provide mutual support, as was the British practice. The trenches were also said to be rougher and less comfortable than those in the Granezza sector.

Despite these various reservations the front line of the British sector, like the rest of the Allied line on the plateau, gave reasonable defensive positions with good views over no-man's-land to the Austrian front line and rear areas. There was, however, one grave disadvantage, namely the positions had very little depth. Behind the front line it was a distance of little more than 3 miles to the line of summits, 300 metres or so higher up, which formed the rim of the plateau, and from which the ground dropped steeply to the plain. Hence the possibilities for either retirement or manoeuvre were very restricted. Particularly so, as any retirement of the artillery would soon take them down the steep slope behind the reserve line where they would be unable to support the infantry higher up over the lip of the plateau.

The positioning of the artillery also faced other problems not encountered on the Western Front. The guns were generally on higher ground than the front line and had to fire with lower than normal angles of elevation. Hence it was often necessary to clear trees to permit lower trajectories and then to camouflage the sometimes very obvious gaps in the woods.[63] Subsequently, use was also made of the Italian practice of employing reduced charges and suitably adjusted range tables. In addition, the rocky and broken nature of the ground made it difficult to find suitable platforms for the guns, particularly bearing in mind the need to avoid clearing a way through too many trees. Hence, despite the use of rock drills, the guns of a battery were often sited irregularly, making control more difficult and requiring elaborate concentration and position correction tables.

Like the artillery, the signal service faced new problems when they arrived on the plateau. In particular it was their usual practice to bury their telephone cables as a protection against damage, but it was quite impracticable to bury several miles of cable in ground consisting of hard rock covered, if at all, by only a vestige of soil. Therefore, *faute de mieux*, the lines were slung between the trees in the woods. This was easily done, but as the signallers were well aware, the lines were very vulnerable to artillery fire, as the fall of even one tree could disrupt a line completely. Therefore other methods were vital.

Normal type radio links were used to establish communication between division and brigade.[64] Contact between brigade and battalions was maintained by another type of radio link using the now forgotten system of power buzzers depending on electrodes stuck into the earth. These new methods were backed up by visual signalling stations which were very effective, provided of course there was no cloud or mist on the plateau. Finally there remained the age-old but rather slow system of sending runners.

The supply services were also presented with new problems. All supplies had to be transported from railheads in the plain to the rim of the plateau 1200 metres above, and then distributed to the troops lower down on the north-facing slopes. As in the Piave sector, the standard procedure was for the lorries of the divisional supply columns to bring up supplies to transfer points where they were handed over to the divisional trains of horse transport units.[65]

The system soon ran into difficulties because the standard three-ton lorries of the supply columns were not suitable for the mountain roads. They were too wide to pass safely in many places, and too long and with an insufficient steering lock to negotiate all the many hairpin bends without manoeuvring. Moreover, in hot weather all the British vehicles tended to overheat. During the winter, snow, ice and slippery mud made the roads very difficult for the inexperienced drivers, particularly as going off the road might mean not just ditching but a fall of hundreds of feet. It was also found that the heavy draught horses of the divisional trains were not fitted for this sort of terrain. There was not sufficient grazing, water, or space for them on the plateau, and they suffered severely from the cold.

The supply arrangements eventually employed are described by Lieut.-Colonel Barnett the Quartermaster of the 48th Division which served in both the Carriola and Granezza sectors.[66] The small 30 cwt Fiat lorries used by the Italian army provided the best solution, but these were in short supply and only a limited number could be made available. There were at least four Italian aerial cableways to move supplies in the British sector, but the British had troubles with the machinery, and with loads either falling off or being "lifted off". Moreover, the cableways were usually required for the transport of ammunition. A large part of the supplies appears to have come up in waggons carrying loads of 1600 or 2000 lbs drawn by four or six mules. The distance was too great for the mules to make the return journey in a day, so loads were brought to a halfway station by teams based in the plain and then taken on by teams based on the plateau.

In the Granezza sector there was a good permanent road up from the plain, but in the Carriola sector access was by a less satisfactory war road partly in the adjacent Italian sector. This road had been built near the line of the rack and pinion light railway to Asiago, and the lower section had steep gradients as well as hairpin bends. Therefore some supplies were transferred to the light railway which carried them to the station of Campiello (Map 7) in a narrow valley well above the difficult part of the road and just below the floor of the plateau. Here the loads were transferred to other lorries for distribution to the units. This route was not at all popular, for besides the hassle of transferring the loads, sections of the railway line including the station at Campiello were in range of the Austrian artillery so all movements had to be made at night.

The supply of water also presented problems because the ground was porous, and carried very little surface water above the floor of the plateau. Two or three small pools were used for watering animals but these dried up in summer. Therefore it was necessary to pump water from the River Astico by pipeline to reservoirs, tanks and standpipes on the plateau.

Finally we note that at any time two of the three divisions of the British XIV Corps (the 7th, 23rd and 48th) were maintained on the plateau to hold the front line, while the other was kept in reserve. As there was little space on the rim of the plateau, the reserve division was billeted in the foothills, some miles away and 800 metres lower, near Valdagno north-east of Vicenza.[67] The locations of the three divisions up to the middle of June were as shown below:

From	Carriola	Granezza	Reserve
30 March	7	23	48
23 April	7	48	23
19 May	7	23	48
31 May	48	23	7[68]

5. Preparations

As already described, the plans for an Allied offensive on the Asiago plateau were substantially modified after the start of the German Michael offensive on the Western Front on 21 March, and the subsequent transfer of Allied battalions from Italy to France. Even so, planning for a modified offensive continued, and at the end of March three British divisons had moved to the Asiago area to be part of General Montuori's 6th Army. The 7th and 23rd Divisions took over a section of the front line on the plateau, while the 48th remained in reserve below the plateau in the Valdagno area.

The 7th and 23rd Divisions spent the first three weeks settling down into their new front line, support line and reserve line. Private Gladden recounts how he spent his time: with his Lewis gun in anti-aircraft guard; cleaning up and improving the Italian defence lines; doing work for other services; shifting six inch shells (weighing about one cwt each); practising bayonet fighting and hill climbing, and taking part in exercises in any available clearings in the woods. The weather on the plateau was miserable at first, cold and damp, much worse than on the plain. Gladden describes a visit in April to the divisional baths at the foot of the mountains where the meadows were full of flowers and the sun shone brilliantly. They took their time to walk back, stopping for the night in houses or bivouacs on the hillside. Then during the night a storm broke, with heavy rains and gale-force winds, so a very wet and bedraggled troop arrived back on the plateau to be revived by hot tea and rum.

Meanwhile, in Flanders on 9 April, the Germans launched their offensive against the British First Army. By the second day they had overwhelmed twenty miles of the front to a depth of up to ten miles, and on 12 April Haig issued his famous "backs to the wall" Order of the Day. Also on 12 April, the CIGS (Wilson) telegraphed Cavan expressing doubts about the proposed Asiago offensive because of the now reduced number of French and British divisions, and because of the serious situation on the Western Front.[69] He was also greatly concerned about the great shortage of men. (For the first time, in contradiction to previous pledges, the age limit for front line British troops had been reduced from 19 to 18 years.[70]) Nevertheless, Wilson said that he had no objection to some plan which could be carried out at small cost in order to improve local conditions on the front, if this would permit some economy of men in the future.[71] Otherwise, however, any offensive should be postponed.

Cavan had already come to the opinion that some limited offensive was desirable: to obtain more depth to his position; to anticipate any Austrian offensive; and to raise the morale of the Italian Army. However, before Cavan replied to Wilson he consulted Diaz, who agreed with Wilson on the overriding need to conserve men. Cavan then wrote to Wilson on 15 April saying that the offensive would be postponed, but that the Comando Supremo still intended to attack at Asiago if the Austrians sent strong reinforcements to France or attacked Italy elsewhere.[72]

Also on 15 April Cavan held a conference with his divisional commanders where he issued some somewhat ambiguous instructions. He impressed on them that, though they were not to slacken their efforts as regards preparations for an offensive, those for the defensive would from now onwards have precedence.[73] General Fanshawe (48th Division) later commented that "the competition between "Attack" and "Defence" Plans . . . caused me a great deal of thought at the time as a Divisional Commander as to how best to combine".[74]

There now followed a period of uncertainty during which the troops continued to prepare for both defence and attack as best they could. Since arriving on the plateau the British divisions had made their presence felt by establishing a forward line 500 to 1000 yards beyond the front line, consisting of positions in hollows in the ground covered by loose wire, and also a few hillocks occupied by day as observation posts.[75] Sporadic raids on the enemy trenches every few days continued to harass the Austrians and give valuable experience to a large number of "raw and inexperienced drafts" which had come out from Britain to join the 7th Division.[76]

On 23 April the 48th Division went up to Granezza to take over from the 23rd Division. They arrived in sleet and snow, after which the snow continued incessantly for four days and was then replaced by rain and fog until the sun eventually appeared on 30 April. The winter snow then began to melt, and the division was soon engaged in clearing up the accumulated filth and stench which had been left on the rocky ground either unburied or unburnt.[77]

By 24 April Cavan had come to agree with Diaz that the offensive at Asiago should only be launched if the Austrians sent strong reinforcements to France.[78] However, on 30 April Cavan heard that the French Premier and War Minister, Clemenceau, had ordered General Graziani (the French general now in charge of the French troops in Italy) to press for an offensive at Asiago.[79] Then on 1 May General Montuori told his corps commanders that an Austrian offensive should be considered highly probable, and that the Italian 11th Division would be attached to the British for training.[80]

Cavan was now much concerned by the general atmosphere of uncertainty and indecision, and on 10 May set out his views in a letter to the CIGS.[81] He disagreed with the French view favouring an Asiago offensive, because any local result would not ease the position in France. Cavan also stated that Diaz appeared to agree, although he had hopes of great results from Czech propaganda in Austria, and was anxious to launch an attack if opportunity presented. Cavan's letter ends by saying that he faced two difficulties. (a) His views were different from those of the French commander. (b) His troops were being kept in a state of constant tension. Reliefs were difficult for in this mountainous country with few roads the relief of a division took five days. Moreover, preparations for an offensive conflicted with labour demands for defensive works.

The position became clearer as the threat from the German offensive in Flanders died down. On 7 May Foch wrote to Diaz requesting an offensive.[82] and Diaz replied on 14 May that an offensive at Asiago had now been decided on.[83] Finally, on 16 May, Cavan attended a conference of corps commanders called by General Montuori and was told to be ready to launch an attack by 31 May.[84]

The XIVth Corps under Lord Cavan was to initiate the attack with the 7th and 23rd British Divisions and the attached 11th Italian Division, while the British 48th and the attached Italian 57th and 60th Divisions remained in reserve. The plan was first to gain the enemy positions about 1500 yards ahead on the left and about 300 yards ahead on the right, and then go forward to reach the line Monte Longara – Monte Moschiagh about 3 miles further on (Map 5, p.42). However, on 25 May Cavan wrote to Wilson saying that there were rumours of an impending Austrian attack and ending, "my fear is that dread of an Austrian offensive may paralyse the preparations for our offensive".[85]

On 27 May Cavan wrote again to Wilson saying that he had heard from General Montuori that a Czech deserter had given news, thought to be reliable, of an impending Austrian offensive on the lower Piave.[86] Montuori had also passed on news that ten German divisions were on their way to the Austrian front, although the evidence was not conclusive. Cavan was sceptical, but on the same day sent a second letter telling of some signs of corroborative evidence of the information given by a Czech deserter (an officer).

By 28 May Diaz was sufficiently concerned at the prospect of an Austrian offensive that he wrote to Foch asking him to envisage the situation where the strength of the effort of the Austrian Armies would necessitate sending over new Allied divisions to Italy.[87] On 29 May Cavan wrote to the CIGS that prisoners and documents captured by the Italians indicated that the Austrians were concentrating behind the lower Piave and the Austrian Vth Army facing the Italian 3rd Army had been reinforced by four or five divisions, but there was no confirmation of the presence of German divisions.

Cavan wrote to Wilson again on 3 June saying that reports from prisoners and deserters constantly referred to an approaching Austrian offensive on the lower Piave, and that British air reconnaissance reported an increase in activity on airfields east of the Piave. Meanwhile the Comando Supremo was making plans for a series of minor actions along the front to disturb any enemy preparations. By 10 June it had been agreed that the French would mount an assault on Monte Sisemol on 18 June, and at the same time the British would advance to the southern edge of Val d'Assa.[88]

Next day, 11 June, the position changed again when Lord Cavan attended a conference at the Comando Supremo. Diaz had received reports from an Italian officer, dropped by plane behind the enemy lines, that Austrian troops in position for an attack on the Piave were now marching away from the river, probably either to the Brenta or the Trentino. Diaz took this to indicate, incorrectly as it turned out, that the attack across the lower Piave had been abandoned. He therefore decided to strike at the enemy, while his forces were still on the move, by a French attack at Asiago up the Val di Nos (east of Monte Sisemol) which would then spread out on either side.[89]

The same day at 16.00 Cavan conferred with the French General Graziani, who agreed to the proposed attack provided that his flanks were duly protected. Both generals then went on to a conference at 6th Army HQ where General Montuori suggested that this operation should be extended. He proposed that it start with a British attack across the Ghelpac stream at the same time as a French attack near Monte Sisemol, the objectives being for the British to capture Monte Catz, about 3 miles north of Asiago, and for the French to advance to Bosco di Gallio north of Gallio. These objectives were somewhat similar to those in the plan of 15 May, but in that plan the three British divisions were to have been supported by three attached Italian divisions, and these had already been withdrawn. Hence, Cavan now considered the move impossible, and after "reasoned argument" Montuori agreed that the attack now set for 18 June would be limited to reach the southern edge of Val d'Assa and Monte Sisemol, and this was agreed by the Comando Supremo on 14 June.[90]

During the last few days the French Government and GHQ had continued to press for a full Italian offensive. On 9 June the Germans opened their offensive south of Noyon and Clemenceau asked Foch whether he approved of the Italian inaction. Then on 12 June Foch wrote to Diaz saying that he observed no sign of an Italian attack and that the answer to Austria's uncertain intentions was "to attack with resolution". Foch ended by asking Diaz to let him know as soon as possible "the approximate date at which you think able to launch your offensive operations".[91] However, on 15 June all these discussions and preparations were forestalled by the opening of the main Austrian offensive along all the front from Asiago to the sea.

6. The Air Force

By the end of 1917 the air forces of all the principal powers were playing some significant part in the war. Their principal role was primarily in reconnaissance and for this it was necessary to obtain as much control of the air space as possible. In addition, a considerable fraction of the effort went into bombing strategic and tactical targets, such as bridges, installations, and concentrations of troops. German air power had played an important role at Caporetto by establishing control of the Austro-German air space, which did much to conceal the concentration of troops before the battle. However, this section deals only briefly with the British contribution by the squadrons sent out to assist the British Army and the Italian Air Force. A more detailed account of the British effort is given by Jones.[92]

The Italian Air Force had a difficult time during the retreat from the Isonzo, as it had to abandon virtually all its front-line airfields. Even so, by March 1918 the front-line strength had risen to 450 aircraft, 213 fighters, 250 reconnaissance planes and forty-six bombers. To these numbers the Royal Flying Corps and the French Air Force initially made a notable addition of 138 French and ninety British fighter and reconnaissance planes. Then in April a further 158 Italian aircraft came into action, and eighty French and twenty British planes were able to leave for France.[93]

From April onwards the British force consisted of three squadrons of Sopwith Camel fighters, two squadrons of RE 8 army reconnaissance planes, normally escorted by Camels, and two Balloon Companies. Besides constant day-by-day activity, described in some detail by Jones and Macmillan, the RFC now renamed the RAF, played a significant role during the Austrian June offensive and the battle of Vittorio Veneto. At the time of the Austrian offensive the RAF was operating in support of the British divisions holding part of the Allied line at Asiago. However, when the Austrians delivered their attack on the morning of 15 June the ground was enveloped in rain and mist, and the pilots could do little to help. When the weather became worse in the afternoon the squadrons were diverted to assist the Italians on the Piave front. Here they performed valuable services in bringing back information on the large numbers of Austrians crossing the river, and also by bombing and machine-gunning troops crossing in boats and by pontoon bridges. In all 350 bombs were dropped during the day, reinforcing the attacks made by the Italian airmen, and imposing some delay on the enemy advance. These attacks continued throughout the next day, but then clouds and rain intervened. However, on 23 June when the Austrians were in retreat the whole RAF strength was deployed to reinforce the Italian bombing squadrons, as many as fifty British airplanes being engaged at one time (forty-four Sopwith Camels and six RE 8s).[94]

During the battle of Vittorio Veneto the RAF was in support of the two British divisions on the Piave. No photographs of the enemy sector were available, so despite unfavourable weather conditions, the photographic unit obtained and distributed some 5000 prints in time for the first crossing (Section 8.1). Then, in the closing stages of the battle, the whole force turned its attack on the Austrian columns retreating from the Piave (Section 8.8).

The Austrian Offensive, June 1918

As the Allies continued to lay plans for 1918 the Austrians were making their own preparations for an offensive. We now outline these preparations and the fighting which ensued in June 1918, as set out in the official accounts and by Pieropan[1] and Fiala.[2]

1. The Austrian Plan

In January 1918 the Austrian High Command began to consider how they would deploy their armies in the coming year when they hoped that the signing of a Peace Treaty with Russia would release troops from the Eastern Front. The commanders of the two Austrian Army Groups on the Italian front took rather different views of the situation. Field Marshal Boroevic, in command of the Vth and VIth Armies on the Piave, was cautious, and believed that the best course for Austria was to remain on the defensive and let Germany win the war on the Western Front. However, this was not a realistic possibility. The Austrian High Command was fully aware of Austria's indebtedness to Germany for the very considerable military assistance received during the previous years of the war. No doubt the Austrians also thought that if their troops were not fully employed on the Italian Front they would come under pressure to send units to fight in the West.

The other Army Group Commander was Field Marshal Conrad, now no longer Chief of Staff. His command comprised the Xth Army between the Stelvio Pass and the Adige River, and the XIth Army between the Adige and the Brenta. He was much concerned that the Allies might launch an offensive on the Trentino, and at the end of January urged that all the available resources be concentrated for a general attack at Asiago and on Grappa.

In mid-February while the Austrian High Command was considering the various possibilities, Conrad changed his mind and proposed that there should also be a subsidiary attack across the Piave, provided sufficient troops would first be available to meet his own requirements.[3] Discussions continued during February and March, perhaps encouraged by the hope that the coming German offensive in France would ensure that all the French and British troops in Italy would return to the Western Front. The Austrian plans eventually crystallized into a two-pronged attack, by Conrad at Asiago and Grappa, and by Boroevic across the Piave. Boroevic and Conrad each claimed a full share of the available divisions, so General Arz, the Chief of the Austrian Staff, allotted the available divisions equally between them.[4]

On 21 March Germany launched its Michael offensive against the 3rd and 5th British Armies in France and two days later the Austrian High Command issued orders to Boroevic and Conrad to prepare offensives on the lines indicated above. In addition Conrad was ordered to pre-pare a diversionary subsidiary attack across the Tonale Pass on the western edge of the Trentino (Map 1). At the end of April the Michael offensive had been brought to a halt, and General Ludendorff at German GHQ observed sadly that French and British troops were still in Italy, and that Italy had sent troops to the Western Front.[5] He appealed to Austria for some military action and on 15 June the Austrians launched an offensive from Asiago to the sea, their largest operation yet against Italy.

The resulting battle, known in Italy as the 2nd Battle of the Piave, involved most of the Italian Army. The French and British divisions at Asiago played their part in the action as described in Chapter 6. In this chapter we give only a brief summary of how the fighting progressed along the whole front. We begin by describing the diversionary attack which the Austrians launched at the Tonale Pass on 12 June.

2. Tonale

The road over the Tonale Pass (1183m) provides the best, and least difficult, east-west route through the mountains between the Trentino and Lombardy. In 1915 the frontier between Austria and Italy in this region ran approximately north-south and crossed the road at the summit of the pass. At that time and for many years previously each side maintained various fortifications in the region around the pass to deny any enemy incursion across the frontier.

Although the road on either side of the Pass rises quite steeply to the summit, the summit itself is unusually spacious. For nearly a mile the road is relatively level as it passes through a broad saddle with a flat floor up to a half a mile wide. The ground to the north slopes up to a line of rocky summits which stand 1000m or more higher than the Pass, and run parallel to the road for about three miles on either side of the summit. To the south of the road the ground near the road rises more steeply to the rock ridge of the Monticelli, about 800m above the road and dominating the Pass. Then, beyond and further to the south, the ground continues to rise to the rock and snow peaks at the northern end of the Adamello range (which also run parallel to the road for about three miles on either side of the summit).

Since 1915 both sides had maintained positions both on the Pass and up to the summits on either side. The Austrians held particularly good defence positions on the Monticelli, and the Italians had attempted to displace them by approaching from the glaciers and rock peaks which lay to the south. In particular, a remarkable attack in 1916 across the glaciers by a force of about 4000 alpini had appreciably improved the Italian tactical position.[6] Then in May 1918 the Italians launched a well-prepared attack by five alpini battalions and a group of arditi, and in two days (25,26 May) drove the Austrians off many of their positions on the higher peaks south of the Pass, and off the Monticelli except at the east end.[7]

The Italians then began to prepare for a further assault on the Austrian positions. This was intended to be a diversionary attack which would form part of the projected Allied offensive at Asiago being planned for June. The immediate objective at Tonale was to dislodge the Austrians from the mountains on either side of the road, thus extending Italian control for three miles or so on the Austrian side of the pass. This was quite an ambitious aim in view of the difficult nature of the ground , but the attack was to be delivered by some twenty alpini battalions and an assault battalion.[8] On 12 June the Comando Supremo gave orders that the operation would be launched on 16 June,[9] but events decided otherwise.

Meanwhile, quite independently of the Italian plans, the Austrians had also been planning a major offensive in June (Section 5.1) and this included a diversionary effort at Tonale just before the main attack. This diversionary operation known as Lawine (Avalanche) was to be something of a mirror image of the Italian plan, and was to be carried out by two divisions, the 1st and the 22nd. The aim was the capture of the summits lying north and south of the road on the Italian side of the frontier, and then a descent to Ponte di Legno at the foot of the pass, and on to Val Camonica and Valtellina.[10]

It appears that each side was largely unaware of the activities of the other until the Austrians opened their attack with a heavy artillery bombardment on 12 June. Accounts of the subsequent events are given by the IOH and Viazzi.[11] The bombardment continued during the night of 12/13 June and intensified at 03.30. Then at 05.45 the troops of the Austrian 1st Division began to move up the pass and along the mountain slopes on either side of the road. At first they had some local success in taking Italian outposts, but these were nearly all reversed during the day by Italian counter-attacks well supported by the artillery. Thus by daybreak on 14 June the Austrians still held no more than the east summit of the Monticelli. The attack had failed completely, and was then abandoned.

The Austrians appear to have thought that their two divisions would provide a considerable superiority in numbers, but this was not the case. The 22nd Austrian Division had been kept in reserve lower down the valley, waiting to follow up after an initial breakthrough had been achieved. Only the 1st Division had been engaged, and was opposed by a greater number of units than had been expected. According to Viazzi the Italian losses were 320 dead and wounded, and the corresponding Austrian losses were estimated, "probably with exaggeration", at 2300. The Italians are said to have taken 185 prisoners.[12]

3. Asiago

When the Austrians launched their offensive on 15 June the line at Asiago between the Astico and the Brenta was held by the right of the Italian X Corps, the British XIV Corps, the French XII Corps, and the Italian XIII and XX Corps.[13] During the previous days the French and British forces had been preparing for their limited attack on 18 June. It was not until 13 June that the Italian intellegence services received information, both from a trusted informer and from deserters, that an offensive would almost certainly be launched on the Asiago plateau on the morning of 15 June. Further confirmation was given by the interception of messages from a radio station on Monte Grappa saying that the attack would start at 03.00 on 15 June with a gas bombardment for one hour, followed by three hours of high explosives. The next day, 14 June, Badoglio informed the 6th Army that an attack was very probable, and General Cavan told General Fanshawe and General Babington, in command of the 48th and 23rd Divisions respectively, that the intelligence pointed to an attack on the French and the Italian sector on their right, but not on the British sector, although they might be bombarded with both HE and gas.

The artillery of the 6th Army was commanded by General Segre, an able officer trusted by the Allies, who according to Pieropan had succeeded in the delicate task of coordinating the Italian and Franco-British artillery. On 14 June he was concerned about an order received the previous day from the army commander, General Montuori, saying that the artillery was to begin counter-preparation fire half an hour after the enemy had opened fire.[14] Segre had not yet passed this order on, because if the enemy was going to attack, why should the 6th Army troops wait supinely for half an hour? He eventually talked with Montuori and then at 22.00 gave orders for counter-preparation fire.

Although the IOH gives a lengthy discussion of the direction of the

1. Contemporary view of the summit of Monte Grappa and its ridges looking from the west across Val Brenta. (*Vienna K24431a*)

2. Italian reserve troops on the top of Monte Grappa during an action. (*BL 9084H7*)

3. The Piave viewed from British trenches on the Montello. (*IWM Q26185*)

4. The Asiago plateau from near Monte Sisemol looking north.

5. The southern edge of the Asiago plateau. The Allied lines lay in and below the
lower edge of the woods in the left half of the picture.

6. View from Monte Interotto showing the head of the Assa gorge with the road
bridge just visible.

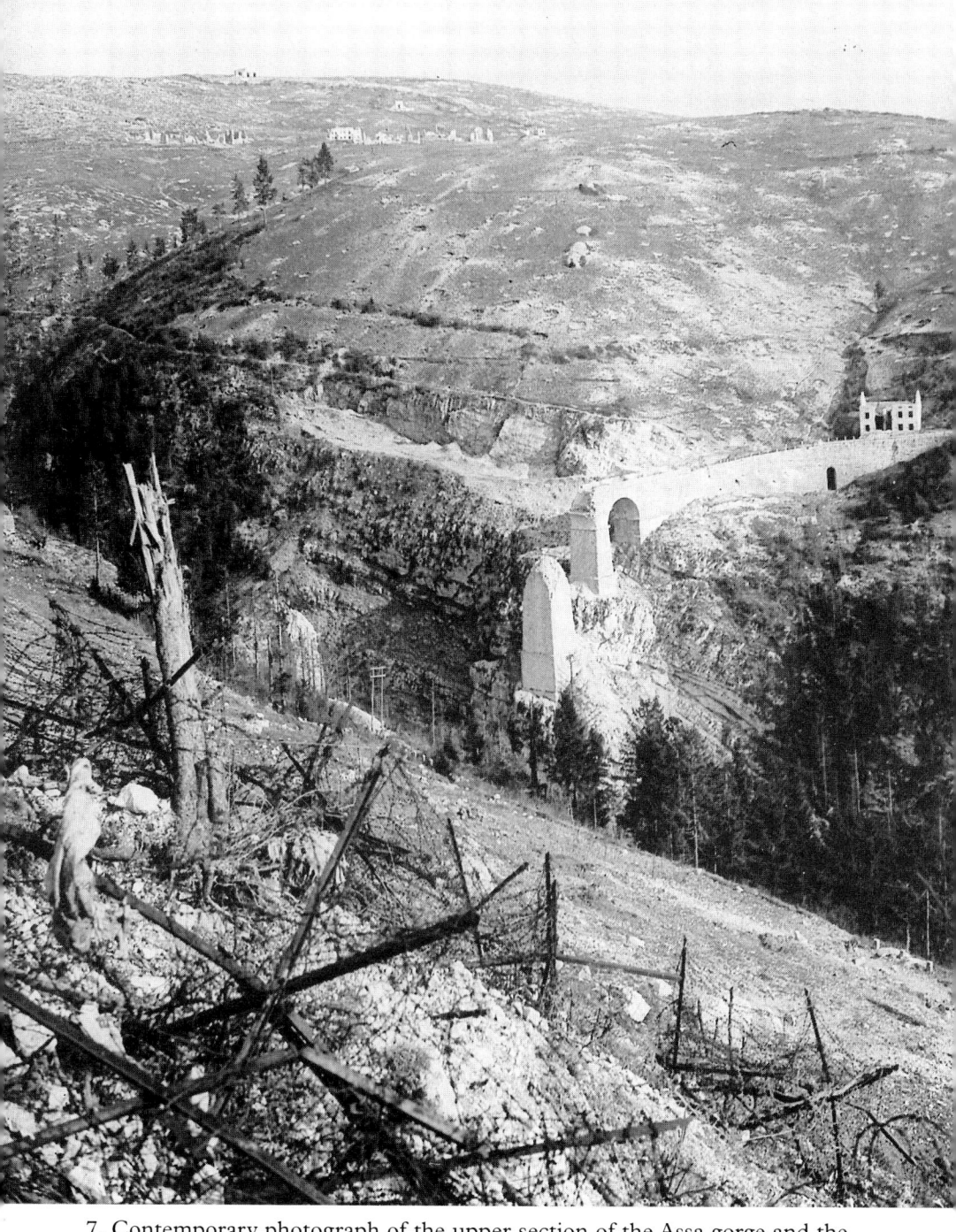

7. Contemporary photograph of the upper section of the Assa gorge and the broken road bridge. (*IWM Q25981*)

8. British troops in the woods at Asiago. (*IWM Q26670*)

9. Rocky ground at Asiago. (*IWM Q26671*)

10. In the woods near Asiago. (*IWM Q25994*)

11. A flood-retaining embankment on the Piave, with firing positions on the left. (*IWM Q26393*)

12. A Piave boat. (*IWM Q26394*)

13. A captured Austrian dug-out on the Piave. (*IWM Q26391*)

14. Construction of a trestle bridge at the end of a pontoon bridge on the Piave. (*IWM Q26695*)

15. View of a similar completed bridge on the Piave, with prisoners returning. (*IWM Q26704*)

artillery and the subsequent polemics,[15] it remains difficult to obtain a detailed picture of the actions of the artillery. It appears however, that following General Segre's orders, the 67th Group of heavy artillery directly under his command began a violent counter-preparation fire at 23.25 on likely regions of concentration and assembly, and were soon joined by the 2nd and 3rd units of heavy artillery tactically dependent upon the French XIIth and the Italian XXth Corps.[16] On the other hand, references to the guns of the British XIV Corps mention only counter-battery work between 23.00 and 24.00, and between 02.00 and 03.00.[17] Eventually the Austrian bombardment began at 03.00, and was then followed by a general response including British counter-preparation fire at 03.20. Finally, between 06.00 and 08.00 the Austrian infantry began their attack all along the front.

The most westerly attack, that on the British XIV Corps produced a pocket a mile wide and up to 700 yards deep in the front of the 48th Division. This ground was partially recovered by 14.00, and totally recovered by 08.15 the next day. The XII French Corps was also strongly attacked, but here the Austrians made no progress at all and suffered heavy losses. Further details are given in the next chapter.

To the east of the French Corps the Italian XIII Corps was holding the line Pennar – Col Rosso – Col d'Ecchele – Val Frenzela (Map 5). This line was strongly assailed and, despite two counter-attacks in the afternoon, the line east of Pennar was forced back, and by the end of the day the Austrians had advanced up to a mile beyond the line Valbella – Col d'Ecchele. After fierce fighting the next day, the Italians retook some ground towards Col Rosso, and then further ground on 18 June. On 24 June the Italians regained the crest of Monte Valbella but could not hold it, but on 29 and 30 June, aided by French batteries and a French detachment as a flank guard, they repossessed all the positions lost on 15 June. Meanwhile the XXth Italian Corps, in positions astride the valley of the Brenta, held firm at Rivalta in spite of enemy attempts aiming at Col Moschin.

Both sides suffered considerable casualties, particularly the Austrians. The losses on the Allied side for the period 15 to 24 June are given as

	Missing	Dead	Wounded
Italian	21	1690	2722
French	96	481	15
British	270	1124	365

giving a total Allied figure of 7,184.[18] The Austrian figure is less certain, but Pieropan[19] quotes a figure of 30,181 (dead, wounded and missing). The final outcome was very clear. In spite of heavy losses the Austrians had made no gains whatsoever.

4. Grappa

The Austrians aimed to secure control of the whole Grappa massif by occupying the line of summits, Asolone – Monte Grappa – Tomba (Map 4). As already mentioned, the Allied positions at Asiago had a weakness in that there were only three miles of ground for a possible retirement between the front line and the edge of the plateau. However, on Grappa much of the line along the summits from Col Moschin to Monfenera was immediately above the plain. Therefore the Austrians had hopes of pushing the Italians right off the mountain.

The Italian line on Grappa was held by the 4th Army, now under General Giardino, and was divided into four sectors. On the left IX Corps with two divisions held the line from Val Brenta to Asolone; VI Corps with two divisions from Asolone to Monte Grappa; XVIII Corps with two divisons from Monte Grappa to Monfenera; while the line from Monfenera down to the Piave was held by one division of I Corps; in all a total of 120 battalions and over 1000 guns.

The defence works on Grappa had been much extended since the fighting in 1917. The summit of Monte Grappa, the so-called *nave*, is a ridge about 350 yards long running north and south, perpendicular to the southern edge of the massif. This area had been transformed into a massive fortress by a system of large tunnels leading to gun positions looking out on either side of the *nave*. Three miles of tunnels gave access to positions for ninety-two guns, mainly of 70, 75 and 105 mm calibre, and to posts for some seventy machine guns, all with commanding positions. In addition much work had been done along the main defence line to provide trenches, cut mainly in the solid rock, and also some secondary lines of defence.[20]

The Austrians launched their offensive on 15 June with six divisions plus two in reserve. Their immediate objectives for the different sectors of the front may be summarized as follows, reading from west to east. *A*: From their positions near Col Caprile to take Fenilon and Col Moschin overlooking Val Brenta. *B*: From the rear of Asolone to advance up to the main ridge, and then down its southern slopes. *C*: To make straight up the valley north of Asolone towards Coston and Monte Grappa. *D*: From Monte Pertica to advance on either side of the ridge to Monte Grappa. *E*: From the head of Val Stizzone to make up the north ridge of Monte Grappa. *F*: A series of attacks from the Austrian positions on Fontanasecca and Spinoncia against the head of the Col dell'Orso salient.[21]

84

After an artillery bombardment beginning at 03.00, the Austrian infantry advanced at about 07.00. At the western end of the front, Fenilon and Col Moschin were taken by 10.00 and Fagheron by 13.00. The move from behind Asolone towards Coston took the Italian positions at Point 1478m on Asolone, but was then blocked below Coston. However, units from either side of Asolone succeeded in infiltrating to the south down into Val San Lorenzo with an advanced party reaching Ponte San Lorenzo on the Strada Cadorna, the main Italian supply route. From Pertica, Austrian assault troops took Point 1581m below Grappa, and further east other units occupied the first line of the Italian defences on Solarol at the head of the Col dell'Orso salient.

By noon the Austrians had made substantial gains, but were now meeting considerable resistance, including artillery fire on the ground they had recently captured. From the other side of Val Brenta, guns of the 6th Army on the Asiago plateau gave support by bringing fire down on Col Moschin, Fenelon and Fagheron, thus permitting 4th Army guns to switch to other targets, including enemy reserves waiting in rear areas. The Austrian advance down the San Lorenzo valley was halted by a great concentration of fire at Ponte San Lorenzo at about 13.00, while the Abruzzi Brigade was ordered to positions on the so-called *linea inglese* (Section 3.6), to block the lower end of the valley.[22]

The IOH, Pieropan, and Giardino (Vol.2) give detailed accounts of these actions and the subsequent counter-attacks. We note here only that the situation was reversed by Italian counter-attacks launched from 15.00 onwards.[23] At the west end of the front, overlooking Val Brenta, Monte Fagheron was soon recaptured, and Fenilon by 23.00. Col Moschin was retaken by 07.00 the next day, 16 June, and Col di Miglio north of Fenilon by midnight on 16 June. Point 1503m which had been lost on Asolone was retaken, and during the night of 15/16 June another counter-attack regained Point 1581m under Monte Grappa. In the Col dell'Orso salient, counter-attacks supported by heavy artillery were launched at 16.00, and by 21.00 all positions lost on Solarol had been regained. (There is some suggestion that the Austrians had also planned an assault on Tomba. If so, their preparations were disrupted completely by the Italian artillery in the early hours of 15 June.[24])

By midnight on 16 June the Italians had regained nearly all their lost ground. This was virtually the end of the battle. The Austrians had made little or no progress, had suffered heavy losses, and made no further attempt to continue their offensive. During the next two weeks the Italians carried out some limited local actions which restored their line almost to its original position.

The Italian casualties for the period from 15 to 24 June are given as 918 killed, 3,697 wounded, 9,374 missing; 13,989 in all.[25] The corresponding Austrian losses (for an unstated period) are given as 18,782.[26]

5. Montello

The attacks described in the previous sections were delivered by Conrad's Army Group. We now outline the concurrent operations by the VIth and Vth Armies forming Boroevic's Army Group, and begin with the attack of the VIth Army across the Piave towards the hill of the Montello. (The topography of the Montello was briefly outlined in Section 4.1, and we only mention here that the abundance of trees and scrub, plus a scarcity of any very characteristic features, would have made it difficult to maintain direction and orientation.[27])

The Montello was defended by the Italian 8th Army, whose front extended from Pederobba to Palazzon about three miles below Ponte di Priula (Map 2). The sector from Pederobba to a point somewhat east of Crocetta was held by XXVII Corps (66 and 51 Division), and from there to Palazzon by VIII Corps (58 and 48 Division).[28] The attack began on 15 June with the 31, 13 and 17 Divisions of the Austrian XXIV Corps striking across the river on either side of Falze (Map 3).

Aided by surprise, and by smoke and mist, the Austrians were soon across the river. Reaching the right bank, they turned upstream and downstream along the road at the foot of the Montello, and then moved up and across the hill along the numerous transverse tracks. The 58th Italian Division was surprised and overcome, with the loss of many guns and some 4000 prisoners.[29] Hence, by the end of 15 June the whole north-east corner of the Montello, including Nervesa, had been occupied by some twenty Austrian battalions.[30] Fortunately, however, the enemy pocket had been contained by the remains of the 58th Division, by XXVII Corps on the left, and by the energetic and able action of the 48th Division south of Nervesa.

The next day, 16 June, the Italians rapidly set up counter-attacks, on the left with the 51st and 66th Divisions, and on the right with the 13th Division of the General Reserve. But all failed to push the Austrians back, and by the evening three Austrian divisions were across the river, although food and ammunition were in short supply.

On 17 June the fighting continued, with the main Austrian effort centred on an attempt to take the Italian strongpoint at Villa Berti just south of Nervesa, in order to extend their front along the Piave to Ponte di Priula. Three regiments of the Austrian 17 Division delivered an attack in this region at 13.15, but were held by the Italians. The following day, 18 June, the Austrians continued their attacks with some success, and the Italians were forced to draw back their line so that it only returned to the river near Ponte di Priula.

The weather had by now turned wet and the Piave was rising, running faster and flooding. Since the start of their offensive the Austrians had encountered difficulties in supplying their troops across the river in the face of strong artillery fire and bombing from the air by British and Italian planes. On 18 June all the bridges were damaged by the flood and temporarily out of action, and the supply of food and ammunition brought to a halt.

Meanwhile the generals on either side had been reviewing the situation. The Commander of the VIth Austrian Army, the Archduke Joseph, had already been concerned at the slow rate of progress, and on 18 June informed the Army Group Commander Field Marshal Boroevic that the bridgehead must either be reinforced with another three divisions of infantry plus four artillery brigades, or be evacuated. On the Italian side Diaz was concerned at the scant success experienced by the various Italian counter-attacks. He therefore brought up two fresh corps, the XXXth and the XXIInd, each of two divisions, and gave orders for a well-prepared and coordinated counter-attack.

The attack by XXX Corps was launched at 13.00 the next day, 19 June, against the eastern half of the Austrian salient. No significant gain was achieved, despite much fighting and many casualties. The two divisions of XXII Corps on the right made insignificant progress, and units of VIII Corps did no better, despite hard and intense fighting in the ruins of Nervesa. The actions continued until nightfall and resumed the next day, 20 June, but with little result, and at 17.30 the Army Commander, General Pennella, ordered the suspension of the counter-offensive.

Meanwhile discussions had been proceeding all day at the Austrian GHQ, and at 19.16 the Emperor Karl ordered Boroevic to withdraw all his troops to the left bank of the Piave. The artillery, the wounded, and any infantry not essential for defence were to cross on the night of 21/22, and the rest on the night 22/23. For the next two days, 21 and 22 June, the front remained very quiet, and during the two nights the Austrians retired across the river apparently unobserved. According to the IOH, the 8th Army Command first learnt of this retirement in a telephone call from XXX Corps at 08.15 on 23 June stating that an Austrian prisoner had said that the Austrians were now in full retreat.[31]

The Austrian withdrawal marked the end of the June battle on the Montello. The Austrians had lost some 17,000 men (dead, wounded and missing), and the Italians 1,810 dead, 7,934 wounded and 13,455 missing; 23,209 in all.[32] The Austrians had gained nothing from their attack except a decisive rebuff.

6. Lower Piave

While the VIth Army of Boroevic's Group was attacking the Montello, the Vth Army was engaged in a general offensive across the lower reaches of the Piave, extending from Papadopoli Island to Intestadura below San Dona, at the junction of the Piave and the Old Piave (Map 2). The initial attack on 15 June was launched by eight infantry divisions and a cavalry division grouped into four Corps, and supported by a reserve division in each corps. They were opposed by the Italian 3rd Army with seven infantry divisions grouped into three corps. In addition, the Italian XXVth and XXVIth Corps, each of two divisions and part of the Comando Supremo reserve, were stationed in or near the rear areas of the 3rd Army.[33]

The Austrians failed in their attempt to establish two bridgeheads from Papadopoli Island, but by the evening of 15 June they had succeeded in crossing the river in eight or more places.[34] Thus they were now in possession of a ten-mile strip of land on the right bank extending from Saletto to the junction of the Piave and the Old Piave, except for a mile or so opposite Noventa. At some points this strip was no more than about 500 yards wide, but near Ponte di Piave was about two miles wide, and opposite San Dona almost four miles.

Fighting continued for the next four days all along the edge of this strip. During 16 and 17 June the Austrians gained some ground by advancing in places up to a mile or so,[35] but not enough to put their bridges beyond the range of the Italian artillery. Moreover, there still remained a wide gap separating the bridgeheads from those of the VIth Army on the Montello. The fighting on 18 and 19 June failed to produce any decisive change. The Italians now had the advantage that the whole area behind the Piave formed part of the entrenched camp of Treviso, set up in 1916 during the Strafexpedition. This system with three concentric lines of trenches and wire behind the Piave and around Treviso had been a reassuring factor at the time of Caporetto, and would present a serious obstacle to the Austrians. (The Italian line on 17 June as shown in Carta 35 of the IOH coincides quite closely with the outer line of the Treviso defence system shown in Carta 18.)

The day of 18 June was particularly difficult for the Austrians, as flood waters in the early hours brought down trees and other debris which further damaged or carried away their bridges across the Piave, already damaged by Italian artillery fire. A report by British air observers stated that all the bridges had been swept away except for two near San Dona, but that two more were nearing completion.[36] Hence, as on the Montello, there was a serious interruption to the flow of food and ammunition.

The end of the fighting came on 20 June with Karl's orders to

88

Boroevic to suspend all operations by the Army Group on the Piave. As on the Montello, the next day was quiet and the Austrians managed to withdraw during the nights of 21 and 22 June with little difficulty. This was the end of the fighting on the lower Piave, save for a subsidiary operation from 2 to 5 July when the Italians reoccupied the ground between the Piave and the Old Piave taken by the Austrians during the Arrestamento in 1917.

Although there had been little movement in the battle, both sides on the lower Piave had made a great effort, the losses in this sector being much greater than those at Asiago, on Grappa, or on the Montello. The Austrian losses are quoted as 4,200 dead, 38,000 wounded, 9,700 missing; 51,900 in all.[37] The corresponding figures for the Italians were 2,596 dead, 12,727 wounded, 25,915 missing; 41,238 in all.[38]

7.   The Outcome of the Offensive

The Austrians had gathered together all the forces they could muster for a conclusive attack on the Italians. Yet at Tonale the battle began on 12 June and was all over by 14 June. At Asiago the Austrian attack began on 15 June and made some limited gains, but was called off on 16 June, and all the Allied line was regained by 30 June. On Grappa some ground was gained on 15 June, but almost all was recovered by the Italians by 17 June. Bridgeheads were established across the Piave on 15 June both on the Montello and further downstream, but the Austrians were unable to break out from these bridgeheads and had withdrawn completely by 23 June.

The Austrian losses had been grievous. The Austrian Official History quotes 11,643 dead, 80,852 wounded and 25,547 missing; in all 118,042, plus 24,508 out of action through sickness (perhaps mostly due to influenza).[39] Nothing had been gained. The Italians had also suffered severe losses, but less than the Austrians (about 6,000 dead, 28,000 wounded, 52,000 missing; 86,000 in all). In fact the outcome was a disaster from which the Austrian Army never recovered.

Naturally the success of the Italian Army was greatly welcomed in Italy and did much "to sustain the morale of a country undoubtedly tired and anxious".[40] Even so the Comando Supremo was much concerned with some aspects of the Italian defence. However, these concerns were not made public until the relevant volumes of the Official History appeared in 1980 and 1988.

In discussing the battle the IOH refers to Italian "deficiencies in the direction and execution [of operations] which had made the final outcome more perilous and uncertain".[41] The IOH is particularly critical of how quickly some Italian front positions were surprised and overrun on Grappa and the Montello, and of the lack of expertise shown in various Italian counter-attacks. It concludes that "following long periods in the trenches in defensive positions, units had lost the capacity to march and manoeuvre and to deal with the problems of maintaining contact between units during combat".[42]

The Command of the 8th Army on the Montello is strongly criticized on several grounds, the first of which concerns the dispositions of its units prior to the Austrian attack. The main weight of this attack fell on the VIII Corps sector held by the 58th and 48th Divisions, each nominally of two brigades. Yet movements and rearrangements which the IOH describes as "somewhat capricious"[43] had transferred brigades from division to division, and regiments from brigade to brigade, to such an extent that the habitual chains of command in each unit had been severely disrupted. Perhaps as a result, the positions of some divisions and brigades on 15 June are shown differently on Carta 34 and Carta 39 of the IOH. The IOH also states that the actual dispositions differed from that shown on Carta 34, even though this was a map held by the Comando Supremo.[44]

The IOH also refers to counter-attacks on the Montello on 16 June by the reserve 13th Italian Division allocated to VIII Corps. The scope of the operation was laid down by the Corps Commander in an order issued at 08.00 on 16 June, and the Army Commander, General Pennella, set the start time as between 10.00 and 11.00.[45] At 05.00 that morning the Division was in their rear area some twenty kms away and ready to move by lorry to the Montello. In fact due to delays with the motor transport the troops only arrived at the foot of the Montello between 09.50 and 14.30. The Divisional Commander made representations that the start of the attack be deferred to at least 17.00 to give time to allow some reconnaissance of the ground (especially as no maps were available), to make contact with the adjacent corps, to take up new positions, to replenish ammunition and to refresh the troops (some not even having received their bread ration).[46]

General Pennella replied at 13.00 with an order giving the new start time as 14.00, adding that even a minute later would be "considered an act of disobedience in the face of the enemy by whosoever transgresses this order".[47] The Corps Commander then made "a kind of compromise which could not fail to have a negative influence on the outcome of the operation" and fixed the time for 15.30.[48] The counter-attack was made but without success, and at 22.30 the troops were ordered back to their start line. (The IOH criticizes the command for "extreme arrogance" and "ignoring the basic elements of human dignity".[49])

The IOH goes into considerable detail of other events on the Montello, of which we note only two. On 17 June General Di Giorgio commanding XXVII Corps gave instructions to his divisions for the defence of their positions, ending with the totally disconnected remark that "the divisions must consider themselves in a FULL WAR OF MOVEMENT" (sic).[50] It is unclear how the divisions were expected to respond to this order, but it certainly alarmed the adjacent I Corps on the right of the 4th Army who received a copy and took it to mean that Di Giorgio was planning to retreat.[51]

On 19 June various counter-attacks by XXII and XXX Corps were hurriedly prepared and failed in their purpose. The detailed account in the IOH refers to "a moment of indescribable confusion and mix up which implied a grave crisis and an enormous disorder, while the Army Commander continued to rage, with grave threats, in order to ensure that the action proceeded without delay".[52]

On 20 June, after little movement had been achieved by the Italian counter-attacks, General Pennella decided on a new approach and issued orders for all his units to halt the offensive and to hold firmly to their present positions. Then on 21 June, in contrast to his previous haste, he gave orders for a full reorganization and preparation for a renewed offensive on either 27 or 28 June,[53] that is after a pause of almost a week! Meanwhile on the nights of 21 and 22 June the Austrians stole silently away and crossed the river to the far bank, neither hindered nor harassed by the 8th Army. On 24 June General Pennella was transferred to the command of the 9th Reserve Army and was replaced by General Caviglia.

Besides the above strictures on the higher command, the IOH makes other more general points concerning organization and supply. These include inadequate time and attention given to the preparation of the logistics of actions, including the provision of adequate supplies of ammunition, and the high numbers of guns and gun carriages out of service.[54] Finally, there was concern at the very large number of Italians taken prisoner.[55] (Perhaps many by surprise, as were 4000 troops of the 58th Division on the Montello on the first day of the offensive.)

There was most clearly a need for General Diaz and the Comando Supremo to continue their efforts to ensure further reorganization and retraining. Yet the overall outcome was clear. The Austrian Army had been decisively defeated, and the Italian Army had shown that it had recovered from the legacy of Caporetto.

The French and British Forces
June 15–16

1   The Attack on the French Sector

We now outline the part played by the French and British divisions in more detail, beginning with the French divisions. The Allied front line on the Asiago plateau, running from Val d'Assa to Val Frenzela was shown in Map 5. The more detailed Map 7 (see over) sets out the dispositions of the French and British units before the battle. On the left the X Italian Corps straddled Val d'Astico with its 12th Division on the west edge of the plateau. Then reading from left to right, the line was held by the British XIV Corps with the 48th Division on the left and the 23rd Division on the right, and the 7th Division in reserve lower down near the edge of the plain. On the right of the British, the French XII Corps of two divisions (the 24th and 23rd) held a narrower front on more open ground. Finally the XIII Italian Corps of two divisions extended from the French positions to Val Frenzela, and the XX Italian Corps of three divisions from there to join up with the 4th Army at Col Moschin on the east side of Val Brenta.

As early as 6 June the 23rd French Division had captured some twenty prisoners during a raid on the Austrian salient at Bertigo about a mile east of Pennar, and at the same time saw signs of preparations for an attack. Hence they were not surprised by the offensive of 15 June and were well prepared.[1] Following General Segre's orders to the 6th Army artillery the French batteries opened fire at 23.45 on 14 June on regions of concentration and assembly. At 03.00 the Austrian artillery began to seek out the French guns but failed to silence them and they replied energetically. Then, between 03.45 and 04.00, just before the expected time of the attack as revealed by deserters, the French guns switched their fire back to the enemy's preparation and assembly points.

The French Corps had a narrow front of only about two miles and each division was set out in depth with only two battalions in the front line. The most prominent feature of their sector was the Pennar Salient jutting out from the front towards the enemy and, as the counter-preparation began, this salient was quietly evacuated. The Austrian infantry attack began at 06.00 when the enemy left their trenches, supported by violent artillery fire from both flanks. They soon reached and occupied the deserted positions at Pennar, and then moved forward into a trap with the French on either side of them.

For the rest of the day the Austrians struggled to make some progress. During the morning six different attacks were broken up by fire and according to the French Official Account the Austrians did not even approach the main French front line. At one stage enemy reserves were seen approaching from the village of Bertigo, and others were observed rushing down the slopes of Monte Sisemol about a mile north of Bertigo. These troops were targeted by the French artillery and retired in disorder, mingling in confusion with lines of other attacking troops held down by the fire. All attempts by the enemy to infiltrate the French positions were repulsed, as was a final attack in force in the evening by battalions debouching from the region of Pennar.[2]

The Austrians had held high hopes for their offensive. Information found on captured prisoners showed that their objectives for the first day had been the line of the summits on the edge of the plateau, about four miles behind the French front line. In fact no progress at all had been made in this sector. According to the French Official Account their arrest had been bloody and complete. At the same time the French had been able to assist the Italian 14th Division on their right which had been under pressure in the region of Cima Eckar to the east of the Pennar salient. On 17 June General Graziani in command of the French Corps reported that during the battle 230 prisoners had been taken near Pennar, and remarked also that although the Austrians claimed to have taken several thousand prisoners at Asiago, only four French soldiers were missing of whom three had been liaison agents with adjacent divisions and one a forward observer.[3]

2.   The Attack on the British 23rd Division

The no-man's-land between the British and Austrian lines was up to a mile or more wide, so both the 23rd and 48th Divisions maintained outposts there during the hours of darkness, some at a considerable distance in advance of their front line. Hence, there was always a possibility that a sudden emergency S.O.S. call for artillery fire to deal with a surprise attack on the front line might result in fire falling behind these outposts. This possibility was addressed in April 1918 when Lieut.-Colonel Sandilands, the GSO1 of the 23rd Division, attended a meeting at British GHQ.[4] Some of the officers present thought that the outposts would not stand firm if a barrage was put down behind them. The more ruthless argued that there was no need to inform the outposts of such

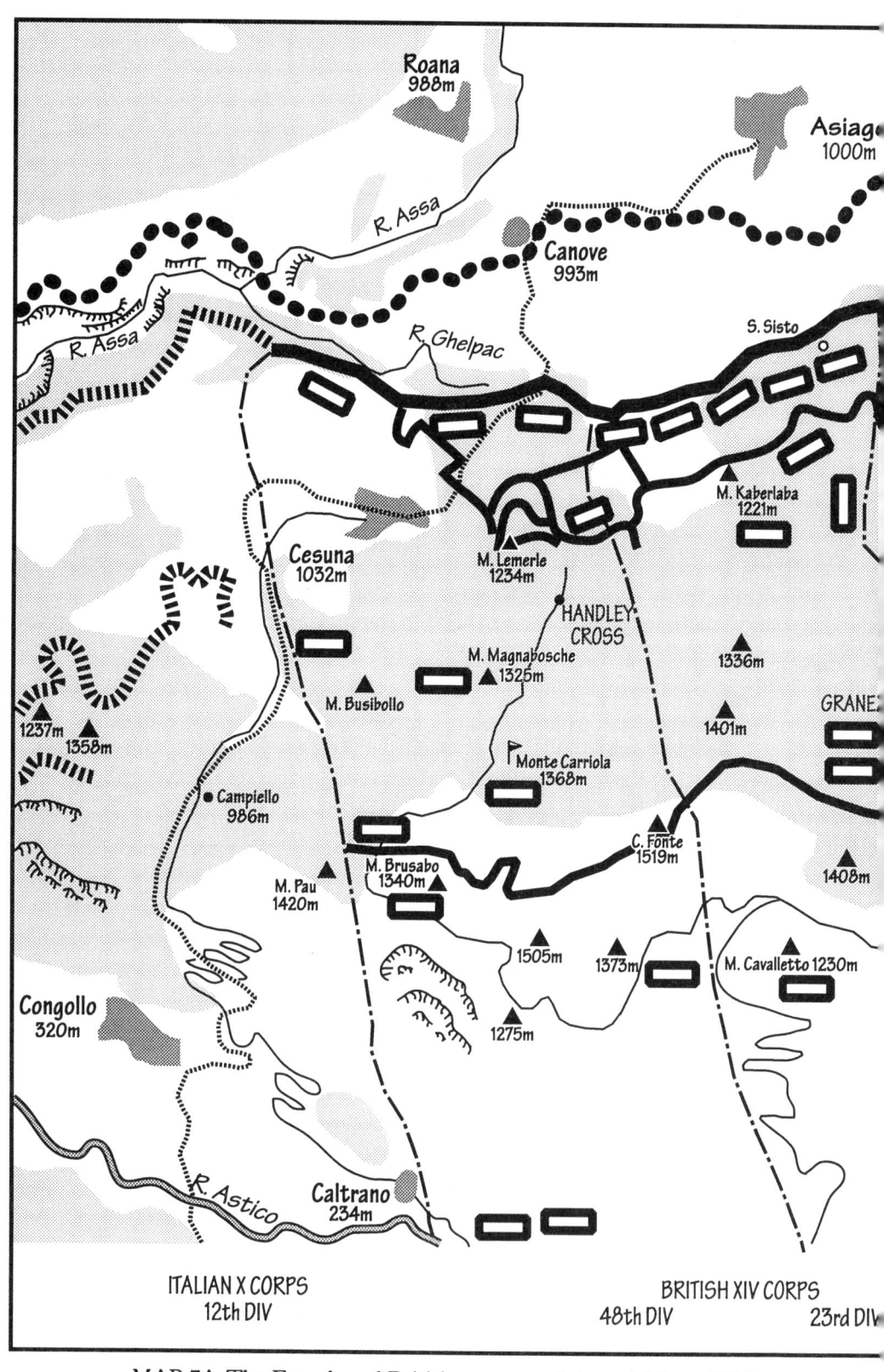

MAP 7A. The French and British sectors at Asiago, 14 June 1918.

Roana
988m

Asiago
1000m

R. Assa

Canove
993m

R. Assa

R. Ghelpac

S. Sisto

M. Kaberlaba
1221m

Cesuna
1032m

M. Lemerle
1234m

HANDLEY
CROSS

1336m

M. Magnabosche
M. Busibollo   1325m

1401m

GRANE

1237m   1358m

Monte Carriola
1368m

Campiello
986m

C. Fonte
1519m

1408m

M. Pau
1420m

M. Brusabo
1340m

1505m   1373m

M. Cavalletto 1230m

Congollo
320m

1275m

R. Astico

Caltrano
234m

ITALIAN X CORPS
12th DIV

BRITISH XIV CORPS
48th DIV   23rd DIV

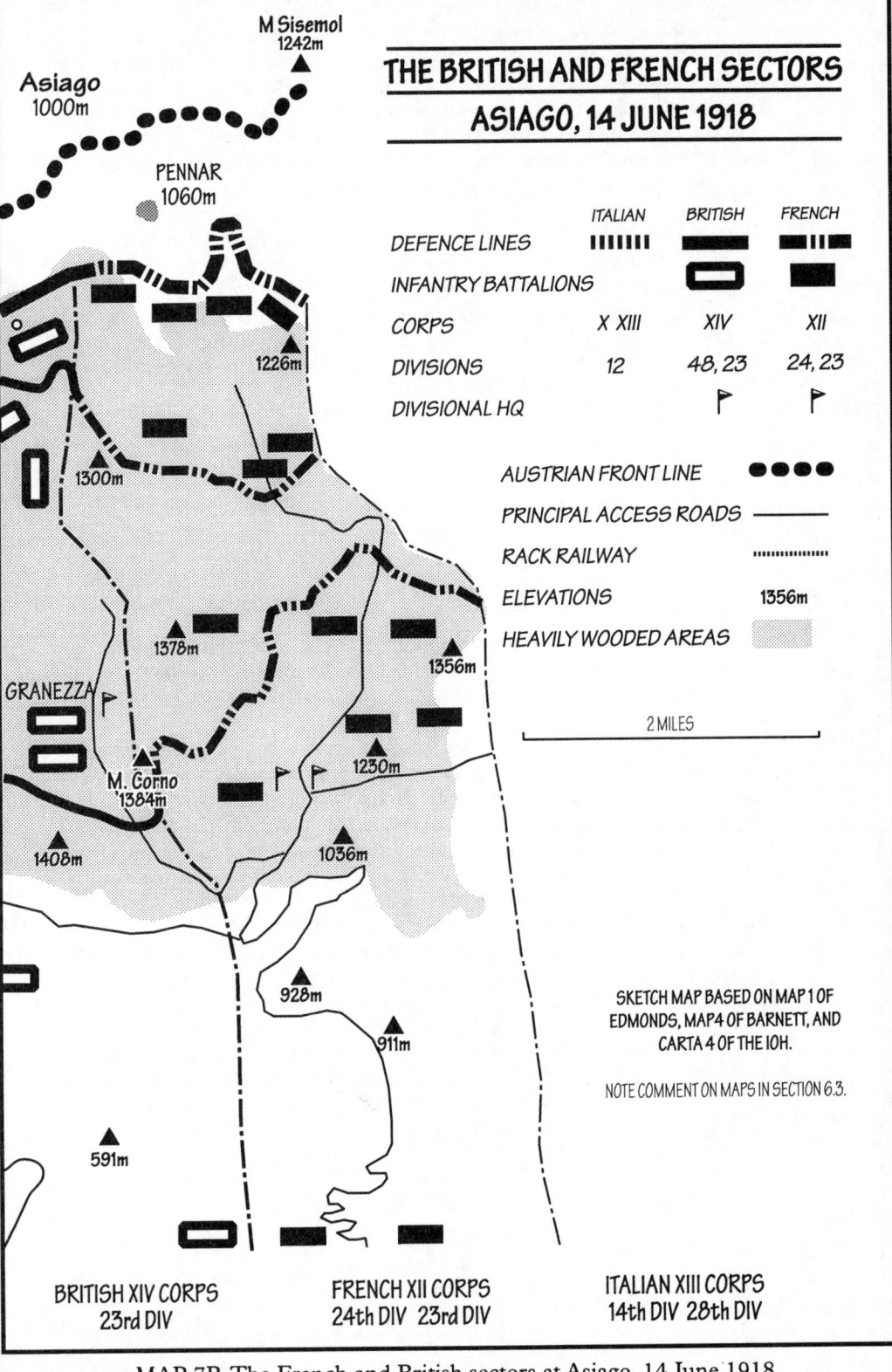

MAP 7B. The French and British sectors at Asiago, 14 June 1918.

an arrangement. On the other hand, Sandilands regarded this approach as a betrayal, and very bad for morale if found out. In his view it was essential that the troops should be informed, and furthermore he believed that they would then stand their ground. Eventually a compromise was reached and it was decided that the outposts would be given time to withdraw before putting down the barrage.

On the morning of 14 June the British divisions, preparing for the planned Allied offensive on 18 June, were told that an Austrian offensive was expected the next day, that reliable information had said that the attack would fall only on the French and Italian sectors, but that the British should expect a bombardment. At this time the 23rd Division was holding the right hand sector of the British line with two brigades at the front and one brigade in reserve. The table below shows the dispositions of the battalions in the two forward brigades:

	68 Brigade			70 Brigade	
Front line					
	11th NF	12th DLI	13th DLI	9th Y&L	11th SF
Second line					
				8th Y&L	
Brg. reserve					
		10th NF		8th KOYLI	

(DLI:Durham Light Infantry; KOYLI:King's Own Yorkshire Light Infantry; NF:Northumberland Fusiliers; SF: Sherwood Foresters; Y&L:York and Lancaster Regiment.)[5]

The night of June 14/15 appears to have begun relatively quietly with the divisional artillery engaged only in some counter-battery work. Then at about 03.00, just before daybreak, an intense bombardment of gas, shrapnel and high explosive shells descended on the whole of the British front, on battery positions, on divisional and brigade headquarters and other centres. At 03.20 the British GHQ ordered both divisions to withdraw their outposts. Edmonds states that these orders got through and that the outposts were all withdrawn.

At the same time British GHQ informed the artillery that "counter-preparation" could begin within the outpost line at 05.00.[6]This was a curious order as counter-preparation involved fire on the enemy areas of preparation and concentration, and perhaps counter-battery work, and there were no such targets within the outpost line. Edmonds comments that "There was evidently some misunderstanding at GHQ", and that what was meant was obviously "a defensive barrage". However, the intention was understood and at 03.30 Brigadier Wardrop in command of the artillery at British GHQ ordered counter-preparation beyond the outpost line and after 05.00 a defensive barrage to deal with any forces creeping up to attack.[7]

Unfortunately the fierce enemy bombardment since 03.00 was already creating havoc with the communications in both the British divisions. As mentioned in Section 4.4 all the telephone wires had been slung between trees because the ground was rock hard, and under the shelling trees were coming down in abundance breaking the wires as they fell. The only sure means of communication were now the runners (or cyclists where possible) even between the gunners and their observation posts. Moreover, as dawn broke thick mist hung about the woods obscuring the view. Hence all the battery commanders had generally to rely on their own initiative. According to Sandilands they did not even have sure information that the Austrian infantry was attacking, and were naturally nervous of bringing down a close barrage in case any outposts had not been withdrawn.

A good first hand account of the enemy bombardment and subsequent attack as seen from the receiving end is given by Gladden, who was then a member of a Lewis-gun team in a front line trench held by the 11th Battalion Northumberland Fusiliers immediately to the right of the 48th Division. Taking what shelter they could during the bombardment these troops wondered why there was no sign of their own artillery responding. Meanwhile, two night patrols sent out by the 68th Brigade on the left detected an assembly of infantry and a report was sent back.

At about 07.00 the Austrians launched infantry attacks against both the British divisions. One of the main thrusts of the attack was directed largely against the 4th battalion of the Oxfordshire and Buckinghamshire Light Infantry of the 48th Division, immediately on the left of the Northumberland Fusiliers. As Gladden was still wondering what the shelling was about there was a shout "Stand to ! He is coming over". Rushing to the firing step, he saw an officer on horseback marshalling troops into the long tongue of wood to the left, which ran forward about a thousand yards into no-man's-land. With a grandstand view of the action, Gladden saw grey lines of the enemy disappearing into the wood, sounds of rifle fire from within the wood, and a red S.O.S. flare shooting into the sky, but "still our artillery maintained their extraordinary silence".[8]

As Gladden watched, the Austrians continued to work their way up through the wood, then shots were heard coming from the left, and bullets began to fly along the length of his own trench. The Fusiliers now saw that their own positions were threatened but still appeared to have no artillery support. Soon enemy troops were in the gully in front of them, where the curve of the ground gave cover until they were quite close to the Northumberland's wire, and a small party managed to place a tube or bomb in the wire to blow a gap in the defences. Under cover of the dense smoke from the explosion an enemy party were through the gap and in the front trench in a matter of seconds. At the same time an Austrian carrying a heavy flame-thrower staggered above the brow of the curving ground only twenty-five yards away. The flame thrower was instantly shot down but it was not clear what was happening in the trench. Gladden could only see missiles, probably grenades, being lobbed from one section to another, but wounded remnants of the left platoon began to stagger back. The enemy appeared to be gaining ground, but at this moment the company commander, Captain Stirling appeared behind Gladden's trench and called for volunteers to counter-attack the captured length of trench.

Very soon Captain Stirling and his Sergeant Major were leading a line of riflemen with fixed bayonets to storm the enemy-occupied trench from the rear. Covered by fire from the Lewis gun section the party moved towards the rear of the captured section with Captain Stirling and the Sergeant Major hurling hand grenades into the trench. The enemy did not wait to receive them but fled into the woods. So far the Northumberlands' casualties had been light, but now tragedy occurred. Elated by their success, the riflemen having occupied the trench leapt on to the parapet to pursue the retreating enemy, but Austrians in the adjacent woods opened fire and some fusiliers were shot dead. But the front line was once again secure. (Next day Captain Stirling was much pleased to find Gladden still alive, as he thought he had seen him lying dead on the top of the trench. This was a great surprise to Gladden who had not hitherto supposed that Stirling had any interest in him! For their part in the battle, Captain Stirling and the battalion commander Lieut.-Colonel St Hill were awarded the DSO, and Sergeant-Major Rhodes a bar to his MM.)

The Northumberland Fusiliers were further threatened by an Austrian attack at about 08.00 which broke through the 48th Division's front immediately to the left of the 23rd Division. The Fusiliers responded by a realignment which protected their flank and which also prevented any enemy penetration, as described further in Section 6.3. This realignment was subsequently reinforced by a company of the 10th Northumberland Fusiliers and two companies of the 8th York and Lancasters, and held firm for the rest of the day. Thus the 11th Northumberland Fusiliers maintained the line all through the day against both frontal and flank attacks, though at a cost of 104 casualties, a fifth of their strength.[9]

Although the whole length of the 23rd Division line came under attack, another main thrust occurred at the east end held by the 11th Battalion Sherwood Foresters with the 9th Battalion York and Lancaster Regiment on their left. The Sherwood Foresters' line ran along the foot of the so-called San Sisto ridge, a long knoll on the rising ground behind the front line trenches, with its length running parallel with the front line. From the ridge line the ground to the north fell towards the frontline trench, and to the south fell to a shallow valley before rising again towards Monte Kaberlaba. This ridge was a particularly important feature as an enemy party gaining positions on the ridge would be able to enfilade the trenches on either side.

As described by Sandilands[10] one of the first effects of the bombardment had been to produce numerous casualties among the Sherwood Foresters, and to tear gaps in the otherwise formidable wire obstacles in front of them. Hence, by a very determined attack, some 200 Austrians gained a footing in 150 yards of the front line trench. Then parties of these troops, with machine guns and flame-throwers, made their way up the slope of the San Sisto ridge and established themselves on the crest.

The commander of the Sherwood Foresters, Lieut.-Colonel Hudson, had sited his HQ at the foot of the southern slope of the San Sisto ridge and at about 08.45 was informed that the Austrians had reached the ridge. He immediately prepared a counter-attack with the HQ personnel and a few Italian trench-mortar gunners. Advancing at the head of this small party, he stormed the ridge, took twenty prisoners and drove the remainder back down the north slope to the front line.

With a sergeant and only three men Hudson carried on down the slope towards the front line. Coming up towards the trench the sergeant saw that it was occupied and made for cover, but Hudson revolver in hand, ran forward firing, and demanded their surrender. Thinking that many more men were behind Hudson, the Austrians held up their hands and an officer came forward to surrender. Then someone in the trench threw a bomb, killing the officer and severely wounding Hudson who fell into a communication trench. The Austrians made no attempt to fire on him, and he was later recovered by his own troops.Sandilands adds that "though in great pain, before being taken from the field he gave instructions for the counter-attack to be continued". In fact the eventual counter-attack regained the trench by 14.00. Lieut.-Colonel Hudson DSO, MC, was subsequently awarded the Victoria Cross for his "high courage and determination". (He is mentioned, briefly and somewhat unfairly,[11] in Vera Brittain's autobiography *Testament of Youth* when she is seeking information about her brother, Captain Brittain, who served in Hudson's battalion and died during the same action at Asiago.)

The next day was one of mist and drizzle. The front was completely quiet for both the 23rd Division and the adjacent French Divisions. The enemy attack had been completely defeated. The division had captured 230 unwounded prisoners, 137 wounded prisoners, two mountain guns,

24 machine guns and 15 flamethrowers. Its losses were 8 officers and 86 men killed; 24 officers and 388 men wounded; one officer and 48 men missing. In all 33 officers and 522 men.[12]

3.　The Attack on the British 48th Division

The 48th Division held the Carriola sector on the left of the British line with three battalions up front as shown in Map 7, compared with the five battalions in the front line of the 23rd Division, which had a sector of comparable width. This difference was no doubt partly, but only partly, explained by the presence of the Ghelpac gorge which greatly protected the last thousand yards on the left.

Map 8 (p.103) gives a rough sketch of the main and second defence lines on the divisional front. Wyrall in the history of the 5th Battalion the Gloucestershire Regiment comments that the "scarcity of trench maps or information concerning the Divisional front line makes a full description of the front line held by the Gloucesters impossible".[13] The most detailed map is that given by Barnett which outlines the positions of trenches and wired obstacles in some detail. Other maps and sketch maps are given by Edmonds, Carrington, Sandilands, and the Diary of the 48th Division HQ[14], but all exhibit discrepancies with each other. While Map 8 indicates the main features of the second line, the so-called Cesuna Switch, Polygon Trench, the Lemerle Switch and the Boscon Switch, it is important to note that these lines on the ground were not as firm and continuous as the lines in the sketch. Barnett states that the Cesuna and Lemerle Switches were "nothing like complete", and his map indicates that the depth and strength of the second line varied very appreciably from place to place, and was particulary thin near the join of the Cesuna Switch and Polygon Trench.

The initial deployment of the battalions of the 48th Division as given by Edmonds is shown on Map 7 and in the table below. The latter sets out the position at 04.00 on 15 June when the 1st Battalion the Buckinghamshire Regiment had just arrived at its battle positions on the Lemerle Switch.

Front line
143 Brigade (Brig. Sladen)	*145 Bgd (Lt.Col.Reynolds*)*
5th Warwicks	5th Glos 4th Ox & Bucks

Second line
(Cesuna Switch)	(Lemerle/Polderhoek)
	1st Bucks

100

Reserves 6th Warwicks (M.Pau)   4th Berks (Carriola)
        7th Warwicks (Magnaboschi)
        8th Warwicks (M.Busibollo)

Reserve Brigade (144 Lt.Col.Tomkinson*)
          8th Worcs   M. Brusobo
          6th Glos   west of M.Cavalletto
          4th Glos   near Caltrano
          7th Worc   near Caltrano

(Berks: Royal Berkshire Regiment; Bucks: Buckinghamshire
Regiment; Glos: Gloucestershire Regiment; Ox and Bucks:
Oxfordshire and Buckinghamshire Light Infantry; Warwicks:
Royal Warwickshire Regiment; Worcs: Worcestershire
Regiment; * acting GOC)

3.a   The Austrian Advance

The first warning of the Austrian attack came about 03.00, just as it was
getting light, when Lieut.-Colonel Barnett at 48 Division HQ on Monte
Carriola was woken by shells bursting all over the sector, on the slopes
of Monte Pau to the rear, and around the divisonal headquarters. Gas
was being used and was difficult to detect because it was disguised by
the smell of burning pine trees.

At 03.20 orders came from British GHQ to withdraw all outposts from
no-man's-land. These orders got through to the front line, but soon the
bombardment cut the telephone communications between Divisional
HQ and all the forward troops. At 04.45 Brigadier Sladen in command
of 143 Brigade, which had only one battalion in the front line, ordered
up two of his reserve battalions: the 8th Warwicks to the Cesuna Switch
and the 6th Warwicks to a position near his HQ about a mile south-west
of Cesuna.

The Austrians launched their infantry attacks at about 07.00 and
fierce hand-to-hand fighting ensued, often in rough wooded ground
and sometimes in mist. Soon the British line was pierced in four places
by the sheer weight of numbers. (The 4th Ox and Bucks identified seven
different enemy battalions on their section of the front.) These breaks
occurred, reading from left to right, at the junction of the 5th Warwicks
and the 5th Gloucesters, on the right front of the 5th Gloucesters, at the
junction of the 5th Gloucesters and the 4th Ox and Bucks, and at
the junction of the 4th Ox and Bucks and the 11th Northumberland
Fusiliers (23rd Division). By 07.30 the Austrians were advancing
through gaps torn in the front of the 5th Gloucesters into the valley

behind the battalion, cutting communications and overrunning gun positions which had been brought up close behind the front line ready for the Allied offensive planned for two days later.

As all telephone communications to the front had been cut, no news of the attacks arrived at Divisional HQ until about 08.00 when reports came in telling of heavy machine-gun and rifle fire near Perghele, Buco di Cesuna and Pelly Cross (Map 8). Hence, it was only at 08.11 that Brigadier Wardrop, the Commandant Royal Artillery at Corps HQ, gave orders to put down an S.O.S. barrage in front of that part of the line where the attack had taken place, but by then communications to the guns had broken down. Various orders were then given to bring up more reserve units, the 4th Berks from Carriola, the 6th Gloucesters from west of Cavalletto, and the 4th Gloucesters and 7th Worcesters from near Caltrano.

All movements that morning were extremely difficult because of the continuing bombardment, because of fallen trees, and because quite early on the main ammunition dump at Handley Cross, near Magnaboschi (Map 7) had been hit and continued to explode for several hours. This was particularly serious as it had been sited close to the principal road from the rear to the front line. Even so, by 08.30 the 8th Warwicks were on the Cesuna Switch, and by about noon the 4th Berks had two companies supporting the Ox and Bucks, and two companies behind the Oxford Trench. The 6th Gloucesters arrived at Magnaboschi at about 12.30, the 4th Gloucesters and the 7th Worcesters came up from Caltrano by lorry and arrived at Carriola somewhat later during the afternoon.

Meanwhile at 09.30, after receiving a reconnaisance report from the brigade major of 143 Brigade, General Fanshawe had ordered the 7th Warwicks (Lieut.-Colonel Knox) at Magnaboschi to prepare a counter-attack to take and hold the south end of the Cesuna switch (a manoeuvre the battalion had rehearsed a few days previously). At 10.00 Lord Cavan ordered the reserve 7th Division on the plain to warn two battalions of 91 Brigade to be ready to embus to Cima di Fonte between Granezza and Carriola as soon as they received the order.

3.b The Defensive Action

The day was cloudy, mist often obscured the view, and much of the action took place in thickly wooded ground often boulder-strewn, with sudden depressions and rocky outcrops. The rough nature of the terrain made it difficult to recognize features, and to maintain orientation and contact with adjacent units. The artillery played litle part as the gunners could not distingush between friendly and enemy areas in the woods and the battle was fought out by both sides with machine guns and rifles.

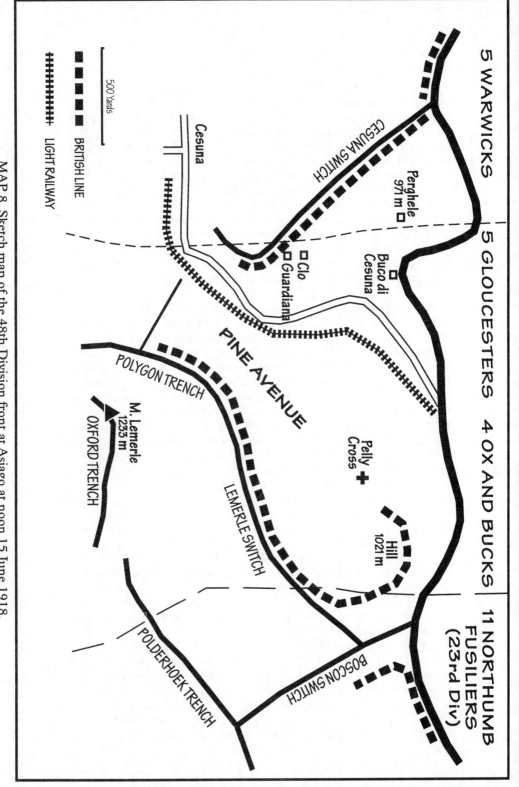

MAP 8. Sketch map of the 48th Division front at Asiago at noon 15 June 1918.

5 WARWICKS   5 GLOUCESTERS   4 OX AND BUCKS   11 NORTHUMB FUSILIERS (23rd Div)

CESUNA SWITCH

Cesuna

Perghele 97 m

Cio Guardiana

Buco di Cesuna

PINE AVENUE

POLYGON TRENCH

M. Lemerle 1233 m

OXFORD TRENCH

LEMERLE SWITCH

Pelly Cross

Hill 1021 m

POLDERHOEK TRENCH

BOSCON SWITCH

500 Yards

BRITISH LINE

LIGHT RAILWAY

Edmonds describes the fighting to halt the Austrian attack as a battalion commanders' and a soldiers' battle, for it was difficult for higher commanders to obtain a clear picture of events.

Accounts of the battle are given in the relevant regimental and battalion histories listed in the bibliography. According to Edmonds the authors of the subsequent Official History had to piece together these previous accounts and found them not always fully consistent. In particular "the exact relation in time of events, even in adjoining battalions' sectors, is not always certain".[15] However, we now outline as best we can how the fighting developed.

Map 8 gives a rough indication of the British positions in the woods at about noon when the Austrians had penetrated the front over a length of about 2500 yards to a depth of up to 800 yards. In the area between the Cesuna and Lemerle switches the British had fallen back along the line of these two switches, but there still remained two gaps in the line. One was at the junction of the 4th Ox and Bucks and the 23rd Division, and the other, larger and more menacing, on either side of the light railway track running from the plain through Campiello to Asiago.

This situation had come about following the Austrian attack on the section of the line held by the 5th Gloucesters. It appears that by about 07.30 two posts on the extreme left of the Gloucesters, where the line was wholly in the woods, had been obliterated by the bombardment, and the Austrians pushed through the resulting gap in large numbers, fanning out behind, and cutting all communications. The left-hand company of the Gloucesters (and the adjacent company of the 5th Warwicks) appear to have been overwhelmed by the force of numbers, despite strong resistance. Shortly afterwards the support company of the Gloucesters, which was sited with Lewis gun posts along a track about 500 yards behind the front line, came under attack and despite fierce resistance including some effective mortar fire was forced to withdraw.

The survivors from the two companies of the Gloucesters, three officers and thirty-seven other ranks, now fell back on to the line of the Cesuna Switch. Here they made contact with a company of the 5th Warwicks supported by two 4.5in howitzers of the 240th Field Battery in place for the offensive on 18 June, and by other gunners, engineers, trench mortar personnel and some Italians. The infantry helped the gunners to pull their guns out of their pits so they could fire straight ahead over open sights. The Austrians were thus checked, but they then proceeded to enfilade the British positions with a machine gun which they had established near a house called Guardiana. However, this was knocked out by a gun of the 12th Battery(XXXV Brigade) of the 7th Division brought up for the offensive, and which had been manhandled down the wooded slopes of Monte Lemerle under the direction of Major

104

Jardine. In the meantime the other two companies of the 5th Gloucesters had been driven out of their positions in the woods by large numbers of Austrians. The survivors retreated to the ground on either side of the railway track uphill to the Lemerle Switch or to the Cesuna Switch.

To the left of the 5th Gloucesters the front line was held by the 5th Warwicks with B Company on the left overlooking the Ghelpac gorge and D Company on the right adjacent to the Gloucesters, with the other two companies in support. The Austrian attack had overwhelmed D Company, taking the company commander prisoner before he could send a message back to Battalion HQ near Perghele. In fact this HQ was quite close to the front line and was soon attacked. The headquarters staff put up a gallant defence. The acting battalion commander was killed, the second in command wounded, and the adjutant captured. Regimental Sergeant-Major Townley took charge of the remaining party of thirteen men, pioneers, cooks and orderlies, and they held out around the huts forming the HQ for about six hours, until the arrival of a company of the 6th Warwicks sent forward at 11.00 to reinforce their position. RSM Townley was subsequently awarded the DCM. (More details of the fighting around the Cesuna Switch are given by Captain Carrington of the 5th Warwicks.[16] Note that Sketch 8 in Edmonds, being on a small scale, drastically oversimplifies the position of the front line near the Cesuna Switch.)

Meanwhile to the left of the battered D Company of the 5th Warwicks, the positions held by B Company overlooking the Ghelpac gorge held firm all day and their mortars continued to be effective against the many Austrians moving up from the gorge. Later an Italian offer to take over 800 yards of the line on the left of the Warwicks' front was accepted by Brigadier Sladen, thus setting free some 5th Warwicks for counter-attacks.

At the right end of the Divisional front, which was held by the 4th Ox and Bucks and was completely in the woods, a long tongue of wood ran forward into no-man's-land for about 1000 yards. Watched by Private Gladden, large numbers of Austrians had pushed through this wood which gave good cover, and then using flame-throwers had broken the Ox and Bucks line near its junction with the 23rd Division. By 09.00 the Ox and Bucks had been forced to abandon their front trench leaving behind two batteries of guns which had been brought up to within a hundred yards of their front. They then established themselves on a line about a hundred yards back running around Hill 1021.

Using clerks, cooks, orderlies, servants and everyone who could use a rifle, the party of Ox and Bucks on Hill 1021 continued to hold out, but the position was serious for contact had been lost with both the 23rd Division on the right and the 1st Bucks on the Lemerle Switch. To fill the gap on the right General Fanshawe sent the 477th Field Company Royal Engineers to the Boscon Switch to establish a connection with the 23rd Division. This could not be achieved so a defence line was formed on the right flank, facing east across the gap, and this line was subsequently held by a second company of the 4th Berks and by patrols of the 1st Bucks coming from the Lemerle Switch. The opposite side of the gap was held by the 11th Northumberland Fusiliers of the 23rd Division who had formed a line facing west. They maintained this position during hard fighting and were reinforced during the morning by a company of the 10th Northumberland Fusiliers and by two companies of the 8th York and Lancasters. Both sides of the gap remained firmly held and no enemy penetration occurred.

It was during this part of the battle that 2nd Lieutenant J.S.Youll of the 11th Northumberland Fusiliers won the VC. He was leading a patrol in the region of the gap when it was caught in an artillery barrrage. Sending his men back to safety, he remained to observe and then found it impossible to rejoin his company. Reporting to a neighbouring unit in the 48th Division sector, he organized a position with men from several different units until troops on the left gave way and an enemy machine gun began to fire from his rear. He then rushed the gun, killed most of the crew himself, and opened fire with the gun inflicting heavy casualties on the enemy. Then, on learning that the enemy had occupied part of the 48th Division front line, he organized and led three separate counter-attacks. On each occasion he drove the enemy back, but each time could not maintain his position because of fire coming from his rear. The citation for the Victoria Cross concludes by referring to "his complete disregard for his personal safety" and "his very gallant leading".[17]

Subsequently a corporal in the Ox and Bucks who had observed Youll in action wrote to him from hospital a letter[18] described by Sandilands as "a humble but human document which must form as glowing a tribute as has ever been paid to a soldier's gallantry":

Dear Sir

    i am writing these few lines to you as i felt i must hoping you wont think me exceeding my duty as officers like you are worthy of the best recommendation and I should like to have one like you in charge of the platoon i was in for you are the sort of scrapper i like i could go anywhere with you and dear sir i think i am right i only heard some of the N.F. talking about different things and I took it you was the officer who come to where i was in charge of a section guarding a gap on our Batt.front when we were cut off on the 15th i believe you came in the Oxf and Bucks front if so you are the same i am pleased to have had the pleasure to see you in

106

action for it puts heart in any man when they have a good officer and I have been in a scrap or two and it is some time since I saw one to equal you and Dear Sir you must excuse my writing as i have got one through the wrist and an explosive bullet in the calf of my leg and it has made a big hole in it and now dear sir i think this is all i remain,

Your obedient Cpl Stratford 18430
A Company 1/4 Ox & Bucks Lt Infantry.

Sir i cant put my address as they keep shifting me all the time.

3.c   The Counter-Attacks

At about 12.00 there were still gaps in the 48th Division's front but the enemy pressure seemed to be easing, and some reinforcements were arriving to help hold the line. The 7th Warwicks arriving at Polygon Trench found that the gap between the Trench and the Cesuna Switch was held by only two guns and a rifle party of the 12th Battery RFA, who were firing at the Austrians about 600 yards away and were themselves under machine-gun fire. Lieut.-Colonel Knox deployed the 7th Warwicks across the gap, made contact with the troops on each side, and opened fire on the Austrians.

There was now no sign of any enemy attempt to press on further but the Austrians maintained themselves stoutly on their positions. Knox's orders at 09.30 had been to mount a counter-attack to drive the enemy back, and then hold the southern end of the Cesuna Switch. Having viewed the situation, Knox decided that he must first consolidate his present position. At 14.00 he himself led a two platoon attack, with support from three guns of the 12th Battery, against machine-gun posts in the small groups of houses called Clo and Guardiana at the south end of the Cesuna Switch. Having dealt with these he tried to advance further but was held up by machine-gun fire and sniping. However, the Austrians appeared to be discouraged by the British fire, and remained halted on a line running approximately along the so-called Pine Avenue.

Meanwhile General Fanshawe had sent for Lieut.-Colonel Tomkinson, acting GOC of the reserve 144 Brigade, and when he arrived at Divisional HQ at 12.20 told him that little news had come in and that the situation was obscure.[19] Tomkinson suggested that he visit Lieut.-Colonel Reynolds (acting GOC 145 Brigade) saying that he was sure that Reynolds would have a good idea of the position in his sector and on his flanks. This was indeed the case. Tomkinson returned in a little over an hour and was then ordered to make a two-battalion attack from the Cesuna Switch to recapture the lost ground. He decided to use the 6th Gloucesters and the 7th Worcesters which were then coming up from their reserve positions.

The 7th Worcesters and 6th Gloucesters were much delayed by heavy artillery fire and the exploding ammunition dump, the Gloucesters arriving at Magnaboschi at about 12.30. An officer of the 6th Gloucesters was sent to contact 143 Brigade, and meeting Colonel Knox of the 7th Warwicks informed him that the battalion was on its way with orders to attack at 18.00, and therefore Knox decided to await the arrival of the Gloucesters before beginning his counter-attack.

It would then appear that the two battalion commanders conferred and decided on a joint counter-attack at 18.00 with the 7th Warwicks on the left and two companies of the 6th Gloucesters on the right along the line of Pine Avenue. Edmonds comments that "It was realized that it would be better to put in all four companies, but anxiety about the gap on the right led to two being kept behind the flank."[20] Edmonds also remarks that "During the afternoon Lord Cavan came up to the 48th Division Headquarters to see if he could be helpful; his presence was encouraging, and he did not interfere with the arrangements that had been made."

The aim of the attack at 18.00 was to pass through the south part of the Cesuna Switch between Polygon Trench and Guardiana to gain touch with the 143 and 145 Brigades on the left and right, and then clear the enemy from the pocket. The attack failed. According to Edmonds, "The troops moved up in what was almost 'artillery formation', lines of small groups of men, followed by echelons of increasingly large bodies, each battalion on a front of two companies. Met by machine-gun and rifle fire the general progress made was not much more than a hundred and fifty yards".[21] B Company of the Gloucesters managed to reach Pelly Cross, but failed to contact the Ox and Bucks around Hill 1021m and had to fall back.

The 7th Warwicks and the 6th Gloucesters were now joined by the support battalion, the 7th Worcesters who had been delayed by the enemy artillery. The three battalions renewed the attack at 20.00, with the Worcesters on the right of the two Gloucester companies somewhere near the line of Pine Avenue. There was now no enemy artillery fire, and the three battalions advanced about 300 yards, but were then stopped by machine-gun fire. However, at about 21.30 a patrol from the 7th Worcesters succeeded in making contact with the 4th Ox and Bucks about 300 yards from Pelly Cross, thus creating an almost continuous line. Meanwhile a detachment from the reserve 6th Warwicks, still stationed behind Cesuna, had tried to retake Perghele but failed under heavy rifle and machine-gun fire.

At 21.30 the commanders of the three battalions engaged in the counter-attack decided to halt on their gains and continue the next morning. At about the same time General Fanshawe talked to Colonel Tomkinson (144 Brigade) about the position on the left of the 4th Ox and Bucks, and approved his suggestion for a further attack to close the gap aided by the 8th Worcesters, the last unallocated battalion of 144 Brigade. Fanshawe then gave orders for an attack involving all three brigades at 04.30 with the object of regaining the whole of the front line.

Although a decision had been taken to suspend the attack until the morning, fighting continued in the woods until midnight, and from 23.00 onwards all movement in the woods became difficult as the Austrian machine guns fired off vast numbers of rounds to create a defensive belt. Fortunately their fire was high and caused relatively few casualties. The British preparations continued throughout the night. The 8th Worcesters came up to the Lemerle Switch, held by the 1st Bucks and the 477th Field Company RE, who were to remain there during the attack as a local reserve. Arrangements were made for machine-gun and heavy trench mortar support, with the artillery mainly searching the enemy back areas, as most of the fighting would still be in the woods.

The attack at 04.30 was delivered by: (reading from left to right) the 6th Warwicks; the 7th Warwicks plus parts of the 8th and 5th Warwicks; the 7th Worcesters; the 6th Gloucesters plus part of the 5th Gloucesters; the 8th Worcesters; and the 4th Ox and Bucks plus part of the 4th Berks. The 1st Bucks at the Lemerle Switch were to act as local reserves and the 4th Gloucesters at Magnaboschi as the divisional reserve. Thus in the next counter-attack almost the whole of the division was to be employed for the first time. By 05.45 the right-hand section of the front line initially held by the Ox and Bucks was reoccupied after only slight resistance. In fact the 1st Bucks found a message on a dead Austrian officer, timed at 02.50, ordering a complete withdrawal to their own original front line.[22] Further to the left there was still much opposition from machine guns and snipers, but after a second combined effort the whole of the old front line was reoccupied by about 08.00 and patrols sent out into no-man's-land.

The Austrians made no attempt to continue. The battle ended with the 48th Division on its original line. All the British guns lost the previous day were regained. The Division took 540 unwounded prisoners, and 188 wounded prisoners, together with 5 mountain guns, 48 machine guns, 5 flame-throwers and a large quantity of rifles, ammunition and equipment of all kinds. The number of Austrian dead found in the British lines and no-man's-land and buried by the British eventually totalled 576. Over 91 corpses were found in front of the position held by Sergeant-Major Townley and his thirteen men. The number of Austrian wounded is not known, but is estimated by Barnett as at least a thousand, giving a total loss of perhaps 2300. The British losses were also heavy: 151 dead, 523 wounded, 246 missing, 920 in all, of which

206 were in the artillery. The 5th Gloucesters who received the full weight of the attack, lost 28 dead, 71 wounded and 120 missing, almost half their strength.[23]

4. General Fanshawe

In twenty-four hours of fighting the 48th Division had completely halted the enemy attack. The Austrians were now back on their start line and unwilling to continue their offensive.

As Edmonds remarks, it had been "a battalion commanders' and soldiers' battle".[24] It had been won by the men on the ground. For example, Major Pickford of the 4th Ox and Bucks was awarded the Military Cross because "He was continually moving between the front line and Battalion Headquarters, and when the situation was critical he personally took a handful of men and placed them exactly where they were required. But for his splendid grasp of the situation and quick initiative the battalion might several times have been surrounded."[25] Lieut.-Colonel Bartlett, the CO of the 4th Ox and Bucks, was awarded the DSO because "By his skilful handling of his Battalion he maintained his position in spite of the line being penetrated on both flanks, thereby checking the enemy's advance, and enabling the line to be completely re-established by counter-attack. By his courage and coolness he set a splendid example to all ranks."[26]

The officers and men of the 48th Division had reason to be proud of their performance. Captain Carrington was to write later that "We all thought that the action of 15–16 June was a brilliant little victory".[27] Yet on 19 June Major-General Fanshawe was ordered to hand over the command of the Division and return to England for duty there. Not unnaturally this recall was taken as some comment on the performance of the Division. Edmonds gives no reason for Fanshawe's posting back to England. The only indication that he left the Division occurs in a subsequent chapter when reference is made to Major-General Sir H.B.Walker "who had taken over command on 4 July".[28] There is, however, more information in the correspondence between Edmonds and various officers of the Division while he was preparing the Official History, and which is now open to inspection. Colonel Tomkinson wrote that Fanshawe "was sacked by Cavan and 48 Div. were for some time mud to GHQ Italy".[29]

All the accounts of the Division in Italy by various members of the Division invariably speak of General Fanshawe's departure with regret and with the suggestion that he had been badly treated and sent home under a cloud. On the other hand the correspondence with Edmonds also shows reservations. Lieut.-Colonel G.W.Howard, the Chief Staff Officer of the 7th Division, wrote "Why the 48th Division should ever have allowed any Austrians to penetrate their positions was always a mystery as it was so strong. Am afraid the look-out could not have been too good. No wonder Fanshawe was sent home."[30] Cavan wrote to Edmonds suggesting that Fanshawe should have "softened the pocket with trench mortars for some hours before his first counter-attack".[31] (Artillery preparations were hardly possible on positions in the woods.) Major Pickford, while supporting Fanshawe, refers to "a controversy that had better not be revived".[32]

It is clear that all the battalions involved acquitted themselves extremely well. It is also possible to see both sides of the controversy, and to appreciate the difficulties faced by the 48th Division, some of which were outside their control. The great influenza epidemic of 1918 had struck at the 23rd and 48th Divisions during the latter part of May and the first part of June. Those taken ill took from three to ten days to recover and by 15 June most of the 23rd Divison had recovered, but the 48th was still badly affected. The maximum fighting strength of its twelve battalions on 15 June, according to Barnett, ranged from 617 down to 379, and "these strengths were still further reduced by men still with their units being affected".[33] Most of the divisional staff except Fanshawe had been on the sick list during the previous week, and it had been necessary for GHQ to send up staff officers to help write the operational orders for the coming offensive.[34] Edmonds also notes, without explanation or comment, that two of the three infantry brigadiers were away and six of the twelve infantry battalions were commanded by majors standing in for colonels.[35]

Virtually all the accounts comment on deficiencies in the trench and defence systems which the British had taken over from the Italians. They were said to be lacking in depth, and without any defence posts behind the front line to serve as rallying points to deal with incursions.[36] The trace of the front line on the ground was largely determined by the contours and was said to limit mutual support by adjacent units. However, trenches cut in rock are not easily modified and the British had arrived only at the beginning of April with the intention of launching an offensive rather than resisting an attack. Moreover, the 48th Division had not previously occupied the Carriola sector and had only moved there two weeks before the battle.

The siting of the main ammunition dump at Handley Cross close to the main route of communications was an error which caused much delay in the bringing up of reserves during the battle. It is not clear who was responsible for this choice. Certainly not the 48th Division who arrived only after it was well established. All that the 48th could do was to note "the folly of making a large dump of high explosives at an important crossroads 2000 yards in rear of front-line trenches". But so much work was needed to prepare for the projected Allied offensive that nothing could be done to move it.[37]

Edmonds also points out that the British had no experience of mountain warfare in Europe.[38] This remark is correct but misleading. The routes up from the plain to the plateau were certainly outside the Division's previous experience, but once on the plateau the ground over which it fought in June was only moderately mountainous. In fact no more so than much ground in Britain, and not to be compared with other regions of the front which the Italian Army took in its stride. On the other hand, the British coming from France had little experience in fighting over wooded ground with all the problems of maintaining contact and communication, and with little assistance from the artillery.

There were, however, other factors which arose from decisions made by the Division. As described above, the 23rd Division had five battalions in the front line, while the 48th Division had only three, and moreover the 23rd Division had three more battalions in positions of close support while the 48th had only one (Map 7). In addition on the evening of 14 June Major Waller, the acting CO of the 5th Gloucesters, was ordered to take over more line from the 4th Ox and Bucks to simplify a handover to 144 Brigade due to take place the following day in preparation for the Allied attack. He pointed out that the battalion was only 400 strong and was too weak to hold this additional line, but was told by Colonel Reynolds that this was an order.[39]

As the battle proceeded on 15 June the reserve battalions were progressively brought forward towards the front (Section 6.3). By 08.30 the 8th Warwicks were on the Cesuna Switch and the 6th Warwicks were at Brigade HQ behind Cesuna. At about this time further units were ordered up; the 4th Berks arrived at the Cesuna Switch at about noon, the 6th Gloucesters at Magnaboschi at 12.30, the 4th Gloucesters at Carriola at 14.00, and the 7th Worcesters at Carriola at 17.00, all delayed to a greater or less extent by the difficult conditions.

The orders for a counter-attack were given at 09.30 but the build-up of strength took some time. The first attack by the 7th Warwicks took place at 14.00. A second attack was made at 18.00 by the 7th Warwicks and 6th Gloucesters, and then both battalions were joined by the 7th Worcesters for a third attack at 20.00. In fact there were never sufficient numbers available to mount a counter-attack effective enough to regain the front line. This was only achieved the following day when almost the whole strength of the Division was eventually employed, and when the Austrians were preparing to withdraw.

In his book *With the 48th Division in Italy* Lieut.-Colonel Barnett, the AA & QMG of the Division, sets out a long list of lessons learnt from the attack.[40] The points made include: the need for the transport lines to have a regular procedure in case of enemy bombardment; enough personnel and animals to get small arms ammunition and grenades to the fighting troops, and water and rations up every 24 hours; reserves of water in petrol cans in case of damaged pipes and tanks; reserves of rations on transport lines for passing personnel; police for battle stragglers, reinforcements for traffic control, escorts for prisoners. Barnett comments that in case of an offensive these points are always provided for and set up beforehand, but "in the case of a sudden enemy offensive, however, they have not always been provided for in the defensive scheme". At the end of this list Barnett's next paragraph begins, "On 19 June Major-General Sir R.Fanshawe was ordered to hand over the command of the Division and proceed to England for duty there".[41]

Although the battle had been won there were some matters which must have concerned GHQ. The enemy attack had not been halted as abruptly as that against the 23rd Division and that against the French Divisions. The cost in casualties had also been greater. The total casualties (dead, wounded and missing) are given as 920 for the 48th Division and 556 for the 23rd Division,[42] whereas the losses of the two French Divisions are given as 592 for the period 5–24June.[43] In 1918 there was a great shortage of manpower and little prospect of further drafts being sent out to Italy. Sandilands in his *History of the 23rd Division* comments that at this stage of the war "to risk incurring casualties lightly or with insufficient reason would be more than ever a crime".[44]

There was also a feeling that the battle had been rather a close run thing. Edmonds states that "British officers who were present think that had the Austrians pressed their attack with determination they would have penetrated far deeper without much difficulty".[45] Certainly, when the Austrians first broke into the British positions, there was quite insufficient strength in the second line to resist a determined attack, as the bulk of the reinforcements were still on their way up to the front. At a conference held by Cavan on 20 June stress was laid on improving the wire protecting the front line and ensuring that it was covered by adequate enfilading fire. It was also necessary to profit from Italian expertise in burying and pegging telegraph lines on the ground, and in using extremely slack cables if slung between poles and trees.[46] Subsequently Lieut.-Colonel Pryor of the 6th Warwicks wrote to Edmonds saying that if the Austrians had had "any initiative at all the Official History would be very difficult to write".[47]

The performance of the British artillery had been disappointing, for the Austrians appear to have made their initial penetrations not greatly hindered by the British guns. Low cloud and dense mist, together with the breakdown of communications, had made great difficulties for the control of the artillery. Indeed Edmonds states that "Battery commanders . . . had to a great extent to act on their own initiative".[48] The actions of the artillery are detailed in the diaries of the Corps and Division artillery but it is difficult to form a clear picture of most of the events. However, an entry at 04.30 in the diary of the CRA 48th Division reads

"Batteries ordered not to fire "S.O.S." unless ordered". In fact the first order for an S.O.S. barrage was only given at 08.12,[49] while the diary of the British Heavy Artillery first reports firing on enemy troops in no-man's-land at 08.10, and an S.O.S. barrage after 08.58.[50]

It was also the case that batteries had been placed very far forward ready for the planned Allied attack, sometimes in the woods and not in good positions to bring defensive fire on an enemy immediately in front of the British trenches. Moreover, some of these guns and their crews were taken by the enemy, a loss of some symbolism, even though the guns were soon recovered. The siting of the guns was primarily the responsibility of Brigadier Wardrop, the Commandant Royal Artillery of XIV Corps, but one point concerning their control did involve Fanshawe.

In his report dated 21 June Fanshawe wrote that "I had directed that the barrage on S.O.S. lines should not be brought down unless the attack was actually seen, as . . . I considered it not at all certain that the enemy would attack, and a S.O.S. barrage would be a great mistake using up our own ammunition and energy uselessly and encouraging the enemy by making him think that he had diverted our artillery from the real attack".[51] In the event, the Austrians began a heavy bombardment at 03.00, followed by an infantry attack at 07.00, and no order was sent until the attack had been under way for about an hour, but by then communications were already cut.

It might also be said that Fanshawe put too much weight on the intelligence reports that the Austrian offensive would extend only to the adjacent French Corps. There was certainly an unfortunate expectation in the Division that they would not be attacked; see for example Greenwell[52] and Morshead[53]. In fact the artillery orders on 14 June were concerned almost entirely with the preparations for the British offensive. Moreover, none of the several accounts of the battle give much impression of Fanshawe playing a forceful role to dominate events. Indeed, on one occasion when Fanshawe had no news on the situation at the front, information was obtained by the initiative of Colonel Tomkinson who himself suggested that he should go forward and talk with Colonel Reynolds.

Clearly there were many points in the battle which might have been better arranged and for which Fanshawe may be criticized. Yet there remain two essential points. The enemy attacks had been completely repulsed, and repulsed by the morale and fighting qualities of the men of the 48th Division, for whom Fanshawe was undoubtedly responsible.

One is struck by the way in which members of the 48th Division in their written accounts all pay tribute to their commander. They were obviously fond of Fanshawe. Colonel Tomkinson refers to "Fanshawe to whom his Division was devoted"[54], and Captain Carrington described

16. Italian troops with mules crossing the Piave. (*IWM Q26698*)

17. Pontoon bridges on the Piave. (*IWM Q26734*)

18. British troops escorting prisoners across the Piave. (*IWM Q26693*)

19. A large trestle bridge across the Piave. (*IWM Q26181*)

20. Italian cavalry crossing the Monticano. (*BL 9084H7*)

21. David Lloyd George.

22. Field Marshal Sir William
Robertson.

23. Marshal Foch.

24. General Luigi Cadorna.

25. General Sir Herbert Plumer.

26. Lieutenant-General the Earl of Cavan.

27. (*Above left*) General Armando Diaz.

28. (*Above*) The Emperor Karl.

29. (*Left*) General Enrico Caviglia.

30. Vittorio Orlando, Prime Minister of Italy 1917-19.

31. President Woodrow Wilson.

him as "the kindest hearted old swashbuckler in the army".[55] Fanshawe had commanded the Division since 1915, and on 24 August 1916 the Division had been in line on the Somme for over three weeks, and the War Record of the 4th Ox and Bucks comments "the men by this time were getting tired and rather war worn, and a visit by the Divisional Commander to every post in and in front of the front line next day greatly cheered everyone".[56] Colonel Howard of the 7th Division writing to Edmonds refers to Fanshawe's habit of "feeding his troops with pieces of chocolate when inspecting the front line early in the morning".[57]

Looking over the written evidence, it appears that the recall of Fanshawe was a judgement that involved balancing several factors. It is not clear how the decision was arrived at, but one further factor may well have played a part.

5. The Italian Assistance

British accounts of the battle generally acknowledge the help given by troops of the adjacent Italian X Corps who took over 800 yards of the British line at the left of the 48th Division front in order to allow troops of the 5th Warwicks to take part in the British counter-attacks. In addition the London *Times* of 17 June carried a short report from GHQ Italy dated 16 June which stated "In the early hours of yesterday when the hostile attack was first launched, invaluable assistance both in infantry and artillery was immediately provided by the Italians on our left, and this assistance was largely responsible for bringing the Austrian infiltration to an immediate halt".[58] Yet no reference to this artillery aid appears in any subsequent British account.

After the war, in 1934, General Caviglia the commander of the Italian X Corps published his book, *Le Tre Battaglie*, in which he refers briefly to the battle at Asiago. He states that "The prompt intervention of the artillery of the Xth Italian Corps (Caviglia) and of its division on the right (12th General Monesi), as well as of the British and Italian artillery of the 6th Army, and the vigorous counter-offensive by the English infantry, restored the situation before the evening".[59] In fact, General Caviglia was on friendly terms with Lord Cavan, having known him since before the war when they both served as military attachés in Japan. Perhaps for this reason further details only appeared much later, in the IOH published in 1980[60], and then in books by Pieropan[61] and Cervone[62].

According to these accounts, early on 15 June Italian artillery observers in the adjacent zone of the 12th Italian Division saw enemy units in considerable strength moving across the Ghelpac and breaking into the British line. On receiving this information General Segre the Commandante d'Artigliere of the 6th Army, telephoned General Cavan who was still without any news from General Fanshawe. Meanwhile General Caviglia had also received the Italian reports, and had ordered the artillery of the Italian 12th Division on the nearby Monte Cengio (Map 3) to fire on the Austrians in the British trenches. He also warned the Casali Brigade of the 12th Division to be ready to counter-attack if necessary to maintain the British positions on their right.

Although the details are not set out precisely, it is clear that there was then a conversation between Caviglia and Cavan in which Cavan protested against artillery fire being directed on to his front line, and Caviglia explained that Austrian troops had occupied that line. Thus Cavan received the first news of the breakthrough from the Italians and not from his own commanders. Given the enemy damage to communications, this failure was understandable, but a further factor must have aggravated the situation for Cavan.

At the start of 1918 the French and British had set up training schools in Italy both for their own troops and to pass on to the Italians the latest methods and techniques which had been developed on the Western Front (Section 4.3). A large training area had been set up near Padua, to quote from Edmonds, "largely in the hope of instilling good doctrine and practice into the Italian Army", and arrangements were made for French and Italian officers to attend the various courses and for British officers to attend French and Italian courses".[63] However, "On 29 May information was received that the Italians proposed to send no more officers and NCOs to British schools. Various reasons were given: (a) the need for all officers to be with their units in the coming time of stress; (b) the fact that, being trained on somewhat different lines to what they were accustomed, officers and NCOs emerged with a lessened faith in their own training and an incomplete knowledge of the British; (c) the intention of starting in the future a large training centre of their own." Lord Cavan "deplored this decision and approached General Badoglio on the subject; but he met with no more success than was represented by a suggestion that the question might be reconsidered in two months".[64] Yet two weeks later at the very start of the British Army's first major engagement in Italy, it was the Italians who brought the first news of the break into the British front to the British GOC and were able to provide infantry and artillery assistance!

(The *Times* report of 17 June was very brief, so brief as to be misleading in saying that the swift Italian intervention was largely responsible for bringing the Austrian infiltration "to an immediate halt". In fact the drive towards the Cesunsa and Lemerle Switches was only halted after several hours by the combined action of the British battalions and of the Italian and British artillery.)

The Summer Recess

1. Italian Plans

After the defeat of the Austrian attack at Asiago the British immediately reoccupied their front line and their forward outposts. On the same day, 16 June, raids on the Austrian front line to the west of Canove (Map 5) met with little resistance and brought back prisoners, many of whom had surrendered readily.

Both Lord Cavan and the French Commander, General Graziani, were eager to move against the defeated Austrians, with the initial aim of securing the enemy line previously set as the first objective for the Allied offensive planned for 18 June. However, Diaz refused to sanction any such attack as he wished to keep all his reserves for any eventuality on the Montello where the Austrians continued their attack until 23 June. Cavan and others were later to maintain that a great opportunity had been lost, but it is by no means clear that the Italian divisions on the flanks of the French and British would have been ready to advance in support. Moreover, the Austrian rear areas behind their front line were still largely intact, and subsequent British patrols soon found a noticeable stiffening of resistance.[1]

The Allied attack for 18 June had been irrevocably disrupted and the Allies had now to decide on future plans. Differences of opinion soon emerged. The French and British were very conscious of the German offensives on the Western Front which had been launched on 21 March and were to continue for four months creating a great salient in the Allied front running from Ypres to Rheims. During this time the Germans took 225,000 prisoners, 2,500 guns and inflicted nearly a million casualties. Moreover the setback coincided with a crisis in Allied manpower, for the great influx of American troops had still to make itself felt. Therefore, with the issue of the war in the balance, the French and British saw the vital necessity of bringing all the available Allied forces to bear on the enemy on all the fronts including the Italian front.

The Italian viewpoint was rather different. The Italian Army had recovered greatly from the disorganization at and after Caporetto, and had decisively seen off the Austrian June offensive. However, General

Diaz was well aware that although the Austrians had been thrown back, the Italian counter-attacks on the Montello had shown up grave deficiencies in the Italian staff work (Section 5.7). Also, although morale had greatly recovered, there was concern at the large number of Italian troops taken prisoner.[2] Therefore, it appears that Diaz's first priority was to avoid any further setbacks or disasters, and for this it was essential the Army be brought to a state of full efficiency, and that the various reforms he had introduced for the welfare of the troops had time to underpin their rising morale. Hence Diaz's cautious, and realistic, aim was to prepare for a final offensive in 1919.

A further thread in the Italian view of the military situation was a continuing belief that Italy was seriously short of manpower. Foch, Robertson and Cavan had never been convinced of this provided that all the available manpower was mobilized and properly used, and thought that Cadorna's appeal for twenty French and British divisions in 1917 had considerably exaggerated Italian needs (Section 2.2). Even so, Italian anxieties continued to lead to some unrealistic discussions. For example, when Diaz visited General Pershing on 6 September he asked that twenty American divisions be sent to Italy! Pershing afterwards wrote that, "as I showed no evidence of surprise, having become accustomed to that sort of thing, he [Diaz] possibly thought that this was a favourable sign, so while the interpreter was translating what he had said he interrupted and raised the number to twenty-five divisions". This was a request "so astonishing that it was difficult to regard it seriously", and Diaz's request was politely declined.[3]

Because of these different views and perspectives the principal activity for the next three months was a discussion of future actions. This interchange had begun immediately after the defeat of the Austrians at Asiago when Cavan and Graziani had wished to push the Austrians back across the plateau. This suggestion was hardly practical, but it was followed by long and courteous exchanges between Diaz and General Foch. (The latter had since 26 March been essentially C. in C. of all the Allied forces on the Western Front, following the success of the German March offensive and Haig's request on 25 March for the immediate support of twenty French divisions.[4])

On 27 June Foch wrote to Diaz stressing the importance of improving the position in the Trentino prior to an offensive on the Piave, saying that this might be achieved by driving up from Feltre (Map 3) through Val Sugana to occupy the region around Trent.[5] This suggestion was followed by an exchange of views during the next three months. On 6 July Diaz requested twenty-five Renault tanks and twenty tonnes of yperite explosive,[6] and on 12 July the Italian Ambassador in Paris asked for the return of the Italian pioneers sent to France earlier in the year to work on defences (Section 4.2).[7] On 17 July Foch replied that they were

118

doing very valuable work and could not be spared.[8] Then on 24 July Signor Nitti the Italian Finance Minister, on a visit to London, pleaded for American divisions to be sent to Italy as she had no resources to meet an emergency. It was pointed out in reply that in case of trouble reinforcements could be sent very quickly by rail, particularly if the Italians put in two or three months' work on the Modane rail route.[9]

On 26 July the Italian Military Attaché in Paris wrote to the President du Conseil saying that Diaz had the intention of doing something ("*quelquechose*") before the autumn, and also asking again for tanks and yperite.[10] Three days later Diaz wrote to Foch saying that he was planning a strong thrust from Asiago which could be launched twenty days "from the moment we have at our disposal the necessary means".[11] Foch responded on 6 August by agreeing to supply some artillery, ammunition charged with yperite and seventy-five assault vehicles, and asking "by what date, as soon as possible, you intend to launch your offensive".[12] On 13 August Diaz replied saying that preparations for the offensive had already begun and should be complete by "about 10 September", after which it should be possible to attack.[13] At the same time he also insisted that he needed more lorries, but on 17 August Foch explained that none could be spared from France. Diaz then prepared a memorandum for the Italian representative on the Allied Executive War Board at Versailles which shows that he had now become lukewarm over the proposed offensive.[14] He was no doubt disappointed at the French response to his various requests, and was probably increasingly aware of the difficulties presented by the strongly fortified ground in the Trentino. In fact on 26 August he asked the 3rd and 8th Armies to draw up plans for possible offensives across the Piave.[15]

On 31 August Diaz visited Foch in Paris where he was received very cordially and encouraged to hasten his offensive.[16] Diaz obtained little from his visit, certainly not twenty or twenty-five American divisions, and refrained from giving any definite commitment. Indeed according to the IOH he was now clearly against any big offensive in 1918, preferring to prepare for an offensive in the spring of 1919.[17]

On 9 September Diaz talked with Cavan who expressed his concern about the delay in taking action,[18] saying that the Austrians were all the time strengthening their line, while his own troops had been standing ready to attack since April. Diaz replied that the Austrians had more divisions than the Italians and were still fighting with stubborn tenacity, and that to take an offensive just for the sake of doing so would be a waste of life. But if in the next week, or even sooner, Foch was to break through the Hindenburg line and take Cambrai or St.Quentin, or both, the Germans would be bound to call on the Austrians for help and in that situation Diaz would attack at once at all costs and, so he said, "it is for this that I want to be ready". Cavan agreed and was much struck by Diaz's evident desire to do all he could to help, while very naturally guarding his country's interests.[19] (Also on 9 September the War Office, in line with current practice on the Western Front, ordered that the number of battalions in each brigade be reduced from four to three and that the nine surplus battalions be sent back to France.[20])

Later, on 23 September, Diaz became seriously concerned at reports of Austrian troop movements to the east of the Piave and ordered some artillery to move from the 1st Army between the Stelvio and Val d'Astico to the 8th Army on the Piave.[21] Then on 26 September he asked General Caviglia, now commanding the 8th Army, to prepare a suitable counter-attack should that become necessary.[22] As the month passed "various signs and silences" suggested to British GHQ that some plans were afoot.[23] Nevertheless, on 24 September Orlando wrote to Foch supporting Diaz in his cautious attitude of preferring to wait to launch his offensive until 1919.[24] Foch replied that there is "no war without risk" and "The question is to know if . . . the Italian Command is ready to run these risks".[25]

At the beginning of August Lord Cavan had proposed that provided the front remained passive, his three divisions should be gradually relieved by three divisions from France who would gain from a comparatively quiet winter in a healthy area.[26] Cavan was away in England for the latter part of Setember and in his absence General Walker suggested to the CIGS that the Comando Supremo should be approached with a view to initiating this rotation. Diaz reluctantly agreed and on 27 September the 23rd Division was relieved by an Italian division and prepared to leave for France. However, Cavan, then in London, urged that as the Italians had now said they were willing to take the offensive, more should be done to cooperate with them, and the orders were rescinded.[27]

On 26 September the French and British launched major offensives on the Western Front which produced immediate successes. The next day Bulgaria requested an armistice. Further successes were reported all along the Western Front on 27 and 28 September. On 1 October the Italian Prime Minister, Orlando, told Foch that he and Diaz had agreed to take the offensive as soon as possible.[28] On 4 October Austria and Germany approached President Wilson to propose an armistice. On 6 October Diaz told Lord Cavan that he meant to take the offensive at an early date and asked him to assume command of a new 10th Army comprising the Italian XIth Corps with the Italian 23rd and 37th Divisions, and the British XIV Corps (Major-General Babington) with the British 7th Division (Major-General Shoubridge) and 23rd Division (Major-General Thuillier). At the same time General Graziani was asked to assume command of a new 12th Army consisting of the Italian I Corps (24th and 70th Divisions), the 52nd alpini Division and the French 23rd

Division.[29] Finally on 14 October Private Gladden found himself leaving the rear billets at Arzignano below the Asiago plateau as part of the move of the 23rd and 7th Divisions to the Piave.

2. At Asiago

None of the discussions described above were known to the British troops on the ground, who continued to hold the Carriola and Granezza sectors from June to October with two divisions up front and one in reserve on the plain. Following General Cavan's conference on 20 June, the 7th Division, which relieved the 48th Division on 26 June, began work to strengthen weak places in the front line, to install fresh wire, and form a picket line in advance of the main line.[30] No further offensive action was taken by the Austrian infantry after 15 June but intermittent artillery exchanges were always an unwelcome hazard on the plateau. The shells from two 430mm Austrian howitzers were particularly unpleasant, smashing into the rocky ground and hurling rock debris in all directions, up to distances of 800 yards. Considerable work was done to improve the deep shelters so as to give better protection against this artillery bombardment, the original Italian ones often having little more than timber and earth as a roof. Italian specialists with power drills aided engineers to make deep shelters in the rocks.[31]

The only offensive actions for the next three months apart from artillery exchanges were a number or raids on the enemy lines by night and some RAF flights by day to help maintain control of the skies. The British Army believed in night raids to dominate the enemy and maintain their own morale, and two of the first raids, on the night of 22 June, were made by reserve units of the 23rd Division who had so far been denied "the opportunity of coming to grips with the enemy". On this occasion one and a half companies of the 10th battalion of the Duke of Wellington's Regiment took thirty-one prisoners and killed fifty or more of the enemy at a cost of one dead, nineteen wounded and three missing. The other raid by 100 men of the 11th West Yorks resulted in a "trench garrison annihilated, no prisoners being taken" at a cost of eight wounded.[32] Accounts of other raids are given by Edmonds and in the regimental and battalion histories by Barnett, Cruttwell, Sandilands and Wright. Although the British casualties were generally relatively light on each occasion, they eventually amounted to a considerable fraction of all the losses on the plateau, as is spelt out on the gravestones and in the cemetery registers in the British cemeteries near Asiago.

By the beginning of August intelligence reports suggested that the Austrians were planning to withdraw their front line opposite the French and British troops to higher ground beyond Asiago, and a deserter said that this withdrawal was planned for 10 August. Therefore on the evening of 5 August General Montuori, commanding the 6th Italian Army, met with Cavan and Graziani, together with General Badoglio the Italian Assistant Chief of Staff, and suggested that the French and British troops should anticipate this move by an earlier attack which would overrun the new line under construction.[33]

Cavan asked for a few hours' adjournment, and when the meeting was resumed later that night Badoglio argued that it was important to give the Austrians some sort of push to show that their retirement was not voluntary. Cavan agreed and was willing to make the attack but stressed that only two thirds of his artillery could be in position in time, and that the new positions could only be supplied across the open and exposed centre part of the plateau, which would be expensive in life and material. Therefore he believed that such positions could only be maintained for a few days, after which it would be essential to advance further to positions commanding the greater part of the plateau. Hence, it was decided after considerable discussion that the most that could be done with the available forces was two large-scale raids, one by the British on the night of 8 August and one by the French on the night of 9 August. The British launched twenty-two companies drawn from all four front-line brigades in eight simultaneous raids supported by British, French and Italian guns. The Austrians lost heavily in killed and wounded, and 355 prisoners were brought back. The total British casualties were 204 including the slightly wounded, all the wounded being brought back. The next night the French captured 241 prisoners with small losses.[34]

Several British accounts show that as August progressed there was a feeling among the British of being left out of the real war which was now being decided on the Western Front. However, towards the end of August senior officers in the divisions were informed, under conditions of strict secrecy, of the proposed offensive in the Trentino. This was an ambitious programme as the way ahead was very mountainous with the few roads well covered by Austrian forts and guns, and the role of the British divisions was to be equally demanding. It was proposed that the 23rd and 7th Divisions would first advance through the new Austrian trench system overlooking Asiago, 1500 yards in depth, to occupy the line Monte Bisa – Monte Interrotto (Map 12,p.169). The 48th Division would then pass through the two leading divisions to occupy Monte Erio to the west. However, Monte Bisa and Monte Erio were on the far side of the deep gorge of Val d'Assa, with no bridges or tracks across it, and rose 700 or 800 metres above the river. Colonel Barnett of the 48th Division describes the plan as "fantastic and contrary to the elements of common sense".[35]

As the Italians finally decided to attack on the Piave and on Grappa nothing became of the above plans except two large raids to find out as much as possible about Austrian intentions. On 24 August small raids were made on enemy outposts at Ave and Sec (just south of Asiago) and captured six prisoners. Then, as it was known that the Austrians generally increased the strength of a garrison after a section of line had been attacked, two nights later on 26 August the 1st Bucks and the 4th Berks battalions of the 48th Division made a much larger attack in the same area. They were supported by a coordinated artillery barrage, and the raid was planned with great care, see for example the orders for the Bucks quoted in full by Wright.[36] This raid brought back 210 prisoners and killed many Austrians at a cost of 169 casualties (dead, wounded and missing). At the same time another raid by the 10th Duke of Wellington's battalion of the 23rd Division killed about 80 men and captured 65 at a cost of 56 casualties.[37]

When the British GHQ left for the Piave on 11 October the 48th Division remained at Asiago under the tactical control of the Italian XII Corps.[38] However, the Division understood that it would shortly be moving to the Piave to join the rest of the British forces, and should begin to evacuate its reserve stores and equipment from the plateau. Then on 19 October General Walker, the new Commander of the 48th Division, received from the Corps Commander, General Pennella, unexpected orders to mount an attack in four days' time, in cooperation with the French, to coincide with the opening of offensives on Grappa and the Piave. But the objectives were similar to those which had been judged impractical at the end of August.[39] General Odry, commanding the French 24th Division, announced that his artillery would take part but that not a single infantryman would leave his lines.[40] General Walker consulted Lord Cavan who got in contact with Diaz and the attack was cancelled.[41] However, a series of raids were ordered for the night of 24 October as some support for the flank of the 4th Army which was to attack on Grappa. Edmonds states that the British raid by the 4th Gloucesters near Ave brought in 229 prisoners for the loss of four wounded; the French on their right captured 761 prisoners and the Italians on their left fourteen prisoners.[42]

3. Austria and Germany

During the summer months the Austrians had shown little inclination for military action for the complete failure of the June offensive had produced a profoundly depressing effect, marking yet another downward step in the fortunes of the Austro-Hungarian Empire.

The Emperor Franz Joseph had come to the throne of the Austrian Empire in 1848 at a time when the empire was at its greatest extent, and shortly before revolutionary movements were to shake many of the old regimes. The young Franz Joseph was then faced with an insurrection in Bohemia (later Czechoslovakia) that was put down by military force.

Yet ideas of nationality and nationhood continued to propagate, and over his long life Franz Joseph had presided over a steadily declining empire. Milan and Lombardy were lost in 1859, and Venice and the Veneto in 1866. In 1867, in order to bind the Hungarian-dominated lands more closely to the Empire, the Hungarians were allowed to set up their own government with its seat in Budapest. However, this was not so great a break as might be supposed, as the Emperor was now accepted by the Austrians as the Emperor of the Austrian lands and by the Hungarians as the Emperor of the Hungarian lands. Hence *de facto* the Empire continued to act as a coherent block, the Austro-Hungarian Empire.

The Empire was also threatened by the nationalist aspirations of the Slavonic races who long ago had marched south from the depths of Russia to settle to the east of the Adriatic, where the Slovenes, Croats, Bosnians, Montenegrins and Serbs had for a long time formed part of either the Austrian or Turkish Empires. Nationalism and resistance to foreign rule were nowhere stronger than in Serbia, which took the lead in moves to free all the southern Slavs from foreign overlords. Eventually, in the Turkish war of 1912, the Serbs together with Greeks, Bulgars and Montenegrins drove the Turks out of almost the whole of their European possessions. By now Austria was much alarmed, for it seemed all too likely that the nationalist movements seeking independence for the southern Slavs would spread to her two Slav states, Slovenia and Croatia. Hence her ill-judged attempt in 1914 to "teach Serbia a lesson".

In June 1914 Franz Joseph was in his 84th year and the heir to the throne was the 50-year old Franz Ferdinand who played a substantial role in conducting the affairs of the Empire. His assassination at Sarejevo, besides precipitating the First World War, unexpectedly projected his 26-year old nephew Karl from a position of relative obscurity to that of heir to the throne. In view of the age of Franz Joseph, Karl was immediately involved in both the civilian administration and military affairs. During the Strafexpedition in Italy in 1916 he was given the command of an Army Corps, and later in Russia he commanded an Army. At other periods he talked frequently with Franz Joseph on the duties of the Emperor. Thus on the death of Franz Joseph on 11 November 1916 Karl had a clear picture of the duties and responsibilities of the Emperor.

Karl had seen at first hand the defeats, setbacks, and failures suffered by the Austrian armies during the war, accompanied by very little in the way of success, and all at a tremendous cost in life and suffering. Moreover, after three years of war Austria was indebted to Germany for assistance on various occasions, and was being asked for repayment either by a new Austrian offensive or by sending units to France. By the time Karl ascended the throne he had seen much to convince him that the war could bring Austria no benefit, and he believed that the war should be ended, on reasonable terms, as soon as possible. In addition he felt it his duty as the Emperor of the two separate Monarchies of Austria and of Hungary to ensure the integrity of the Austro-Hungarian Empire for the future.

Facing these formidable tasks Karl spent much effort in the first half of 1917 exploring the possibility of a negotiated peace with the Allies, using as an intermediary his French brother-in-law, Prince Sixtus of Bourbon, the whole matter being kept secret from his German ally. In the end these various talks came to nothing, except that the details eventually became public and Karl found himself more closely bound to an angry Germany, on whom he depended both for military support and the supply of food which was becoming a critical issue.

By 1918 Karl was also much concerned with the growing signs of unrest in the Empire. The Russian Revolution the previous year encouraged socialist/communist propaganda, all attempting to undermine the established order. But it was not only communists and socialists who gave him cause for concern. On 8 January President Wilson of the United States published his Fourteen Points as a basis for peace discussions, which were followed on 11 February by the Four Principals.[43] These documents laid down that peoples and provinces were no longer to be bartered about from sovereignty to sovereignty, and that every territorial settlement after the war must be made for the interest and benefit of the peoples concerned. (President Wilson also saw this enlightened policy as a means of avoiding a German dominated trading block extending on either side of the recently completed Berlin to Baghdad railway, which would be inimical to American trading interests.[44])

In April, representatives of the southern Slav states met in Rome and set out their aspirations for a single Jugoslav nation, the so-called Pact of Rome.[45] At about the same time Italy began a massive campaign of dropping millions of copies of nationalist propaganda behind the Austrian lines either from aeroplanes, balloons or rockets.[46] In August Britain and France recognized the Czech National Committee in Paris as the Government of their country, and recognition by the United States followed on 3 September. Moreover, the food situation, which had been serious throughout the Empire in 1918 was now aggravated by a poor harvest in July and August. However, events were now to be determined mainly by the Allies' war against Germany on the Western Front.

From March to July the Allies had suffered a succession of disastrous reversals and their line between Arras and Rheims had been forced back to within 40 miles of Paris. The tide only began to turn on 18 July when the French launched a successful offensive between Soissons and Château Thierry (in which two American divisions were in the front line). Then on 8 August a British offensive to push back the German line where it was dangerously close to Amiens produced immediate successes, and for the first time some German divisions were overwhelmed without offering much resistance. In fact the Germans had been over-extended by their four-month offensive which had left them with many losses and few reserves.

General Ludendorff, the First Quartermaster-General of the German Army, was later to describe 8 August as the black day of the German Army. He then came to believe that it was no longer possible for Germany to win the war and that she must concentrate on achieving an acceptable peace.[47] At an Austro-German conference at the German GHQ at Spa on 14 August Karl wanted diplomatic moves to end the war immediately but Ludendorff insisted that it was necessary to wait for a favourable moment. The Austrian delegation including the Chief of Staff, Arz, doubted whether Austria could endure another winter of fighting.[48] Finally on 14 September, against German advice, the Austrian Foreign Minister, Count Burian, made a personal appeal to all the belligerents to agree to some form of round-table conference. This appeared in the Berlin press the following day and was rejected by the United States as soon as it was received because it made no mention of the Fourteen Points. A further blow arrived on 25 September when the Bulgarians requested an Armistice in their war against the Serbs, Greeks, French and British, thus opening the possibility of further attacks along a considerable stretch of the Austro-Hungarian frontier. Two days later the Austrian Crown Council met to discuss the situation and resolved on immediate action to initiate the reforms necessary to meet the Fourteen Points.

Already on 12 September, after the Americans had captured St Mihiel, Ludendorff had showed signs of strain. Not surprisingly, for he had increasingly become not only the director of the German Army but of the whole country as well. The Bulgarian defeat appeared as a final straw, probably involving the loss of the Rumanian oil, and his resolve cracked. Without consulting any other general save Hindenburg he informed the Foreign Minister on 29 September that there was no alternative but to seek an <u>immediate</u> armistice. This was agreed, and telegraphs were sent to Vienna and Constantinople informing their allies of the new situation.[49] Hindenburg, the Kaiser and Ludendorff then signed a decree setting up a new and more representative government intended to be more acceptable to Wilson than the military régime under Ludendorff and Hindenburg.

On 3 October a new German government was formed under Prince Max of Bavaria and the following day Germany, Austria and Turkey sent notes to Wilson asking for negotiations for the restoration of peace, accepting Wilson's speech of 8 January as a basis for negotiation, but without mentioning the Fourteen Points. The next day, 5 October, the Austrians optimistically began assembling an armistice commission at Trent to study the possibility of evacuating the Veneto by a withdrawal without fighting.[50]

President Wilson's reply to the notes of 4 October arrived on 9 October but only asked various questions to clarify the notes. Even so, the Austrians telegraphed to the German GHQ and Foreign Office that they intended to send delegates to the Italian Comando Supremo to treat for an armistice immediately; they were told very early the next morning to hold back. Germany replied to the American queries on the night of 11/12 October, at about the same time that news came through that the liner *Leinster* had been torpedoed with the loss of 450 lives, including 135 women and children and some Americans. Wilson's reply to Germany was handed to the Swiss for transmission late on 14 October and arrived in Berlin at 05.20 on 16 October.

The tone and content of Wilson's reply was a great disappointment to Berlin. So far from offering negotiations on the basis of the Fourteen Points it laid down just three general points. The conditions of the armistice must be left to the military advisers of the US and her Allies, and must provide "absolutely satisfactory safeguards and guarantees of the present military supremacy of the US and the Allies in the field". Illegal and inhumane practices, such as submarines sinking passenger ships at sea, and even the lifeboats making their way to safety, must cease immediately. Finally the note called, if not explicitly for the abdication of the Kaiser, certainly for the replacement of the government of "arbitrary power" which had hitherto controlled the German nation.[51]

Since Ludendorff had first insisted on the despatch of the notes to Wilson on 4 October he had begun to regain confidence and to feel that the military situation was not so desperate as he had supposed. Hence his immediate reaction was to urge rejection of Wilson's reply and carry on the fight. However, the new German government of Prince Max overruled Ludendorff and took stock for themselves of Germany's position. It was all too clear that both the military position and the state of the country left little choice but to accede to Wilson's terms, and a note to this effect was sent on 20 October.

(One should remember that, though it was evident to the government in Berlin that the whole of the German war effort was crumbling, there was virtually no sign of this to the forces of either side still fighting on the ground, especially on the Western Front. Indeed, according to Cruttwell, General Foch was so concerned at the slow progress of the Franco-American offensive between the Meuse and the Argonne that

127

he even considered asking Clemenceau to request that President Wilson dismiss General Pershing.[52] As late as 19 October the British CIGS General Wilson wrote to Lord Cavan in Italy saying, "the Bosch is *not* beaten . . . anything you can do over the Piave will help enormously to Bosch difficulties and Bosch embarrassments".[53])

While Prince Max's government debated in Berlin how best to proceed the Emperor Karl had no doubts, and from now on German and Austrian negotiations proceeded almost independently. On 16 October with the support of the Crown Council Karl issued a Manifesto, stating that his Government had been ordered to provide a new constitution to give autonomy to the different parts of the Empire, each with its own national assembly.[54] In addition, these different parts were to be bonded together by a common Emperor and a new assembly formed from the members of the autonomous parliaments. Thus it was hoped to meet President Wilson's 10th Point which had asked for the peoples of Austria-Hungary "the freest opportunity of autonomous development".

The next day, 18 October, Austria sent Germany a note saying that peace was essential as the fall of Bulgaria laid Hungary open to attack by the Allies through Serbia. Then on 20 October Austria received Wilson's belated reply to their request for an armistice sent on 4 October. This was another great disappointment, for it stated that much had changed during the months since the Fourteen Points had been set out. The gift of autonomy was no longer sufficient because peoples themselves should have the right to choose their own form of government.

There were now clear signs of an Italian offensive in the near future, and in desperation Karl wrote to the Pope on 23 October asking him to persuade the Italians to hold back, but it was then too late.[55]

128

Vittorio Veneto

1. The Revised Plans

The first orders for the October offensive were issued by Diaz on 12 October, and envisaged an attack across a twenty-five mile stretch of the Piave from Pederobba down to and including the island of Papadopoli.[1] The aim of this offensive, subsequently known as the Battle of Vittorio Veneto, was to reach Vittorio Veneto and Sacile (Map 10, p.143), and thus cut the supply lines of the Austrian VIth Army which was holding the left bank of the Piave from just above Pederobba to a point about two miles below Ponte di Priula. These lines all ran back to the east through Vittorio and Sacile, so by taking these centres it was hoped to isolate and capture most of the VIth Austrian Army, and then move up towards Belluno (Map 3) to disrupt the join between the VIth Army and the Austrian Belluno Group on its right. The main weight of the thrust was to be delivered by the 8th Italian Army under General Caviglia with four infantry corps (XXVII, XXII, VIII, XVIII), twelve divisions in all plus an assault corps of two divisions.

The thrust of the 8th Army was to be supported on its left by the advance of the 12th Army. The Italian I Corps was to move up the right bank of the Piave under Monte Grappa, while to its right the French 23rd Division and the Italian 52nd Alpini Division attacked across the river. The right flank of the 8th Army was to be covered by the advance of the 10th Army under Lord Cavan against the Austrian Vth Army, with the British XIV Corps (7th and 23rd Divisions) and the Italian XI Corps (23rd and 37th Divisions). The 12th and 10th Armies were to move across the river at the same time as the 8th Army, while other Italian Armies, the 6th at Asiago, the 4th on Monte Grappa, and the 3rd on the Lower Piave, were to await developments. The 6th and 3rd Armies were warned to be prepared for possible enemy reactions and to be ready to advance should the order be given by the Comando Supremo. The 4th Army on Grappa was to support the flank of the 12th Army by artillery fire and, after the eventual advance of the 12th Army, to follow up to the line Primolano – Arten. The date for the attack was to be decided by the Comando Supremo on the advice of the Commander of the 8th Army bearing in mind the weather and the state of the Piave.

The crossing of the Piave presented substantial hazards. All along this stretch of the Piave, the river meandered across a wide gravel bed in several channels. Many of these are fordable but the main channel or channels could only be crossed by bridging, usually by laying a deck on a line of pontoons anchored across the stream. Such work is not too difficult for trained engineers provided, and this is a considerable proviso, that the river is not high and running fast, and that the site is not under enemy fire.

Besides the hazards presented by the waters of the Piave, the flat stony bed, generally about 1000 yds wide, offered a fine field of fire for the Austrians in their lines of defence and surveillance on the far bank. In these circumstances it was essential to attack under cover of darkness and to achieve the maximum amount of surprise so that the enemy could not make any prior concentration at the crossing points. Therefore particular care was taken to choose starting positions on the right bank with sufficient trees and other cover to conceal the build-up of supplies and troops prior to the crossing. In addition, it was desirable that there was some ground in front of the defences on the far bank where the initial landing parties could first establish themselves. The final decision was for the 8th Army to throw eight principal bridges: near Vidor, Fontana Buoro (three bridges), Falze, Nervesa (two bridges) and Ponte di Priula; while the 12th Army would throw two bridges at Pederobba and the 10th Army two bridges at Papadopoli Island. In addition to these main bridges there were to be a number of passerella, or light footbridges, including three in the 8th Army sector.[2]

A small but important change to the plan was suggested by General Babington, commanding the 23rd British Division, during a conference at 10th Army HQ on 14 October.[3] The British were faced with a difficult operation because at their crossing points the bed of the Piave was almost two miles wide, with the mile-wide Papadopoli Island in the centre held by the Austrians. However, General Babington pointed out that the most difficult part of the whole crossing would probably be the crossing of the main stream which ran between Papadopoli Island and the right bank (Map 9, p.134). He therefore proposed that it would be desirable to cross this main stream and capture the island on the night prior to the main attack, so as to be well placed to reach the far bank of the Piave as soon as the main attack began.

Such a modification would obviously be advantageous for the 10th Army but General Caviglia was concerned that it might warn the Austrians that some larger attack was imminent.[4] However, as Lord Cavan pointed out, statements by a prisoner and a deserter showed that the enemy were already expecting an attack.[5] Caviglia was also concerned that the move might lead to a diversion of effort from the main attack, and possibly an undue concentration of enemy artillery on Papadopoli, but he agreed nevertheless for the crossing to the island to be made on the night before the main attack.[6]

Much preparation was necessary. Besides the vast quantities of stores and ammunition always needed for a large offensive, the bridging of the Piave, and in due course the rivers beyond, would need an immense amount of additional material. The supplies for the Piave front included supplies for over 18 kilometres of bridging of various types, and 20,000 cubic metres of wood for the construction of trestle bridges and the repair of broken permament bridges.[7] Between June and October the specialist battalions of Italian boatmen, the pontieri, were built up from a total of thirteen to twenty-one companies (as well as increasing the number of boatmen on the lagoons near the mouth of the Piave from one to two battalions).[8]

Various precautions were taken to achieve the maximum surprise. Great efforts were made to hide and camouflage the concentrations of stores and equipment. The two British divisions to be moved to the Piave were sent as late as possible, beginning on 18 October. All the British officers sent to reconnoitre wore Italian uniforms, and all British troops likely to be seen beforehand were ordered to wear Italian greatcoats and helmets. The British artillery achieved surprise by employing a technique used on the Western Front at the battle of Cambrai in November 1917. One gun in each battery was calibrated by live firing behind the lines so that it could then be laid on target using maps provided by the RE survey section. Then as the relative performances of the other guns was known to the battery commanders from prior comparisons, all the guns could be laid accurately on a target. Hence the guns could remain completely silent without any previous registration until the battle began. In fact the batteries were only moved into position on the Piave just before the battle and then produced an accurate barrage without having previously revealed their positions.[9]

The four squadrons of the 14th Wing of the RAF at Asiago remained there until they moved to the Treviso area on 22 October. Here high-flying fighters were permitted to take off, but all the low flying RE 8s used for artillery spotting were grounded until the start of the battle. Owing to bad weather no recent air reconnaisances of the Papadopoli area were available, but on 22 October the whole of the XIV Corps area was photographed by 139 Squadron flying Bristol fighter reconnaissance planes. By working through the night, the photographic section produced 5000 prints which were then delivered directly to the units concerned.[10]

Unfortunately, when Diaz issued his orders on 12 October the Piave was high and flowing fast[11], and then continued to rise, thus ruling out

131

any chance of a successful crossing. By 15 October there was some decline in the level of the river, but it was still high and needed to drop still further. The same day, 15 October, the Italian Ambassador in Paris, Signor Bonin, wrote a long letter to the Prime Minister, Orlando, setting out his great concern at the deterioration in relations between Paris and Rome.[12]

Signor Bonin referred in his letter to various incidents which had previously soured relations between France and Italy. The Italian request in July for the repatriation of Italian military pioneers from the Western Front (page 118), at a time when the French and British armies had been very pressed by the Germans, had much embittered the French Prime Minister Clemenceau. Italian attempts to obtain American troops for Italy had not been " suitably conducted" (cf. Diaz's talk with Pershing described on page 118), and were regarded by Clemenceau as "underground methods of those politics described as Machiavellian".[13]

Most importantly, the main French concern was the lack of any Italian offensive action. In May 1918 Italy had refused to accept a unified command of all the Allied forces under General Foch,[14] and was now seen to be the only major ally not actively engaged in a major offensive, even though the enemy still occupied a large part of Italy.[15] Hence the Ambassador foresaw the "gravest danger" to Italian interests unless some military action were taken immediately. Even a partial success would be of use.

In addition to the above disturbing report from Paris, by 17 October Orlando had received news of mutinies among some German troops.[16] Hence, fearing that the end of the war was now very close, he wrote to Diaz at 11.15 on 18 October saying, *inter alia*, that in the present situation "our military inaction represents a real disaster", and concluding that "there are times in which it is necessary to be bold and to stake everything for everything".[17] This was no doubt very true but, as Colonel Girard the French Liason Officer at the Comando Supremo reported to Foch, the bad weather was continuing and the high flow of the Piave forbad, perhaps for a week, any possibility of making a crossing.[18] Therefore, to ensure at least some action, Diaz decided that the 4th Army should initiate a major offensive on Monte Grappa as soon as possible.[19]

On 18 October Diaz issued directive N.14273[20] setting out the form of an offfensive to be launched by the 4th Army with flank support by the 6th and 12th Armies on day X to be announced later. The 4th Army was to be reinforced by three divisions and some 400 guns from the other Italian armies, thus creating a considerable force consisting of the IX, VI, and XXX Corps, some nine divisions in all. It was laid down that this Army was to attack on the morning of day X with the aim of clearing the Austrians off Grappa and reaching the line Val Cismon – Arten – Feltre (Maps 3,4).

The weather now showed some signs of improvement so on 21 October Diaz issued his final orders[21] for an offensive along the whole front from Val Brenta to Papadopoli by the 4th, 12th, 8th and 10th Armies. The flanks on either side were to be covered by the 3rd Army on the lower Piave and the 6th Army at Asiago (extending from Val Brenta to Val d'Astico). The attack by the 4th Army would begin on the morning of 24 October and be followed by the attack across the Piave on the following night (24/25 October). The action on the Piave was to be coordinated by General Caviglia, whose view of the general development of the battle was set out in a letter of 25 October to the Duke of Aosta commanding the 3rd Army. His main thrust would be across the Piave led by the 8th Army with the 10th Army as a flank guard.[22]

The 6th Army on the Asiago plateau was to support the 4th Army (a) by counter-battery work against enemy guns in action against the 4th Army on Grappa, and (b) by the infantry of XX Corps advancing up Val Brenta to the village of Cismon. In addition, the 6th Army received rather vague orders to develop an intense activity on the rest of their front to hold down all the enemy forces on the plateau. At the other end of the front, the 3rd Army was ordered to be ready to provide fire to support the 10th Army, and to advance with them to the River Livenza. However, a proviso was added that this latter move was not to be made until the 3rd Army Command thought it possible in the light of the events which emerged on its left.[23]

(Figures given by Edmonds[24] and Pieropan[25] suggest that the forces deployed by each side on the whole front from the Stelvio to the sea were comparable, as were the numbers on the Grappa and Piave fronts, there being approximately 57 Italian divisions in all, with 20 involved in the Piave offensive and 13 in the Grappa offensive. Some accounts give quite detailed analyses of the relative strengths of the opposing forces but these comparisons are generally unaccompanied by any detailed information on the establishments of the divisions, on the number of troops actually in place, and the efficiency of the divisions.)

2. The Landing on Papadopoli

We now outline the course of the offensive, which is described at length in the IOH and more briefly by Pieropan. The part played by the British units is described by Edmonds, in the histories of the 23rd and 7th Divisions by Sandilands and Atkinson, in an account by Crosse, the Senior Chaplain of the 7th Division, and in the various regimental accounts.

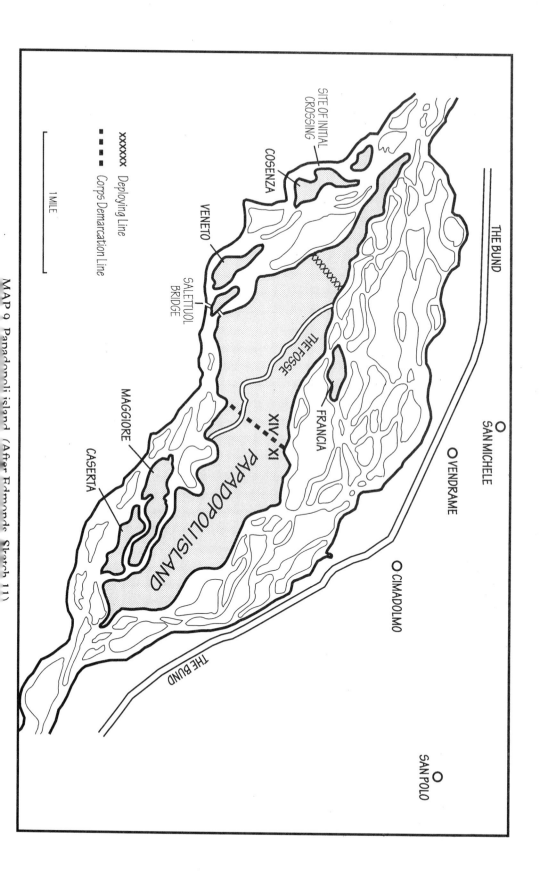

MAP 9 Papadopoli island. (After Edmonds, Sketch 11)

The initial move of the whole offensive was for the 10th Army to occupy Papadopoli Island in the middle of the Piave (Maps 2,9) on the night of 23 October. At this point the bed of the Piave is about two miles wide and the water meanders in several channels among beds of sand and gravel, either bare or covered with scrub, rising not much above the water level. The various channels divide the bed into a great number of islands of various size whose boundaries vary over the years due to changes brought about by exceptionally heavy flows during flood conditions. Today the area is much changed by drainage and consolidation works but Map 9 shows the area as it was in 1918. Much the largest of the islands, the Grave di Papadopoli, or Papadopoli Island, is about 4 miles long and about 2000 yards wide at its centre, narrowing down at each end. It lies nearer to the right bank at a distance varying from about 300 to 800 yards, whereas the left bank is up to a mile from the far side of the island. The river on either side of the island was divided into several streams, the principal main stream of the Piave being between the island and right bank. All round the island there were stretches of sand and gravel which were under water when the river was in flood.

The whole area of Papadopoli Island was, and is, quite flat and not much above high water level. The central area was thickly overgrown with low-lying scrub which gave quite good cover by day for a man lying quiet, and by night made it difficult for members of a unit to keep touch with one another. In peacetime the eastern half of the island had been cultivated with vine and maize and included the remains of twelve small houses. The centre part was covered with scrub, the most conspicuous topographical feature being a fosse about 3 ft deep and 10 ft wide. The upstream end of the island consisted only of sand, gravel or marsh.

The Austrian defences on the island consisted of two lines of trenches, a front line near the southern edge of the island, and a support line running roughly along the centre line of the island. These trenches were dug as deep as possible without striking water, about three feet, and there was also a plentiful supply of low barrow-like shelters for the garrison. The Austrians had installed numerous strong defensive posts, and in places considerable belts of barbed wire now thickly overgrown with long grass and rushes. Intelligence sources reported that the Austrians had a garrison of three companies which could be easily reinforced from the far bank. (In fact events showed that the island was initially held by eight companies, subsequently reinforced to fifteen.[26])

The aim of the 10th Army was to seize the whole of Papadopoli by an attack with the British XIV Corps on the left, and the Italian 37th Division of XI Corps on the right of the demarcation line shown on Map 9. Reconnaisances on previous nights by British patrols had failed to find any crossings to the island which were completely fordable. Cosenza

Island was already connected to the right bank by two footbridges, but was separated from Papadopoli Island by the main channel of the Piave which was not fordable. There appeared to be no possibility of constructing a pontoon bridge as all the feasible sites were too exposed to the view of the Austrians on the island. Hence it was decided that the first troops should cross in boats from Cosenza, while at the same time a footbridge would be constructed somewhat upstream. The only boats available were twelve Italian flat-bottomed pontoons with curved ends designed for bridge-building. Each was guided by two Italian boatmen of the 18th Company Pontieri who manoeuvred the boats with poles so that they were carried downstream by the river to the required landing place. All this called for much specialized expertise, as had been shown by British practice attempts on a smaller and slower river some days earlier.

The attack was made on the night of 23 October by two battalions of 22 Brigade of the 7th Division: the 1st Battalion Honourable Artillery Company and the 1st Battalion Royal Welch Fusiliers, each of three companies of about 100 other ranks. The whole operation on the island was in charge of Lieut.-Colonel O'Connor of the H.A.C. (later General Sir Richard O'Connor). The first move was made at 19.00 when an officer and three other ranks set off by boat from Cosenza to reconnoitre the passage to Papadopoli. They found that three main streams had to be negotiated.

The first stream was 70 yards wide, swift and unfordable; the second was 50 yards wide, even swifter and also unfordable; the third was 100 yards wide but only two or three feet deep and fordable. Between these streams it would be necessary to haul the boats over banks of sand and shingle, a noisy operation fortunately completely masked by the roar of the river as it raced over its stony bed. At 20.15 the first two platoons started to cross to the island with the aid of the twelve boats each able to carry seven men besides the two boatmen. Ten of the twelve boats landed safely a hundred yards or so below the point of embarkation, but the other two were swept down stream.

The first seventy men pushed inland and found a defence line manned only at a few points, and within minutes these posts were taken with the bayonet and twelve Hungarian prisoners captured. At 20.45, while the rest of the leading company together with the second company were still waiting to cross, Austrian S.O.S. flares were seen to go up from the downstream end of the island, presumably in response to an attempt by the Italian 37th Division to reach Maggiore Island (Map 9). This flare was followed by machine-gun and artillery fire on the British embarkation area, while a searchlight to the north swept the right bank. At about the same time the moon, hitherto obscured, broke through the clouds. There were a fair number of casualties but no boats were hit and the crossings continued.

While the troops were ferried across by boat the remainder of the Pontieri Company and the 101st Field Company RE (23 Division) were constructing two footbridges across the unfordable parts of the river about 400 yards upstream. These were made of boats about 20 feet apart joined by extra strong duckboards. As soon as they were finished all the rest of the two forward battalions were able to cross over, but as the site was completely exposed to view the bridges had to be taken down and hidden in bushes during the hours of daylight.

By about 23.00 the first two companies of the HAC had reached Papadopoli, had formed up facing south east, and had begun to advance between the two lines of Austrian trenches. The right-hand company and part of the left pressed straight on and surprised Hungarian troops by a flank attack which met with little resistance and by 24.00 most of the two companies had reached their objective opposite Salettuol. Meanwhile the left-hand platoon and the support company had drifted off to the left and eventually came opposite Francia Island. Here they recovered their direction and moved to rejoin the main group, subduing on the way a strongpoint of three officers and sixty men.

The HAC Battalion then set about clearing its front and completing the British line across the island. They were now supported by the 1st Company of the Welch Fusiliers who had arrived with instructions to protect the rear of the HAC, to prevent enemy reinforcements crossing to the island, and to clear up enemy pockets in the captured area. Very soon the other two companies of the Welch Fusiliers reached the island either by boat or footbridge. They were met by the Battalion HQ and one platoon of the HAC who had moved north-west across the island to join them, and on their way had surprised and captured eight Hungarian officers and about 200 troops, only two posts offering any real resistance. By 05.00 on 24 October all the objectives for the British troops had been achieved, and 330 Hungarians captured at small cost in casualties and with all the wounded evacuated back to the right bank.

On the right of the British the Italian 37th Division of XI Corps had the objectives of occupying the islands of Caserta and Maggiore, and if time permitted of pushing on to Papadopoli and then towards the demarcation line. In fact, the 37th Division had reached Caserta by an existing footbridge but failed to cross to Maggiore Island both because of enemy fire and the depth of the water.

3.   Postponement on the Piave

The offensive on Grappa was launched as planned on the morning of 24 October, but before describing this attack, we first follow the progress of the offensive across the Piave by the 12th, 8th and 10th Armies. This offensive was due to commence on the night of 24 October, but on

22 October the river was too high to permit bridging and appeared unlikely to fall to a safe level in less than 48 hours.[27] In fact rain fell heavily all day on the 24th, so Diaz had no choice but to postpone the Piave offensive. On the 25th the weather improved and the flow on the Piave began to decrease, and on 26 October at 18.00 Diaz gave the order for the offensive to begin that night.[28] We now describe how the British troops of XIV Corps spent the period of waiting.

The men of 22 Brigade who had arrived on the island in the early hours of 24 October had a miserable time. The weather was bad throughout 24 October and they were all soaking wet amidst the debris of the previous night's fighting. The Austrians were shelling the island but fortunately their fire was concentrated mainly on their old trenches which the British had wisely avoided. However, it was impossible to dig much protection as the water level was so close to the surface. The enemy also fired gas shells but the British masks appear to have been completely effective.

Facing their second night on the island the troops found themselves in a precarious position. It was quite likely that they would be attacked either from the south-east end of the island or from the far bank of the river. In either case rapid reinforcement was impossible. Communications with the right bank were bad. The rain had silenced the power buzzers, the state of the river made it impossible to lay a telephone cable, and the flat nature of the ground plus the mist and the rain made lamp signalling quite useless except at rare intervals. The only certain means of communication was by runners crossing by boat under machine-gun fire.

The troops had carried 24 hours of rations, and further rations had been brought across during the night, but the beach was now under fairly continuous fire and the river was rising rapidly. In the evening two officers from Divisional HQ brought the news that the offensive had been postponed, together with a warning that the Brigade might now be cut off. As these officers climbed into the boat for their return journey they enquired of the two Italian pontieri, *"Croyez-vous que nous pouvons gagner l'autre côté?"*, and one replied *"Peut-être, probablement non".*[29]

There were as yet no bridges suitable for artillery or wheeled vehicles, so orders were given to start work that night (24/25 October) on a pontoon bridge. The best site appeared to be about 300 yards above Salettuol where the main stream came close against the right bank with the deepest part nearest to the bank. Work began under Lieut.-Colonel Kerrich, the CRE of the 7th Division, with three field companies of engineers from the Division, one company from the 23rd Division and one company of Army troops, assisted by those Italian pontieri not required for ferrying troops and constructing the footbridges from Cosenza Island. The conditions were daunting. The main stream about

138

250 yards wide was flowing fast, and the RE companies had little or no experience of using pontoons, having previously been principally engaged in trench warfare.

A start was made by positioning a cable across the main stream to be held in place by twelve anchors along its length. Four volunteers, dressed ready to swim, set out in a boat to get the cable across the river. Two of the men were to punt the boat across, one was to keep the head of the boat straight, and the fourth to pay out the cable fixed to the home beach, but immediately the boat was launched it was swept downstream at a great pace and soon came to the end of the 250-yard cable. No land was yet visible. The boat began to fill rapidly with water and was in danger of capsizing, so the crew had no choice but to abandon the boat, hoping that they could find their feet on the river bottom. This was just possible and they dragged the boat first into shallower water and then back to a point roughly opposite their start point where the cable was secured to a multiple picket of several stakes supporting each other. Finally the boat was pulled back to the mainland hand over hand along the cable, and then during the night all twelve anchors were transported and laid before daybreak despite enemy shell fire.

The next day, 25 October, the rain had stopped and the weather was sunny, bright and warm, but the Piave was still high and forbade the launch of the main offensive. However, this delay gave the British the opportunity to capture the eastern half of Papadopoli Island, in order that the Italian 37th Division could move to the island ready for the main offensive. Therefore the commander of the 7th Division, General Shoubridge, visited the HQ of 22 Brigade on the right bank of the Piave, and ordered the 2nd Battalion R.Warwicks to join the two battalions already on the island and act in support of an attack that night. The battalion moved to the island as soon as darkness made it possible to cross by boat and to erect the footbridges. (During the afternoon Brigadier Steele, commanding 22 Brigade, had a narrow escape crossing the river when his boat came under machine-gun fire and one boatman was wounded and the other drowned. The lining of the brigadier's helmet was torn by a bullet and he himself somewhat concussed but he reached the island at a second attempt.)

As night came (25/26 October), the river had begun to fall, and the 2nd Warwicks started to cross from Cosenza Island first by boat and then by the footbridges. The Austrians had positioned a searchlight to reveal any attackers but this was blanketed by an Italian searchlight at a point about 500 yards upstream which threw its beam along the Austrian-held bank, and allowed the troops to pass unhindered.

The attack on the east end of the island was timed to start at 21.30 (25 October) when the HAC were to push forward towards the east, while the Welch Fusiliers protected their rear by taking up positions on the north edge of the island. The 2nd Warwicks were to remain in reserve. Enemy shelling of the island began at 21.00 and continued until 22.30 as if the Austrians were expecting an attack, but this did not cause any disruption of the plan. The HAC advanced easily at first, helped by some moonlight, but after about half a mile encountered exceptionally heavy machine-gun fire from the houses near Capanna Bassetto opposite Salettuol. Even so, by 05.15 the British troops urged on by Colonel O'Connor had occupied the whole island and taken 130 prisoners. Then at 05.30 two determined counter-attacks were launched by four companies of Hungarian troops, one against the HAC across bridges from the left bank of the river, and the other against a company of the Fusiliers across fordable channels. The Hungarians obtained only a small area near their bridges, and were soon expelled by the HAC, fifty being killed, 110 captured, and the rest escaping.

By 09.00 (26 October) the British had gained possession of the whole island. The rain had stopped, and the advance guard of the Italian 37th Division now began to cross over their bridges from Maggiore Island. The hazardous operation of driving the Austrians from the island was a notable success for 22 Brigade, achieved with a relatively small number of casualties. However, it must be remembered that the whole operation had been dependent on the courageous expertise of the Italian pontieri.

During the night work had continued on the bridge at Salettuol. To cross the first and deepest part of the main stream the 18th Company Pontieri brought up and positioned their own pontoons. These boats were larger and better designed for this type of work than the smaller British boats, but even so in the hands of any but absolute experts they would turn round and round in the current and eventually capsize. During the evening of 25 October the Italians placed four pontoons in position across about two-thirds of the deepest part of the main stream, the anchors to hold each boat being placed at the last moment as the pontoons were guided into position. To one British observer the whole operation was "a miracle of skill" quite outside British experience.[30] but there was still a long way to go to reach the island.

The next day, 26 October, the weather continued to improve and the river continued to fall. Except for a brief hour about noon the day was misty and the bridge was hidden from enemy view and fire, so work proceeded steadily all day, mainly unharassed by the enemy.[31] After the fourth Italian pontoon had been placed in position the RE had lowered a man from it to determine the depth of the next part of the stream. Although the sapper could not stand he could just touch the bottom, so it was decided that bridging by trestles would probably be possible. The engineers positioned three bays of trestles ahead of the Italian pontoons and then continued the bridge in shallower and slacker water using ten

British pontoons. As the day progressed it became clear that the bridge at Salettuol would not be finished by nightfall so the last part was completed as a temporary footbridge of duckboards on wooden bridging trestles.

Meanwhile most of the British troops due to take part in the offensive from Papadopoli Island were still waiting on the right bank in miserable conditions. The 20 and 91 brigades of the 7th Division had left billets in the region of Treviso on the morning of 22 October and marched to the village of Maseradi near the Piave, in time for a full day's rest before taking up their positions for the attack across the river set for the early hours of 25 October. In fact there were no billets available at Maseradi and both brigades had to bivouac among vineyards, with a ban on fires and tents in order to conceal their positions. Next morning, 23 October, the bivouacs were struck in order to avoid observation and then about midday the rain came down in torrents. There was no sun, no dry grass, no canteen, no card games. The cigarette supply had stopped two weeks earlier. There was nothing to do but walk up and down to keep warm as the hard surface of the fields turned to slush and quagmire.[32]

When the offensive was eventually postponed on the evening of 24 October there was talk of returning to billets for a day or so, but this would have meant a day's march there and a similar march back. Hence it was finally decided to hang on in the wet and in the complete boredom of inertia. However, the next day the rain stopped, the sun came out and everyone felt happier. (Crosse also comments that "strangely enough this very damp episode coincided with the end of the influenza epidemic in the Division".)

During this time the 23rd Division was also on the right bank and once again Private Gladden has left an account of events as seen from the lowest rung of the ladder. Although not always precise on details of time and place (the reference on page 164 to 25 October must be a misprint for 24 October) Gladden presents a succession of vignettes of some interest.[33] His battalion marched through Treviso on 22 October and spent the night in billets two or three miles further on. Soon after setting off next morning news came through that the battalion was to stand to for an immediate attack across the Piave. According to Gladden, this order came as a shock, for the war in the west seemed to be going so well that no one had expected any call for further effort. It was said that the officers were very pessimistic and that Captain Stirling had even told his batman that he would prefer to be going home on leave.

By the evening of 23 October the battalion had come up close to the Piave and could hear the intimidating roar of the swollen waters rushing over the shingle beaches. The prospect of an attack across the river appeared very daunting even to the usually imperturbable Gladden. He felt that his good fortune in coming unscathed through the Somme and

Passchendaele could not last for much longer, and that he was not being allowed his fair share of service with the reserves behind the front line.

"I felt that my run of fortune had been phenomenal and could not possibly extend any further. Surely my number was up this time! I took the very unmilitary step of pointing this out to the machine-gun sergeant, and it is characteristic of the change in attitude then widely in evidence that he listened sympathetically – it happened that he was not coming in himself – and made some representations on my behalf but the outcome was a foregone conclusion. Experienced Lewis gunners could not be spared, particularly as the company's complement of guns had recently been doubled. This was true enough and I should have known better. It was cowardly even to try but the roar of the torrent struck additional terror in my soul."[34] The night was spent in an open field near the river and in the morning they heard that a party of strong swimmers had failed to find any fordable passages and that one had been swept away.

4.   Across the Piave (27 October)

The days 22 to 26 October were anxious times for the Comando Supremo. On 22 October the Piave was in flood and running too fast for success, yet there was an urgent need to start the offensive as soon as possible. After the postponement on 24 October it was hoped that conditions would improve within the next two days, as the Piave could rise and fall quite rapidly. In fact conditions began to improve on 26 October, so Diaz gave the order to advance that night. However, rain fell during the night, and conditions on the river proved extremely difficult. We now summarize the outcome of the first 24 hours for each Army in turn, relying principally on the IOH, Edmonds and the British divisional accounts.

The 8th Army

XXVII Corps was to cross at Vidor, but all attempts to build a bridge were foiled by the speed of the water. By daylight on 27 October, out of the Corps' three divisions only the Cuneo Brigade had reached the left bank, and this by using one of the bridges thrown by XXII Corps.

XXII Corps was to throw three bridges (B,C,D) near Fontana Buoro. Here the ground on the left bank of the river was liable to flooding, so the Austrian lines of observation were some hundreds of yards back from the river, leaving a space not under observation at night.[35] The 5th Pontieri Company, aided by darkness and heavy rain, ferried squads of assault troops (arditi) across the river in ten or so barges to seize ground for the projected bridgeheads. It appears that they were able to land unopposed and take their first objective, a surveillance line on the shore manned by only a few sentries who were quickly overcome or captured.

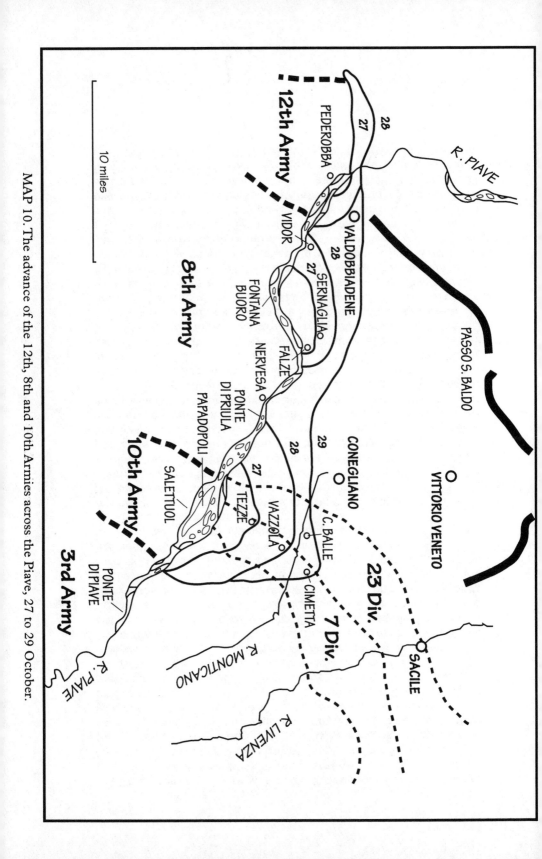

MAP 10. The advance of the 12th, 8th and 10th Armies across the Piave, 27 to 29 October.

At the same time work was going forward on the three bridges. Conditions were very difficult, but thanks to good fortune and the tenacity of the pontieri bridge B was completed by 23.00, and units of the 1st Assault Division began crossing to the left bank, followed by the Cuneo Brigade. About this time the alarm was raised on the Austrian side and their artillery opened up; some damage was caused to the bridge during the night but it was soon repaired. About 03.00 the Mantova Brigade of 57 Division began to cross and was followed about 04.00 by the Pisa Brigade of the same division.[36]

Work continued on the other two bridges at Fontana Buoro and sometime after midnight the 4th Company Pontieri had completed bridge D despite severe losses. The 30th Infantry Regiment of the Pisa Brigade and two battalions of the Piedmonte Brigade then began to cross to the other side. But all attempts to construct bridge C were foiled by the flow of the river and the attempt was abandoned. Nor was any success obtained at throwing a bridge at Falze, or in throwing any of the light footbridges which had been proposed. However, the main body of the 1st Assault Division had been crossing over bridges B and D, and by 03.00 had overcome the first enemy defence line, and by 04.00 had reached the main enemy defences in front of the villages of Sernaglia (Map 10) and Moriago about a mile to the south west.[37]

From now on the bridges were constantly threatened both by the swirling water of the Piave and by the enemy's artillery. At about 07.30 part of bridge B failed while the 29th Infantry Regiment was crossing, and by 09.30 both bridges B and D had been seriously damaged and were entirely out of action. It was now full daylight but the pontieri continued to ferry some troops across the river. On the left bank the now sizeable force continued to push forward to consolidate the bridgehead up to the line through Moriago and Sernaglia. During the day some 3200 prisoners and 200 machine guns were captured, the prisoners being gathered on the left bank to await transport across the river.

VIII Corps was to have thrown three main bridges during the night, two at Nervesa and one at Ponte di Priula, but had no success at all, primarily because of the flooded state of the river. The next day any work on the bridges was fully visible to the Austrian artillery. Attempts were made to ferry assault squads across, some reached the other side but remained isolated, one section on a pontoon which went adrift ended up on Papadopoli Island.[38]

Thus by the end of 27 October the 8th Army had only been able to pass its units over two of the projected seven main bridges, and these two bridges were now broken. Yet, a sizeable bridgehead had been established on the far bank and was held by almost all of the 1st Assault Division and the 57th Division (Pisa and Mantova Brigades) as well as the Cuneo Brigade of XXVII Corps and two battalions of the Piedmonte

Brigade. But the bridgehead was not yet large enough to push the enemy artillery out of range of the bridges, and since 09.00 it had been impossible to work on them, or cross by boat in any significant numbers.

The 12th Army

The construction of two bridges at Pederobba began at about 18.00 on 26 October. The pontoons for one bridge were carried away by the current, but by about 02.30 on 27 October three French battalions and parts of four alpini battalions had crossed over to the far bank. Then, at about 06.00 as three more French battalions were about to cross, the bridge was hit by Austrian fire and broke away. More water coming down the river after a storm three hours earlier made it impossible to repair the bridge in daylight. Nevertheless, the five battalions already across extended the bridgehead to about 2000 yards from the river and repulsed several enemy counter-attacks. More pontoons were sent for to repair the bridge but their arrival was delayed by the mass of traffic on the roads.[39] (The other part of the 12th Army, I Corps stationed above Pederobba, did not take part in the crossing but attacked towards the Alano basin (Map 5) as part of the offensive on Grappa.)

The 10th Army

The task of the 10th Army was to establish a bridgehead opposite to Papadopoli Island where they were already in position with bridges behind them to the right bank. Between the north side of the island and the far bank lay one to two thousand yards of river bed, largely shoals of sand and gravel giving little or no cover. Over this bed the river flowed in perhaps two to six main channels which were thought to be fordable but might be waist deep, and the river was still flowing fast. Once having crossed the river, the troops would then face the main Austrian defence line known as the Bund (Map 9). This was based on a flood containment wall rather like a railway embankment, about 10 foot high and 6 foot wide at the top, standing between 20 and 200 yards back from the edge of the river bed. The ground between the Bund and the river was protected by strong belts of wire and showed traces of the remains of various trenches and posts for machine guns and snipers. It was clear that the Bund would present a formidable defence if manned by determined troops with a dozen well placed machine guns.[40]

Lord Cavan's orders laid down that the 10th Army would advance from Papadopoli Island with the British 23rd and 7th Divisions on the left and right of XIV Corps, and would be supported on the right by the Italian 37th Division of XI Corps followed by the Italian 23rd Division of XI Corps. On 26 October, the 22 Brigade of the 7th Division, and some advance troops of the British 23rd Division and the Italian 37th Division, were already on the island. At 18.30 the 68 and 69 Brigades of the British 23rd Division began to move through the darkness to Cosenza Island by the existing footbridges, and then to

Papadopoli, first by ferry boats and then by the footbridges which the engineers and the pontieri had re-erected by about 22.30.[41] As on the previous night the enemy searchlight was blanketed and initially there was not much opposition from the enemy artillery. However, by the time Private Gladden passed over the first footbridge it was under enemy fire, but the noise of this shelling was overshadowed by that of the British artillery and even more by the noise of the swollen Piave. Close by, a member of Gladden's platoon was hit and disappeared into the murk. The next stream was even worse, its noisy swirling waters only just visible in the dark. Gladden was much impressed by the Italian pontiere in charge of the security of the bridge who sat smoking cigarettes apparently ignoring the bursting of the shells in the vicinity.

At the same time, 20 and 91 Brigades of the 7th Division were crossing to Papadopoli over the bridge at Salettuol. Marching in single file, battalion by battalion, they had to wade only one small stream, and were in position on the right of the 23rd Division by 24.00. To the right of the 7th Division the pontieri of the 37th Italian Division had bridged the main stream for the Italians to pass over to Papadopoli by way of Caserta and Maggiore Islands.

The British artillery had begun their bombardment of the enemy positions at 22.30. The guns had been brought up secretly, and to ensure surprise had carried out no previous registration, relying only on accurate surveys of the enemy positions by units of the Royal Engineers. The main targets of this preliminary bombardment were the lines of wire defending the Bund. The Austrian artillery made some reply against the island and towards the bridges but without damaging them.

By about 03.30 on 27 October virtually all the troops had taken up their start positions on the island, and were seeking what protection they could against the enemy artillery which was firing both shell and shrapnel and producing some casualties. At 05.00 a heavy rainstorm left all the troops soaking wet. At 05.30 while it was still dark some units began to creep forward to get as close as possible to the first channels before the attack began. Finally at 06.25 the British 18-pounder guns opened up to provide an advancing barrage,[42] which though not particularly heavy, was designed to give accurate and well-positioned fire which would be used to coordinate the advance of the infantry.

At 06.45 the barrage reached the enemy front line and then jumped forward to make way for the infantry assault. Sandilands[43] and Gladden[44] record how the 68 and 69 brigades of the 23rd Division moved off in darkness, bitter cold and heavy rain, their officers finding direction by compass bearings. In order to ford the flooded channels it was necesary to link arms and struggle against the flow of the water, in places waist deep. Several were swept from their feet and drowned under the weight of their equipment. The two brigades of the 7th

Division had a similar experience, the 22nd Manchesters having a particularly difficult time, coming under heavy fire as they struggled in the deeper channels.

Having forced the river, the first objective, the Bund, was soon gained. The 69 Brigade on the right of the 23rd Division stormed ahead, overwhelmed the garrison and occupied the front line by 07.00. The 68th Brigade on the left of the 69th met stronger resistance because of uncut wire, but by soon after 07.00 were on the Bund. The 11th Northumberland Fusiliers and the 12th Durham Light Infantry had a particularly difficult time. The CO of the Northumberland Fusiliers, Lieut.-Colonel St Hill, was killed and also Captain Stirling and Lieutenant Youll. All the other officers in the battalion above the rank of subaltern became casulaties and the command fell to a lieutenant. Once again Gladden came through unscathed.

The 20 and 91 brigades of the 7th Division on the right of the 23rd made good progress. The South Staffords and the Manchesters were held up by wire but only for a short time. When they finally stormed the Bund "not many Austrians stayed to fight, the majority, surprised and dismayed at the failure of the wire to hold up the attack, streamed back inland in disorder, almost too fast to give riflemen and Lewis gunners much chance to shoot them down. Those who did show fight were soon disposed of, several prisoners being taken."[45]

By soon after 07.00 both divisions of XIV Corps were established on the Bund. (It was then apparent that the position was not as strong as had been supposed. There were few machine-gun posts and the only dugouts were on the far side of the Bund acting as shelters.) Although XIV Corps had now obtained its first objective, the position on its two flanks was less satisfactory. To the left, the adjacent 58th Italian Division of VIII Corps in the 8th Army had failed to get any troops across the river, and on the right the 37th Italian Division, held back by the flow of water down the river and by considerable enemy resistance, were not yet across.

The objective for the day for XIV Corps was a road through a line of villages about 3000 yards beyond the Bund across sparsely cultivated fields. At 07.10 the barrage lifted and the troops moved towards the next intermediate objective, a well-wired line of trenches. Some of the enemy appear to have been demoralized by the shock of the first attack and were not prepared to stand and fight.Most of the resistance was encountered on the exposed flanks of the corps front, particularly by 68 Brigade (23 Division) on the left who came under machine-gun and sniper fire. Nevertheless all the immediate objectives of the 23rd Division were secured by 08.10.[46]

The 7th Division advancing over similar ground also came up to their line on time, although 91 Brigade encountered machine-gun posts and

147

snipers in the villages of Cimadolmo, Vendrame, and San Michele (Map 9). At one stage some of the 2nd Gordons went ahead too fast, and their CO Lieut.-Colonel Ross and five other officers were killed, apparently by the British barrage. But the division reached its second objectives and took many prisoners.[47] There was at first no sign of the Italian 37th Division on the right but a company of the 8th Devonshires sent to make contact found the 281st Regiment about half a mile further back.

After another short pause the barrage moved on again followed by the infantry of both divisions towards the final objective for the day, the road from San Polo to Tezze (about a mile north of Vendrame), now some 1000 yards or so ahead. The 23rd Division encountered little resistance until approaching the road when "a few minutes sharp fighting" were needed to storm farm buildings and trench lines, but all the objectives were gained by 12.00. Then at 13.00 the Austrians counterattacked. The British found themselves short of ammunition and were forced to withdraw from the buildings. A company of the 11th West Yorks, the Brigade reserve, was ordered to retake the position and by 16.00 most of the Austrians had been killed or captured.[48]

On the right of the Corps front, held by the 7th Division, 91 Brigade reached the final line near Tezze by 11.00, and 20 Brigade which was held up by strong points in four farms arrived just short of this line by the evening.[49] The right flank of the Division should have been covered by the Italian XI Corps whose 37th and 23rd Divisions encountered considerable resistance which delayed their advance.[50] Therefore the 8th Devonshires on the right of the 7th Division were diverted to form a flank line bending back a mile or so to maintain contact.[51] However, by the late afternoon the left of the 37th Division had reached San Polo, and formed a line stretching back to the river with the VI Bersaglieri Brigade of the Italian 23rd Division on their right. The losses in these two Italian divisions are given by the IOH as 155 dead, 356 wounded, and 104 missing almost all drowned.[52]

The position on the left flank of the 10th Army was less satisfactory, for no 8th Army troops had succeeded in crossing the river, and a good deal of enemy mortar and machine-gun fire was coming in from this side. However, this was eventually silenced by the 10th Northumberland Fusiliers, supported by three 18-pounder batteries RFA, together with the howitzer batteries already covering the flank.

Throughout the day the front-line troops had been supported by the supply, signals, and engineer units who faced the considerable problems presented by the crossing of the Piave. The engineers had the urgent task of rebuilding the temporary end of the bridge at Salettuol with pontoons so that it could take heavy traffic, and this was finished by midday. Others bridged the channels between the island and the far bank. Sandilands, in the history of the 23rd Division, emphasizes the part

148

played by the Divisional Signal Company.[53] Despite the flow of the water and the enemy fire, a telephone cable was laid across the swollen Piave to link the Divisional and Brigade Headquarters, and to permit two observing officers in each artillery brigade, well forward with the infantry, direct contact with their Brigade HQ.

The Official Air Force History[54] notes that the artillery had been aided by six spotter planes from No 34 Squadron. These planes had been fiercely attacked and the two flight commanders had been lost, one wounded and one missing. On the other hand three enemy spotter planes had been shot down, and 5000 rounds of small arms ammunition had been dropped by parachute to hard-pressed troops on the ground. (The history also states that the bridge at Salettuol was bombed as well as shelled by the enemy, and that although there were appreciable casualties the bridge remained intact, but there is no reference to any air response to these bombing attacks, perhaps because No.45 Squadron of fighter planes had returned to France in September.)

By nightfall on 27 October the 10th Army salient extended to the line shown on Map 10. The 7th and 23rd Divisions had crossed the Piave from Papadopoli, and advanced 3000 yards from the far bank. The 7th Division had taken 1690 prisoners and twenty-five guns; the 23rd Division 1830 prisoners and twenty-nine guns[55]; the 37th and 23rd Italian Divisions 2146 prisoners.[56]

5.   The Austrian Army

On the morning of 28 October the Allies on the Piave faced a difficult situation. The 12th Army had established a bridgehead opposite Pederobba, but its bridges had been destroyed. The 8th Army had established a bridgehead between Fontana Buoro and Falze, but had failed to cross at Vidor and Nervesa. Because of the heavy flow of water down the river and the enemy artillery, all seven projected 8th Army bridges were out of action. Thus all the units of the 8th and 12th Armies which had succeeded in reaching the far bank were now cut off from supplies and reinforcements. The only satisfactory position was that of the 10th Army which had established a substantial bridgehead with supply lines back over Papadopoli Island to the right bank.

However, unknown to the Allies, the Austrian Army faced very serious difficulties quite apart from those presented by the Allied offensive. The decisive defeat of the Austrian offensive in June had been a serious blow to the Army. Subsequently there was a poor harvest which during July and August led to a food shortage in Austria, exacerbated by poor distribution and profiteering. The Austrian Official History refers to real hunger in the country, although the front-line troops did better than the rest.[57] In September more bread became available but meat was still scarce. The Official History also states that the morale of the troops at the front was still satisfactory, but refers also to a lack of enthusiasm, and a feeling that the Army was no longer supported by the country as a whole.[58] The troops were said to be not fit to fight an offensive.

As described in Section 7, Austria was eager for an armistice and had assembled an Armistice Commission at Trent as early as 5 October, and on 9 October had proposed discussions with the Comando Supremo. Although this last suggestion was immediately vetoed by Germany, on 11 October the Austrian GHQ ordered Field Marshal Boroevic, now commanding the Army Group holding Grappa and the Piave, to send all not indispensable war material back to Austria, as preparation for a retreat from the Veneto.[59] However, at a meeting of GHQ at Baden, near Vienna, on 14 October this order was cancelled on the grounds that if the troops in the rear saw all the material going back to Austria it would be difficult to stop them going too.[60]

Even more serious difficulties were developing as the result of the political situation evolving in the Empire. The Army of the Austro-Hungarian Empire was a remarkable organization. Besides its two principal partners, Austria and Hungary, it welded into a coherent whole units of what are now the Czech Republic, Slovakia, part of Poland, the Trentino in Italy, Slovenia,Croatia and Bosnia, all speaking their own languages. It might seem surprising that such a polyglot army could succeed at all, but the citizens of all continental countries in 1914 expected to be conscripted into the army. If you lived in the Empire you accepted conscription into the Army of the Empire, and the Austro-Hungarian Army was in fact tolerably though not outstandingly efficient.

The Emperor Karl was anxious to end the war but on the basis of leaving the overall structure and institutions of the Empire intact. However, the publication of his manifesto of 17 October had led to the setting up of National Councils in the different ethnic parts of the Empire, and these Councils soon wished to take control of their armed forces. By 19 October Ruthenian Poles had assembled a National Council at Lemberg (Lwow), and a Czech Council in Prague joined with the Slovaks to form the state of Czechoslovakia. The Hungarians talked of a fully independent national state with its own foreign policy and its own army. (Although they also assumed that other peoples within their lands would be satisfied with some lesser form of autonomy.) Therefore high-ranking Austrian officers were sent to talk to the Councils to encourage them to avoid the break-up of the Imperial Army, at least until the troops had returned home. These appeals made litle impression and the Empire was clearly in no good position to resist an Allied attack.

150

On 21 October General Arz, the Austrian Chief of Staff, warned the Austrian Crown Council that if peace were not obtained in two weeks there would be Bolshevism in the Army. He also stated that the military situation made it impossible to repatriate the Hungarian troops.[61] On 22 October the commander of the army in the Asiago region reported that the morale of his troops was still good, but he did not think it possible to expose the troops to a long retreat such as would be involved in evacuating the Veneto.[62] Then on 23 October came news of mutinies.

On 23 October units of the 83rd Croatian Brigade in the 42nd Hungarian Division on Grappa refused to go up to the front line on Monte Asolone.[63] Two companies of Bosnians mutinied and were joined by a third company which had been sent to keep order. Eventually they were all disarmed by two new battalions, but a court-martial then declared that the war was over.[64] The spirit of disobedience then spread to all the reserve units in the Belluno Group. There was also trouble from Slovene troops of the 44th Division at Codroipo.[65]

On 25 October, units of the 27th and 38th Hungarian Divisions at Asiago asked to return to Hungary which they said, they were ready to defend. A Hungarian battalion in the 27th Division refused to take part in an attack at Asiago and demanded to be sent home. It was joined by two other battalions of the regiment, and another regiment decided that they too would leave at the same time. In Val Sugana a regiment of the 38th Hungarian Division established itself in the village of Levico, refused to go up to the line at Asiago, and covered all approaches to the village with machine guns.[66]

The Commander of the Army Group from Asiago to the Stelvio, the Archduke Joseph, was known to have Hungarian sympathies. He reported on 26 October that there was no alternative but to send the 27th and 38th Divisions back to Hungary where he hoped they could be disciplined. He also suggested that all other Hungarian troops be sent home as fast as transport was available in order to save the Army from a fatal collapse and to ensure that it would "be in a position to maintain tranquillty in the interior with its more reliable units". Finally he implored Karl to end the war as soon as possible.[67] News that the 27th Division went home unpunished spread rapidly and soon other Hungarian units were refusing to fight.[68]

Despite the troubles at Asiago, Austrian and Hungarian troops of the Belluno Group in the front line on Monte Grappa had stoutly resisted formidable Italian attacks for three days (24, 25 and 26 October), and on 27 October had launched an energetic counter-attack. But there was trouble on the Piave on 27 October when the British crossed the river and moved against the 29th, 7th and 64th Austrian Divisions. According to the Austrian Official History the Hungarian and southern Slavs of the 7th Division did not stand up to the attack and some units of the reserve brigade refused to go into battle. The History also states that the appearance of the British produced a general panic in the division, and that the two adjacent divisions were involved in its retreat.[69]

At 09.00 on 28 October Boroevic reported to the Austrian High Command that he was receiving many accounts of weakening resistance by Polish, Hungarian, Czech, Slovak and southern Slav troops. The number of mutinies was rising and he had no power to quell them. At 13.00 he was informed that the Austrian Government had asked President Wilson for an Armistice, and commented that this news would hardly raise morale.[70] Boroevic now believed that the only way to keep his armies intact was for them to retire steadily, evacuating the Veneto in an orderly way, keeping the Italians at bay by suitable rearguards. But there was an immediate danger that the VIth Army might be cut off from their supply lines by the Allied advance towards Vittorio Veneto and Sacile. Therefore to counter this threat he ordered up four fresh reserve divisions for a major attempt to halt the advancing Allies. The Austrian 34th Division, ordered to Falze, refused to march, but the 10th, 24th and 26th divisions directed towards the British sector of the front reached the line of the Monticano River (Map 10) by the evening of 28 October.

6. The Advance from the Piave (28–29 October)

28 October

Although the Austrian Commands were now seriously concerned about the morale of their armies, the Allies faced a difficult day.

In the 12th Army sector the French had worked all through the night of 27/28 October to repair one of the broken bridges by 05.00, and the 138 French Regiment crossed over to reinforce the five battalions on the far side. They were followed by Italian alpini but at about 08.00 the bridge was again broken by shell, and ammunitions and rations had to be sent over by boat. Even so the bridgehead was expanded to a depth of about 2000 yards during the day, the French capturing 18 guns and 700 prisoners.[71]

In the 8th Army the XXVII Corps which had failed to cross at Vidor the previous day was able to send only one battalion across by boat to the bridgehead opposite Fontana Buoro. During the day XXII Corps was able to make repairs to one of the bridges at Fontana Buoro so that the 60th Italian Division was able to cross, but then the bridge was broken again by shelling. Some of the subordinate generals on the far bank were then so concerned at the shortage of ammunition, rations, and poor communications to the rear that they suggested reducing the size of the bridgehead in order to make it more viable against an enemy counterattack. Whereupon the commanders of the 12th, 57th, and 1st Assault Divisions were summoned to Corps Headquarters on the right bank where the Corps Commander, General Vaccari, spelt out the imperative need of not retreating a single step because air reconnaissance had reported enemy movements northwards away from the river. In fact the two Brigades of the recently arrived 60th Division pushed forward to meet only scarce resistance, and by the end of the day the size of the bridgehead had been appreciably extended (Map 10).[72]

On the right wing of the 8th Army renewed attempts by VIII Corps to bridge the Piave at Nervesa and Ponte di Priula were all unsuccessful and the Corps remained immobilized on the right bank. Fortunately General Caviglia had foreseen that the 8th Army might be held up and his orders on 19 October had already referred to the possibility of passing 8th Army troops across the 10th Army bridges.[73] Hence, on the morning of 27 October, the reserve XVIII Corps of the 8th Army was allocated temporarily to the 10th Army in order to cross by the British bridges.[74] During the day the two divisions of XVIII Corps moved up to the river to be ready to cross that night, the 33rd Division by the Cosenza footbridges, and the 56th Division at Salettuol.

The road to Salettuol was extremely congested and the Italians suffered casualties by shelling and bombing (fifty killed and many wounded). The bridge itself was under artillery fire but remained intact. The British plans for passing their own transport and supplies over the Salettuol bridge were considerably disrupted. Sandilands[75] gives a graphic description of the scene at sunset on 27 October as troops and pack mules made their way across the bridge and then across the fords to the far bank. As the gunners struggled with the waggon trains carrying the 6 inch mortars through water running waist deep, the Italians of XVIII Corps arrived and "confusion reigned once more", some Italians being swept away and nearly drowned. However, by the morning of 28 October the Como Brigade of the 56th Division and one regiment of the Bisagno Brigade of the 33rd Division had arrived on the left bank.

After a general bombardment starting at 05.00, the Como Brigade went forward at 09.00 supported by a moving barrage fired by the British artillery, a form of support not previously experienced.[76] The enemy resisted tenaciously at first but by 12.30 the Brigade had come into line on the left of the 23rd Division, and the leading regiment of the Bisagno Brigade had taken up positions on the left of the Como Brigade, thus extending the front by about 3000 yards. Then the other regiment of the Bisagno Brigade took up a flank position between the first regiment and the river.

The 10th Army renewed its advance at 12.30 after the arrival of the two Italian brigades. Detailed accounts of the advance in the British sector are given by Sandilands[77] and Atkinson[78]. The enemy appeared to be retreating covered by rearguards, and the chief opposition came from nests of machine guns in improvised defence posts. The 23rd

Division encountered most opposition on its left flank and Sandilands mentions two platoons of the 10th Northumberland Fusiliers, one of which killed or captured sixty Austrians in a machine-gun post, and the other surrounded and captured 160 prisoners. (Private Wilfred Wood of the Northumberland Fusiliers was subsequently awarded the VC for his action with his Lewis gun which caused 140 enemy to surrender.) On the 7th Division front the day's fighting had not been heavy, and "for the most part the Austrians did not wait to be taken prisoner". By the evening both divisions had come up to their objectives on the line shown on Map 10.

Meanwhile the Como and Bisagno Brigades of XVIII Corps on the left flank of the 10th Army had also made good progress. Lord Cavan in his report refers to "the splendid dash with which they took up the attack with little opportunity for previous reconnaissance".[79] By the evening they had extended the bridgehead along the Piave as far as Ponte di Priula and captured 3000 prisoners, seven guns and 150 machine guns. Thus the enemy had now been cleared from the left bank up to Priula, and the Italian VIII Corps could begin to build its bridges.[80]

On the right flank of the 10th Army the front of the Italian XI Corps was now considerably extended, going back to the Piave where the 3rd Army had not yet moved. The Austrians put up some strong resistance against the 37th Division and mounted a counter-attack, but after further artillery action the Italians were able to advance to the line shown on Map 10.[81]

Unfortunately the all-important bridge at Salettuol was put out of action on the morning of 28 October when a pontoon and three trestle sections were broken by the flow of water. After attempts to make repairs had failed, the 18th Pontieri Company was called in and by 19.00 had rebuilt the bridge 30 yards downstream, and made a second route to Papadopoli by a bridge from Veneto Island. Thus, all through the day, as on 27 October, rations and ammunition for the 10th Army had to be carried on mules negotiating the swollen channels. The evacuation of the wounded on stretchers across the flooded channels to the advance dressing station on the right bank was particularly hazardous and dangerous.

By the end of the day, 28 October, Boroevic saw that the advance of the 10th Army was threatening both the line of retreat of the VIth Army through Sacile and the rear of the Vth Army. He therefore decided that the VIth Army should withdraw during the night towards Conegliano, and that the Vth Army should defend the line of the Monticano on the 29th.[82] The withdrawal began on the night 28/29 October as Boroevic ordered up four fresh divisions to check the Allied advance.

29 October
During the night 28/29 October VIII Corps of the 8th Army had

154

established bridges at Ponte di Priula and Nervesa, and began to cross the Piave in the early morning of 29 October. The Austrians were now retreating and the Italian advance appears to have been largely unopposed. The Corps reached the Susegana – Conegliano road (Map 2) without encountering much opposition, and in the early morning of 30 October a light column of Bersaglieri and cyclists occupied Vittorio Veneto, by then abandoned by the enemy.[83] Meanwhile, following a bombardment of the now demoralized Austrians the XXII and XXVII Corps had little difficulty in advancing from the Sernaglia bridgehead.[84]

Further upstream beyond the 8th Army the 12th Army bridges remained under enemy fire, but the bridgehead was extended by an advance of some 2000 to 4000 yards. On the right bank of the Piave the Italian I Corps was still encountering considerable opposition because the Italian 4th Army on its left was still held up on Grappa, but during the day the Corps advanced about a thousand yards.

Of the four fresh divisions ordered up by Boroevic one refused to march against the Sernaglia bridgehead but the other three, the 10th, 24th and 26th, moved up to halt the advance of the British XIV Corps on the line of the Monticano. The river was only about fifteen yards wide and at the time quite shallow and sluggish, but was enclosed between twenty-foot high embankments, any bridges being of wood at the level of the top of the embankments. These embankments gave good positions overlooking the flat countryside, so the river was an obvious choice for an Austrian stand.

The situation of the 10th Army was by no means ideal. The difficulties and traffic congestions at the Piave bridges had delayed the advance of their artillery, which was not yet in position to support the crossing of the river. Moreover, Lord Cavan was concerned that while the 23rd and 7th Divisions of XIV Corps were at the forefront of the advance, the units on either side had made less progress, as shown in Map 10. On the right flank the Italian XI Corps had to maintain an increasing length of line to keep contact with the 3rd Army which was still on the Piave. On the left flank of the 10th Army, the line of the Italian XVIII Corps was also bent back towards the river, so as to cover the flank left exposed by the failure of VIII Corps to get any units across the Piave on the previous two days. Hence Cavan was concerned that the shape of his front was taking "the form of an umbrella".[85] Nevertheless, on the evening of 28 October he issued orders for the crossing of the Monticano the following day.

The British XIV Corps began its attack at 08.30 on 29 October with the 23rd Division on the left and the 7th on the right. The 23rd Division deployed the 68 and 69 Brigades each with two battalions in the front line, and with the 69 Brigade on the right. At 10.00 the 8th Green Howards, of 69 Brigade, arrived at the bridge north-east of Vazzola, seized an hour or so earlier by a dismounted squadron of the 1st Northamptonshire Yeomanry, and then forced their way across.[86] To the left of the Green Howards the 11th West Yorks had forced a crossing by 09.30 and then advanced to capture Capanna Balle at about 12.00. By now the left flank of 69 Brigade was exposed as 68 Brigade on the left had yet to cross the river, so a company of the 10th Duke of Wellington's was sent to cover this flank.

Turning now to 68 Brigade, the 12th Durham Light Infantry met strong opposition but succeeded in forcing the river by 13.00. But the 10th Northumberland Fusiliers on their left had yet to cross and there was no sign of the 56th Italian Division further to the left. Therefore the reserve battalion, the 11th Northumberland Fusiliers, now reorganized into only two companies after their losses two days earlier, crossed the river behind the 12th Durhams. Then together with part of the Durhams, they moved westwards up the river bank, and despite considerable resistance from machine guns in farm houses and ditches drove the enemy clear of the river, thus allowing the 10th Northumberland Fusiliers to cross.[87] Edmonds records that 68 Brigade was greatly helped by the 146th Italian Mountain Battery attached to the 23rd Division who had carried their guns and ammunition across the Piave and then dragged them forward by hand to support the Brigade.[88]

The 7th Division (91, 20 Brigades) on the right of XIV Corps began their advance with the 2nd Queens of 91 Brigade on its left. The Queens set off for the bridge north-east of Vazzola, believing it to be already held by the 23rd Division. In fact they soon came under fire from the far bank. They first helped troops of the 23rd Division to secure the bridge, and then proceeded to force their own passage across the river somewhat to the right. After an advance of about 500 yards resistance stiffened and contact was lost with 20 Brigade on the right, apparently because the adjacent Italian XI Corps on the right flank was somewhat behind, and the enemy coming from this flank had infiltrated between the two brigades.

To restore the situation the 22nd Manchesters (91 Brigade) waded across the river at about midday, and took up positions as a flank guard for the 2nd Queens. Moving forward again the Queens came against strong resistance near the village of Cimetta, and the remaining battalion of 91 Brigade, the 1st South Staffordshires, was ordered up for a joint attack on Cimetta at 14.30. The village was taken at 15.15 together with 720 prisoners, and contact regained with 20 Brigade on the right. Meanwhile the front of 20 Brigade was held by the 2nd Borders, who had reached the Monticano about midday after some opposition while crossing a tributary, but were not in sufficient strength to force a crossing. An attack was planned for 18.30 but was then cancelled, as it was judged that the advance of 91 Brigade would cause the enemy to withdraw during the night, as indeed he did.

The XIV Corps was now across the Monticano except on the extreme right. The 23rd Division had experienced their hardest day yet[89] and the 7th Division had had to fight hard for Cimetta.[90] The crossing had been achieved despite the traffic and congestion at the Piave bridges, particularly at Salettuol which carried all the heavy transport. All day the Corps had been assisted, as on the previous day, by the RAF which bombed and machine-gunned roads and troops. The Austrian Official History blames the Austrian failure to hold the line of the Monticano on panic in Czech units of 26 Division produced by machine-gunning from the air, a form of attack not previously encountered.[91]

Meanwhile, to the left of XIV Corps, the Bisagno Brigade, on the left of the Italian XVIII Corps, found that the Austrians had disappeared, and were able to reach Susegana by 08.00.[92] At 10.35 the Corps reverted to the 8th Army and continued to push on, apparently meeting little resistance. There are no records of serious fighting except at the end of the day when they encountered determined opposition at the outskirts of Conegliano. On the other side of XIV Corps the 37th Italian Division of XI Corps pushed forward against some opposition, and closed up towards the line set as their objective for the day.

Throughout the day the Austrian Armies, observed and harassed from the air, had been retreating from the Piave, and had largely escaped encirclement. Even so, the Austrian Official History describes 29 October as the decisive day. The last substantial Austrian reserves including three fresh divisions had failed to hold the line on the Monticano, and there was now little prospect of making any further stand to halt the advancing Allies. That evening orders were sent to Corps Commanders to retreat to the Livenza River, and General Boroevic received orders to evacuate the Veneto.

7. The Attack on Grappa (24–29 October)

As already mentioned, a large-scale offensive had been launched by the Italian 4th Army against the Austrian Belluno Group on Monte Grappa on 24 October. But the previous fighting on Grappa had shown that it was very difficult for either side to make significant advances against well-sited and well-defended positions. Therefore, all the discussions during August and September had assumed that any major offensive would be launched on more favourable ground. Hence planning for future action by the 4th Army appears to have been limited to a study dated 2 September of possible minor actions in order to improve local tactical positions by giving more depth to the defence system and by shortening the length of the front.[93]

Given the above background, it was not unexpected that the first orders for the October offensive, issued by the Comando Supremo on

157

12 October, gave only a secondary role to the 4th Army.[94] The main offensive would be made by the 12th, 8th and 10th Armies. The 4th Army was ordered only "to be ready to attack in order to follow up the advance of the 12th Army, with the objective of the line Primolano-Arten" (Map 3), and to provide some artillery support for the left flank of the 12th Army. These orders were passed on to the units of the 4th Army by the Army Commander, General Giardino, on 15 October when he added the comment that the nature of the action would be one of "an impulsive pursuit without too much preoccupation with liaison with adjacent units".[95]

As described above, the plan for the offensive was greatly changed by the Comando Supremo's order of 18 October.[96] The 4th Army was no longer to move forward <u>after</u> the 12th Army had advanced, but was to launch a full-scale offensive against the Austrians on Grappa to reach the line Primolano-Arten-Feltre (Maps 3,4). Although it was to be reinforced by three divisions and some 400 guns, the 4th Army had received a very tough assignment, quite apart from the inherent difficulty of making a large advance over mountainous ground.

The 4th Army had previously been stationed in the mountains of the Dolomites, but had no prior experience of organizing a large-scale offensive in the mountains, or indeed elsewhere. The enemy positions on Grappa were strong, and the Italians were not well informed as to their strength and location. On 18 October the Italian guns, like the Austrian guns, were sited in good defensive positions with considerable depth.[97] Hence a major redeployment of the Italian artillery would be necessary to bring the guns sufficiently forward to support an Italian advance. Moreover, for some days prior to 18 October the 4th Army artillery had been shelling Austrian positions and rear areas with the object of diverting attention from the Italian preparations on the Piave. Therefore there was now little prospect of any Italian attack on Grappa achieving much surprise.[98]

As described above, the pressure of events elsewhere determined that the offensives on both Grappa and the Piave should be launched on 24 October, giving the 4th Army only five clear days to make its preparations. General Giardino was subsequently to write that this period was to be compared with over a month's notice given to the 8th Army, and was quite inadequate.[99] No previous studies had been made for such an action, and there was neither time nor clear weather to make the necessary detailed assessment of all the enemy strong points, machine-gun and artillery positions.[100] Consequently General Giardino's order to the 4th Army on 19 October[101] was not greatly different from the previous order of 15 October. The IOH comments that the objectives for each corps were "practically unchanged" and that "the action continued to be seen on the lines already studied".[102]

There remained little time for units to shift from defensive to offensive positions, and to re-orientate themselves in new positions. Conditions were particularly difficult for the artillery.[103] Some of the additional batteries came from distant parts of the front; twelve batteries reached their positions only on the night before the attack; another seven failed to arrive before the action had started. It was necessary for many of the other batteries to move to new positions, and then bad weather with cloud greatly hampered the necessary re-registration of the guns. Moreover, the initial establishment of the 4th Army had been one appropriate to a defensive posture, so even with the additional three divisions and artillery, its strength was little more than comparable with that of the Austrians.[104] Hence it is hardly surprising that the IOH states that the operation on Grappa started "with little hope of success".[105]

Nevertheless the Italians battled valiantly for six days to gain ground. Both sides suffered heavy casualties. Despite continued Italian attacks and minor advances the Austrians continued to respond stoutly with counter-attacks and artillery fire from well-prepared positions. No significant change of positions was effected by either side. The actions are described in detail in the IOH and summarised there in Schizzo 28 and 34.[106] The Italian losses are given as 2887 dead, 18,560 wounded and 3060 missing. A total of about 25,000, that is about 67% of all the Italian casualties during the battle of Vittorio Veneto.[107]

The IOH praises the performance of the troops in the difficult circumstances in which they found themselves, but also notes various deficiencies in the higher direction of the battle. Already on 24 October Lieut.-Colonel Laviano, a staff officer from the Comando Supremo, had commented adversely on the Army's dispositions and tactics.[108] Units were spread out uniformly along the front without regard for the mountainous nature of the ground. The plan of attack appeared to be no more than successive advances parallel to the original start line, implying that the whole army would move forward together, but without any indication as to how cohesion would be maintained between different units. There was in fact "no concept of manoeuvre for the army as a whole".

After the failure to make any significant progress on 24 and 25 October, General Diaz visited 4th Army HQ on 26 October. There he confirmed General Giardino's intention of making a pause for reorganization during the next day, and advised that there should be longer artillery preparation before attacks. He also advised the Army Commander that attacks along the whole of the front should be renounced in favour of concentrating on points selected with an eye to the final objectives.[109]

(On the same day, 26 October, Diaz sent an order to the 4th, 12th, 8th and 10th Armies stressing that any substitution of troops in action should be by the transfer of whole divisions and that any partial substitution of a division was "absolutely forbidden".[110] Presumably this order was thought necessary in order to avoid the problems which had arisen on the Montello during the Austrian June offensive (Section 5.7).

Back at his HQ on the morning of 27 October, Diaz sent further advice to Giardino regarding an intended attack on Col Berretta. His directive indicated that the attack should proceed by an enveloping movement and added, "This solution has the advantage of avoiding the frontal attacks by IX Corps already repeated too many times".[111] The fighting was renewed at full strength on 28 October, but on 29 October snow and fog made conditions particularly difficult for the artillery. The IOH states that "despite the persistence of our troops and their generous tribute of blood the attack launched on the front of the 4th Army achieved no success"[112], and at 19.00 Diaz ordered that the offensive on Grappa be suspended the next day.[113]

As viewed by the Italians on 29 October, the results of the fighting had been disappointing. Despite the repeated assaults and heavy casualties, only very slight advances had been made, particularly when compared with the projected aims of the offensive. To the Austrians, however, the general position of their Armies appeared quite different. Their front-line troops high up on the wintry ridges of Grappa were still resisting fiercely and holding their ground, but as already described the reserve and support units behind them were becoming increasingly unreliable and mutinous. Moreover, by 29 October the 12th, 8th and 10th Allied Armies had crossed the Piave in strength, and the VIth Austrian Army was threatened with encirclement. The Austrians had now little choice but to retreat, and at 13.40 General von Goglio gave the initial order for the Belluno Group to retire from Grappa.[114]

The IOH comments that "the day of 29 October can be considered the end of the actual battle on Grappa, fought by the 4th Army after a hurried preparation, with great dash and valour, on harsh difficult ground, against a valiant and determined enemy deployed on dominating summits and ridges, made stronger by a most efficient system of fortifications".[115] From now on the 4th Army was to take part in the general pursuit of the Austrians which followed the Allied crossing of the Monticano River.

The attacks on Grappa, though responsible for the greater part of all casualties during the battle of Vittorio Veneto, failed to force back the Austrians until their retreat was imposed by the advance from the Piave. Hence it might perhaps appear that the battle on Grappa was a waste of life and effort, but the fighting there made a significant contribution; first by ensuring that none of the units of the Belluno Group were able to intervene on the Piave, and perhaps more significantly, setting on record the Italian determination to throw out the invader and to do so before other events had concluded the war.

The valiant efforts of the 4th Army both in repelling the Austrian attacks in 1917 and 1918, and during the final battle of Vittorio Veneto, were a source of pride to Italy, and Grappa was to become a symbol of Italian courage and effort, enshrined in the words of the famous song, *La Canzone del Grappa*, *"Monte Grappa, tu sei la mia Patria"* (Monte Grappa, you are my country)".[116]

8. From the Monticano to the Livenza (30–31 October)

By the end of 29 October air reconnaissances had made clear the extent of the Austrian withdrawal from the Piave,[117] and Diaz ordered the 3rd Army to cross the river the next day and advance against the Austrian Vth Army. On all the fronts the battle was now becoming a pursuit of the retreating Austrians, although some rearguards were still resisting.

Units of the 12th Army advanced up either side of the Piave above Pederobba. The 52nd Alpini Division (XI Corps) occupied the high ground running up from Valdobbiadene to Monte Cesen (1569m, Maps 3,10), while the 23rd French Division on their right moved up the left bank of the Piave. On the opposite side of the river, the Italian I Corps of the 12th Army overcame tenacious resistance by Austrian units and occupied the ruins of Alano at the foot of the Grappa massif (Map 4), the Re and Trapani Brigades suffering particularly heavy casualties.[118] This thrust of the Italian I Corps, supported by guns on the high ground behind Valdobbiadene, now threatened Feltre (Map 3), with the possibilty of cutting one of the main Austrian lines of retreat. Therefore on 30 October the Austrian Command ordered a general retreat to a line from Asiago to the Dolomites similar to that held before the battle of Caporetto (Map 1).

The 8th Army moved forward to the line shown in Map 11, encountered little opposition, and were urged on by their Army Commander to "accelerate their advance" by avoiding built up areas.[119] In the 10th Army the British troops of XIV Corps had a trying day for they had now been marching and fighting continuously for three days, and were quite tired. Many were footsore as their boots had got wet in crossing the Piave, and possibly at the Monticano, and had dried hard. They had no change of socks and no blankets; fortunately the weather though cold was fine. According to both Sandilands and Atkinson progress was not rapid. Their line of advance lay through an agricultural area with farms and villages which made the work of the advance guards slow and difficult, even though it was eventually found that the ground was now clear of the enemy.[120]

The head of XIV Corps, including cavalry, a cyclist battalion and a motor machine-gun battery, entered the town of Sacile on the Livenza at about noon. There they surprised about two to three thousand

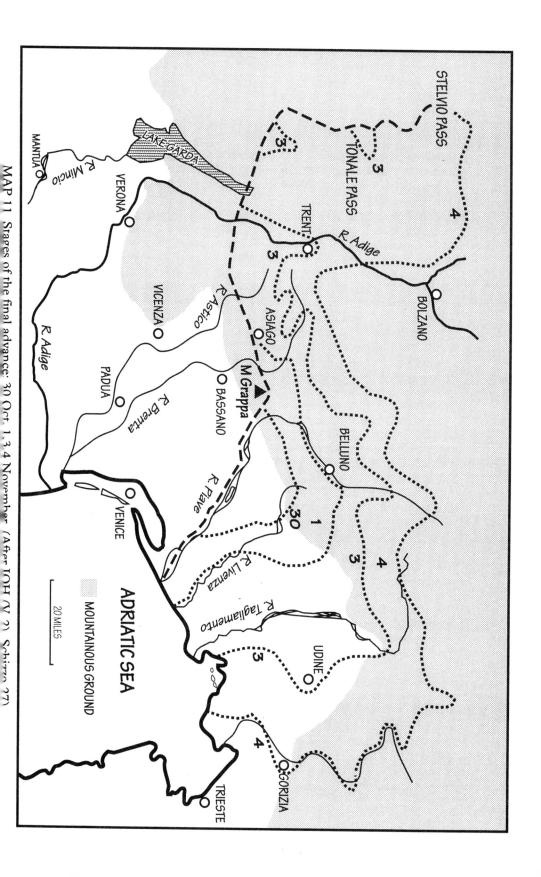

MAP 11 Stages of the final advance: 30 Oct, 1,3,4 November. (After IOH (V.2), Schizzo 27)

Austrians who first surrendered but then realized the small size of the British force and went over to the attack. By about 15.00 the mounted troops were forced to withdraw, but took with them 350 prisoners. They then occupied positions a short distance from the town to await the arrival of the infantry the following day.

Also on 30 October, the 3rd Army on the lower reaches of the Piave opened a bombardment across the river at 04.00 and began to establish bridgeheads both by bridging and by squads crossing in boats.[121] Progress was slow except on the left of the front where the VI Bersaglieri Brigade of the 23rd Italian Division (now transferred from XI Corps of the 10th Army to the 3rd Army) moved down the left bank of the river to Ponte di Piave, clearing out the Austrians, and thus permitting the 53rd Italian Division to cross.[122] Hence by nightfall the right flank of the 10th Army was covered first by the Italian 37th Division and then by the 23rd and 53rd Divisions of the 3rd Army stretching back to the Piave. This was a long flank but presented no threat, for already on the morning of the 30th the Austrians between Papadopoli and the sea had begun to retire.

Diaz's orders for 31 October issued the previous evening laid down that the advance of the 12th, 8th, 10th and 3rd Armies would now be joined by the 4th Army descending from the summits of the Grappa massif (Maps 3,4). During the day units on the left of the 4th Army descended to Cismon in Val Brenta and moved up towards Primolano capturing 4000 prisoners. Other units went northwards from the summits down the much fought-over ridges and valleys of Grappa towards the Fonzaso–Feltre road. By the evening they had reached Seren at the foot of the massif where the Austrians had established their main base, and a party of arditi and alpini entered Feltre and captured 2000 prisoners.

To the right of the 4th Army units of the 12th Army pushed up the Piave valley to the bridge about four miles north-east of Feltre, but arrived too late to prevent it being blown. Units of the French 23rd Division descended from Monte Cesen to Caorera about four miles south-east of Feltre, where they waded the river and joined forces with the 52nd Division on the other side.[123]

To the right of the 12th Army the left wing of the 8th Army was aiming for Belluno (Map 3) to cut off the retreating Austrians. The Mantova Brigade occupied Passo San Baldo (706m, Map 10) in the mountains between Vittorio Veneto and the Piave, and then descended to the Piave about seven miles short of Belluno. At the same time another column moved up the deep valley leading from Vittorio Veneto to Belluno, and encountered strong resistance from an Austrian rearguard in the narrows near Fadalto. Progress was maintained partly by a turning motion on the high and steep east side of the valley, and partly by

163

crossing over Monte Faverghera (1611m) and Col Visentin (1763m) on the west side of the valley to reach the Piave opposite Belluno.

Meanwhile the right wing of the 8th Army was advancing together with the 10th and 3rd Armies towards the Livenza River. For the British 7th Division this was mainly a day for consolidation and for repairing and laying bridges, while the infantry enjoyed a well earned rest, but the 23rd Division had "a more lively day" at Sacile.[124] The 9th Yorks and Lancasters soon made contact with the Austrians at the railway station and by noon had driven them off, had taken 500 prisoners, and had been joined by the other two battalions of their brigade who had come up without opposition. However, the town's wooden bridge over the Livenza had been demolished and the Austrians had taken up positions on the far bank.

Having decided to force a passage by constructing a temporary footbridge over the debris of the broken bridge, it was first necessary to deal with enemy fire from the far bank. The 18-pounder guns of the 102 Brigade RFA silenced an enemy battery, and Stokes guns and 6 inch mortars dealt with two machine guns in nearby houses. Work was then able to start on the footbridge, but almost immediately a machine gun opened fire from the steeple of Sacile church, wounding several of the men. Three direct hits by the artillery silenced the gun and a Pioneer Battalion quickly completed the bridge. The 9th Yorks and Lancasters crossed to the far bank, and after some sharp street fighting the Austrian rearguards drew back in the evening. Finally a single shot rang out in the night, fired probably by a sentry at a shadow, the last shot of the war for the 23rd Division. (The IOH states that the liberation of Sacile was due to the British 23rd Division,[125] in contradiction to an early official claim that Italian cavalry took part.[126] Other details of this episode are given by Edmonds.[127])

During the day the 3rd Army, between the 10th Army and the sea, also came up to the Livenza to find blown bridges and only rearguards defending the river. The Austrians were now in retreat on the whole front from Grappa to the sea and the Austrian Official History refers to the troops withdrawing from the Piave as being in full flight, hungry and in disorder, but not closely pursued.[128] They were, however, harried by intensive bombing by the Italian Air Force, and by three squadrons of the RAF which bombed and machine-gunned the retreating columns on the British front. "In this last advance the British squadrons dropped 20,000 lb.wts of bombs and fired 51,000 rounds of ammunition from low heights at a cost of seven aeroplanes missing." As the advance proceeded the enemy airfields were overrun and all opposition in the air ceased, leaving the Allied planes free to attack the plentiful ground targets. The official RAF historian comments,"It was all attack and no defence, terrible, but mercifully short".[129]

It was now clear that Diaz's offensive to break the enemy front had succeeded. That evening General Diaz ordered a general advance for the next day (1 November), from the Stelvio to the Adriatic, now bringing in the 6th Army at Asiago, the 1st Army between Asiago and Lake Garda, and the 7th Army between Lake Garda and the Stelvio.[130]

9.   The Final Advance

To follow the Allies' final advance to the Austrian frontier we first take note of Austria's efforts to obtain an armistice. Already on 29 October an Austrian Armistice Commission had sent Captain Ruggera of the General Staff across the frontier south of Trent with a white flag, carrying a letter from General Weber, the Head of the Commisssion, to the Italian Comando Supremo, asking for the immediate negotiation of an armistice.[131]

The Austrians appear to have believed that this move would at once halt the hostilities, and had not realized the time scale that would be involved. Not surprisingly, when General Weber's letter arrived at Padua, 90 miles away, the Comando Supremo replied that no negotiations could begin until documents were produced to show that the General was fully accredited by the Austrian Royal and Imperial High Command. On receiving the Italian reply at about 21.00, Captain Ruggera at once declared that all the members of the Commission possessed the necessary powers, and begged that they be received the next day (30 October). The following morning he was told that the Italian reply was addressed to General Weber, and he was asked not to interfere.

As there were no reliable or confidential means of communication between Padua and either Trent or Vienna, Captain Ruggera had now to return and report to General Weber and the other members of the Commission waiting at Rovereto about twelve miles south of Trent. Hence it was only at about 15.00 that General Weber's report of these events reached the Austrian High Command at Baden. Even so, by 16.00 Weber was given the necessary authorization to receive the conditions for an armistice, and was instructed to cross the lines to the Comando Supremo with the members of the Commission.

Meanwhile, the same afternoon a conference of Allied Premiers in Paris, including the American President's representative Colonel House, discussed the terms for an armistice which had already been drafted on 21 October. The terms were finally decided and approved by the Supreme War Council the next afternoon (31 October), and Diaz was empowered to treat with accredited Austrian representatives.

The details of the resulting meetings are summarized by Edmonds and Primicerj and do not concern us here. It is sufficient to note that it took most of 31 October to assemble the Austrian Commission at Padua, where they were informed that the first meeting would be held at 10.00 the following day. After this meeting on 1 November, General Weber sent two officers to Trent to telegraph Baden to say that the armistice conditions were so severe that he did not feel authorized to sign, and since he had been told that no discussion of the terms was allowed he suggested that a complete set of counter-proposals be prepared.

The news from Weber reached Baden at 00.30 on the night 1/2 November. The Emperor was prepared to accept, but was worried by the fact that only three days earlier he had assured the Kaiser that he would never permit Allied troops to pass through Austria to attack Germany, as the armistice terms demanded. However, the General Staff insisted that the military situation was so desperate that an immediate armistice was essential, for if the Allied troops were not granted passage through Austria they would soon be in a position to take it for themselves.[132]

Much of 2 November was spent by the government in Vienna in an unsuccessful attempt to persuade the various new national groups in the Empire to take responsibility for the decision. The Crown Council met in the evening and decided to accept the Allied terms, and a message to this effect (Nr.2100) was sent by radio to General Weber at 01.20 on 3 November. However, the Austrians again underestimated the complexities of arranging an armistice, and the time required to arrange a cease-fire. The message to General Weber had also stated that all Austrian forces had been told to halt hostilities, and at 01.30 both the Army Groups on the Italian Front received telephone communication Nr.2101 from General Waldstatten, the Chief of the Operations Branch, ordering the immediate suspension of all hostilities on land and in the air. Unfortunately the Austrian High Command had still to receive a further message from General Weber which stated that the Allied terms contained a protocol saying that hostilities would cease 24 hours after the signing of the armistice, in order to give time for orders to reach all the troops involved.[133]

Meanwhile back in Vienna the Chairman of the State Council had informed the Prime Minister, Professor Lammasch, and General Arz that he did not have the authority to approve the message to Weber accepting the armistice. This could only be done by the Council of State and it was unlikely to do so. The Emperor then insisted that General Waldstatten send another message annulling the cessation of hostilities.[134] This message arrived at Trent at about 03.00 and was passed on to the Chief of Staff of the 11th Army, General Sundermann, who replied that this was not possible as the previous order had already gone out. In a further conversation with General Waldstatten, Sundermann agreed that the order could be sent out, but only with a disastrous effect on the troops, so it was decided to take no further action.

During the morning (3 November) various inconclusive discussions were held in Vienna, and it was not until 13.00 that General Weber at the Commission's headquarters at Padua learnt of General Waldstatten's order for the immediate cessation of hostilities and of the impossibility of withdrawing this order. Therefore, in the absence of any clear instruction from Vienna, he felt he had no choice but to sign the armistice. A final, and heated, attempt by Weber to obtain the immediate cessation of hostilities was dismissed by General Badoglio who pointed out that it was not the Italians who had asked for the armistice, and that the Italian Army was ready and willing to continue its advance. The armistice was then signed at 15.00 with hostilities to cease at 15.00 the next day (4 November).

While the above discussions followed their meandering course, Diaz had issued orders on 1 November for a general advance of all the Italian Armies. Map 11 shows the progress of the armies on successive days from 30 October. On the Venetian and Friulian plain there was generally little enemy resistance after 30 October, and the rate of progress was determined mainly by the logistics of the advance, by the need to repair broken roads and bridges, by the increasing length of the supply lines, and by the congestion of traffic on the roads. Both Atkinson and Crosse describe roads crowded by débris, dead horses, abandoned waggons and guns, and corpses, all testifying to the "awful carnage caused by aeroplanes a few days earlier".[135]

The advance across the plain was initially led by the infantry of the 10th and 8th Armies but the Italian cavalry now took the lead, and four divisions of the Cavalry Corps pushed ahead of the infantry. Thus, when yeomanry and cyclists forming the advance guard of XIV Corps reached the Tagliamento River on 3 November they saw on the far side units of the 3rd Italian Cavalry Division, apparently fraternizing with a considerable number of Austrian troops. In fact the Italians had crossed on an undemolished bridge (near Bonzico) to be greeted by Austrians bearing white flags who informed them that an armistice had been signed. Therefore, so they said, the Tagliamento was now the line of demarcation beyond which the Italians were not entitled to advance or take prisoners.[136]

Neither the British nor the Italians had received any news or instructions regarding an armistice, and under the conventions of military law were not required to believe any information from an enemy saying that an armistice had been agreed. However, after some discussion and the arrival of senior Italian and British officers, the Austrian division together with another brigade surrendered its arms on the understanding that these would be returned if the report of an armistice turned out to be true.

Most of the Italian cavalry now withdrew to the right bank but one squadron rode on unopposed to Udine. Meanwhile 20 Brigade of the British 7th Division crossed the river unopposed to form a bridgehead on the far side, but 22 Brigade lower down the river on the right were told by the Austrians that further progress would be resisted. Therefore, as 20 Brigade were already across the river, 22 Brigade decided to wait during the night on the right bank.[137] At 03.00 that night (3/4 November) XIV Corps received orders from 10th Army that an armistice had been signed, and that they were to advance to a line about 6 miles beyond the Tagliamento. Next morning both brigades crossed the river, took the surrender of about a division of Austrians, and moved on to their final line, all unopposed. Meanwhile the Italian cavalry were far ahead almost at Gorizia on the Isonzo.

(The Italians had for some months been pressing for American troops to be sent to Italy in order to support offensive operations. However, the first response came only when the 332nd Regiment of Infantry was allocated to the 10th Army, and arrived in time to cross the Piave on 29 October, and the Tagliamento on 3 November.[138])

Meanwhile, on the western half of the Italian front the other Italian Armies from the Stelvio to Lake Garda, Asiago and Grappa had been advancing into the Trentino and towards Bolzano (Map 11). As early as the night of 28 October the Austrians on the Asiago plateau had secretly withdrawn from their front line running through the ruins of Asiago town to the so-called Winterstellung line about two miles back on the slopes of the hills to the north. On 31 October the Austrian guns were heard firing off ammunition, and fires and explosions were observed behind the Austrian lines, as if in preparation for a further withdrawal. The French 24th Division found that Monte Sisemol (Map 12) had been abandoned, and the commander of the 6th Army, General Montuori, issued orders for an advance the next day (1 November).

At this time the British 48th Division was holding the Granezza sector at Asiago as part of XII Corps of the 6th Army, with the 20th Italian Division on its left. To the right of XII Corps the line was held by the Italian XIII Corps comprising the 24th French Division (next to the British 48th Division) and the 14th Italian Division. Their orders[139] stated that XII Corps would advance towards Caldonazzo and Levico in Val Sugana above Trent, supported by XIII Corps in the second line. The 48th Division was to follow the line of the main road up Val d'Assa, with the 20th Division to their left using minor roads through Rotzo and Lavarone. The XIII Corps was to thrust north from Asiago and Gallio and also to follow up XII Corps.

The advance started in the early hours of 1 November. The 24th French Division captured Monte Longara by 08.30 and then continued to advance towards a line running through Monte Sbarbatal and Monte Columbara, with the 14th Italian Division advancing on their right.[140]

168

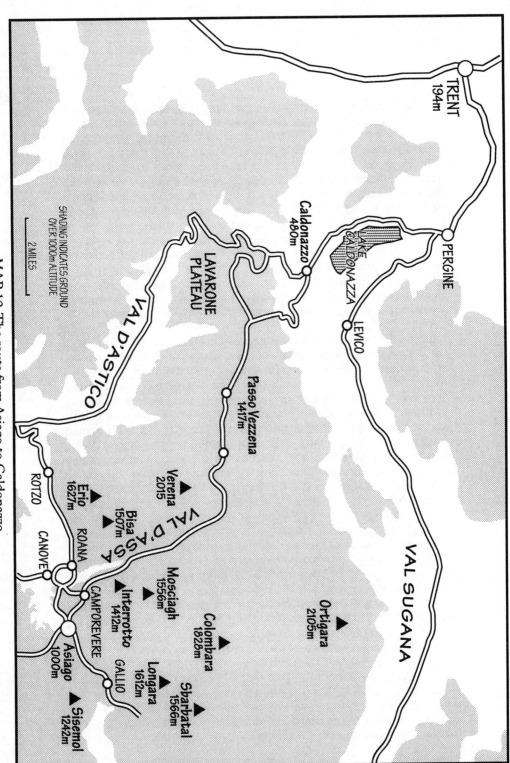

MAP 12. The route from Asiago to Caldonazzo.

The 48th Division, however, was held up by stiff resistance from Austrian troops in and around the fort of Interrotto overlooking the entrance to the upper reaches of Val d'Assa. The 4th and 6th Gloucesters were driven back, one into Camporovere and the other to beyond Bosco about a mile to the east. To the left of the 48th Division, the Italian 20th Division was held up by the formidable task of crossing the deep gorge of the Assa River covered by Austrian machine guns. However, by the end of the day the right-hand brigade of the 48th Division had reached positions near Monte Mosciagh, and the Italians had crossed the Assa and reached the slopes of Monte Erio.[141]

Meanwhile, by 17.30, the Austrians had decided that the progress of XIII Corps was threatening to encircle their forces defending the entrance to Val d'Assa at Interrrotto, and ordered a withdrawal from the line Monte Erio – Monte Mosciagh. The next morning (2 November) a dawn attack by the 48th Division on Monte Interrotto found that many of the Austrians had already gone, and by 08.45 all the rest were forced to decamp. The Division then marched up the narrow and steep sided Val d'Assa, while the Italian 20th Division moved through the mountains on the left, and the Italian 14th Division (now substituted for the French 24th) over the mountains to the right. The 48th Division eventually halted for the night about a mile short of Passo Vezzena, the highest point on the road (1417m), where the advance guard had reported the Austrians to be in considerable strength. Although the march had been largely unopposed the Division had already collected some 3000 prisoners and several hundred guns.[142]

The following morning (3 November) the leading troops moved off in the dark, and although there was some small resistance, parties of ten or twenty Austrians soon appeared carrying torches and coloured lights, coming forward to surrender. Near the summit of the pass a line of troops was drawn up across the road where their Divisional Commander claimed that an armistice had already been signed. However, after ten minutes of discussion all the troops surrendered, about fourteen battalions in all, together with a corps commander and three divisional comanders.

By 08.00 virtually all opposition had ceased, and the leading troops of the 48th Division were descending the narrow zigzag road to the villages of Caldonazzo and Levico, their objectives for the day, almost a thousand metres below. Meanwhile, the Austrians continued to assert the existence of an armistice. Therefore one of the Austrian generals was allowed to go to Divisional HQ to protest against being taken prisoner, and against the continuing advance, and was firmly but politely told that the advance must go on.

The great number of prisoners presented problems. Lieut-Colonel Barnett, the Adjutant and Quartermaster of the 48th Division, drove up

Val d'Assa on the morning of 3 November and saw streams of prisoners "dejected, sullen and footsore" in parties of from 10 to 300 making their way downhill to Asiago. When he arrived at Vezzena he saw a flat area of perhaps a hundred acres "absolutely packed with humanity, moving aimlessly about like a swarm of ants";[143] about 10,000 men, without food, some in a rather truculent mood. However, it was explained to them that there was no food nearer than Granezza, so their only hope of avoiding starvation was to march there quietly under escort. They were then sent off in parties of 500 with a ten-man escort, the 600 or so officers being sent last.

Meanwhile the advance guard of the 48th Division, the 5th Warwicks, continued down the road towards Levico and Caldonazzo. From high up they saw various Austrian columns converging on Levico from all directions as they retired towards Trent. Eventually, passing blazing dumps of stores and ammunition, the first units of the Warwicks reached Caldonazzo at about 12.30, a few hours before units of the Italian 20th Division, which had come up on their left from Rotzo.[144]

Caldonazzo had been the railhead for the Austrian army with a camp of 200 huts and an enormous quantity of stores including 200 guns, 5000 machine guns, and according to Edmonds a million rifles, but now it was a scene of confusion with crowds of hungry Austrians looting the dumps of material. A mounted patrol of the 48th Division pushed on to Levico three miles away, captured another transport column en route, and arrived at 12.50 to find the village practically deserted. During the afternoon six Hungarian battalions arrived at Levico after retreating up Val Sugana pursued by the Italian 14th Division, and finding their way blocked surrendered to the British. Fortunately the main body of the 5th Warwicks arrived soon after on captured Austrian transport and were able to take charge of the 6000 or so prisoners.[145]

Meanwhile units of the Italian 1st Army were converging on Trent. The first to arrive were three squadrons of X Corps cavalry which had come up the Adige valley and entered the town at about 15.15, and were soon followed by the XXIX Assault Group, and the 4th Alpini Group.[146] The town was crammed with Austrian troops in wild confusion, great numbers struggling to get on trains going north. The Italians soon blocked all roads out of the town, thousands of Austrians surrendered without resistance, and the Italian tricolor was hoisted on Castel Buonconsiglio, the forbidding palace of the former Prince Bishops of Trent.[147]

Further troops continued to arrive in Trent. At 17.30 two companies of the Brigata Pistoia (26 Division) went northwards to S.Michele dell'Adige, at the confluence of the Adige and Noce Rivers, to cut off the considerable number of Austrians retreating down the Noce valley towards Bolzano. Somewhat later, units of the 32nd Division arrived in the city, and also the 14th Regiment of the IV Bersaglieri Brigade (69th Division). The Chieti Brigade of the 6th Division descending from Val d'Astico reached Mattarello on the Adige four miles to the south of Trent. Edmonds gives some prominence to the arrival in Trent of two British officers an hour or two before the Italians.[148] This somewhat curious episode did not affect the troop movements on the ground and is described later in Section 9.5.

The next day at 15.00, 4 November, the war against Austria came to an end. The 48th Division moved to an area about five miles north-east of Trent, and on 6 November were informed they would soon be moving back to Granezza, on the first stage of the journey home. Meanwhile the Italians had set up a line across the Adige valley at Gardolo about three miles above Trent, and declared that all the Austrians south of that line were prisoners, while those on the other were free to leave as best they could. In fact there was utter confusion on the main railway line leading back from the Trentino into Austria and the other parts of the Empire.

It was expected that Italy would soon take over all the Trentino and that part of the Tyrol between the Trentino and the Brenner Pass (now the Province of Bolzano). Hence there was a desperate desire by the Austrian troops, of all nationalities, to get back to their homelands as soon as possible. Discipline and order had by now largely disappeared in much of the Austrian Army. The stations and trains on the Brenner railway, the only way out, were overwhelmed. Trains were terribly over-crowded with men clinging to roofs, running boards and buffers. Many either fell off or were knocked off by tunnels and bridges, and the line had to be closed for a time to clear the track of some hundreds of corpses.[149]

The war against Austria had thus finally come to an end. The Allies had gained total victory, and the Austrian Army had collapsed in retreat and disorder. Diaz's communiqué on 4 November announcing the end of hostilities referred to the capture of over 300,000 prisoners, about 4000 guns and a vast quantity of stores.[150] A large part of this haul was taken in the Trentino by the 1st and 6th Armies in the last 36 hours of the war, due to the disastrous orders of the Austrian High Command in the early hours of 3 November. By 11 November the number of prisoners in Italian hands had risen to over 430,000, an increase at least partly due to the complete breakdown of the Austrian supply system along the Brenner railway, which on 5 November led the Command of the Army Group of the Tyrol to advise Austrian GHQ that it was better for the troops to stay put and surrender to the Italians than to starve.[151]

Because of the political collapse of the Austrian Empire, followed by the collapse of the Armies, the Italian casualties in the campaign from 24 October to 4 November, though heavy were not as great as might have been expected, 36,498 killed, wounded and missing.[152] The greater part of the Italian losses, 24,413, were suffered by the 4th Army on Grappa where the Austrian and Hungarian regiments fought strenuously and tenaciously for over a week until their positions were turned by the thrusts across the Piave. In the 10th Army the British losses were 288 dead, 1126 wounded and 208 missing,1622 in all.[153] The corresponding figures for the Italian units in the 10th Army were 443 dead, 1860 wounded and 881 missing, 3184 in all.[154] The losses in the 48th Division in the advance from Asiago were twenty-six dead, 129 wounded and seven missing; 162 in all.[155]

Although the war with Austria was now over, the Italian staff had prepared plans for the invasion of Germany by moving over the Brenner and through Austria to Bavaria. However, on 4 November Lord Cavan was writing to the CIGS in London saying, that although the senior officers of the Italian Army would undertake such operations with zeal, he judged that most of the rank and file would not be enthusiastic about fighting Germany. He himself stressed the difficulties to be faced by any Allied columns encountering German opposition as they emerged from the mountains.[156] In fact by 5 November the German II Bavarian Corps under General Krafft was moving towards Innsbruck.[157] On 6 November a regiment crossed the Brenner and by 8 October 1500 Bavarians had reached the great fortress of Fortezza on the Brenner road.[158] But all these preparations came to nothing with the German surrender on 11 November.

Legacies of the War

By 11 November the First World War had come to an end, but the repercussions were to contine, and we now refer to some of those arising from the Italian theatre. First, however, it will be useful to summarize the military efforts of the Allies in Italy.

1. The Italian Effort

For two and a half years the Italians had fought a series of savage offensives against the Austrians on the Carso, the Bainsizza, and Ortigara, and stood successfully against the massive Austrian offensive at Asiago in the spring of 1916. They had waged a remarkable war in the high mountains of the Alps, even on the ridges and summits of the rock peaks of the Dolomites, and on the peaks and glaciers of the Ortler and Adamello groups. After the Italian offensive on the Bainsizza in 1917, Austria was forced to conclude that her army could not withstand any further onslaughts, and appealed to Germany for assistance. Crack German divisions were then sent to the Isonzo and produced the break-through at Caporetto.

In 1918, following their recovery from Caporetto, the Italians decisively defeated the last attempt by the Austrians to obtain victory by a large scale offensive in June 1918. An Italian corps fought in France and was heavily engaged in the region of Rheims and the Marne in 1918. Finally after Vittorio Veneto the Italians received the complete surrender of Austria.

The Italians had reason to be be well satisfied with this outcome. In a year, their army had recovered from Caporetto, repulsed the June offensive, and advanced triumphantly through and beyond Vittorio Veneto to liberate all the occupied lands. They had taken over 300,000 Austrian prisoners and 4000 guns, and under the Treaty of London they could now expect that the entire Italian Trentino and the largely Italian city of Trieste would become part of Italy. In addition, to ensure protection against future Austrian aggression the German-speaking province of Bolzano would be incorporated into Italy, to give a more defensible frontier along the watershed crossed by the Brenner Pass.

Also, according to the Treaty, they would gain various territories including Dalmatia on the far side of the Adriatic thus denying Austria any control of that sea.

The successful conclusion of the war aginst Austria was quite naturally a source of Italian satisfaction and pride, but it was unfortunate that Italian attention had been so much concentrated on the war against Austria that most Italians were largely unaware of the scale of the war on the Eastern and Western Fronts and elsewhere. Indeed, ever since the end of the war almost any Italian book entitled "The History of the Great War" will be found to deal almost exclusively with Italy's war on its frontier with Austria; the books by Pieropan and Melograni are just two of many examples. There was little appreciation of the defeats suffered by Austria during the Russian offensives in 1914, 1915 and 1916, and in Serbia in 1914. Yet in 1914 the Austrians had lost perhaps 350,000 out of 900,000 men in a campaign against the Russians in Galicia which ended in an Austrian retreat of some 300 miles. Two attempts to invade Serbia in 1914 were repulsed, the first with 40,000 casualties and the second with a loss of 40,000 prisoners.[1] In the Russian Brusilov offensive in 1916, launched to relieve the German pressure on Verdun, the Austrians lost perhaps 260,000 as prisoners, almost a third of their force, an irreparable loss from which Austria never fully recovered.[2]

More than they realized the Italians had become part of a much greater struggle, involving vast numbers from many countries, as shown below.

	Population	Mobilized	Dead
Austro-Hungary	52m	7.8m	1,200,000
Germany	65m	11.0m	1,800,000
Turkey		2.8m	320,000
Bulgaria		1.2m	90,000
France	39m	8.4m	1,400,000
Britain	46m	6.2m	740,000
Brit.Empire		2.7m	170,000
Russia	140m	12.0m	1,700,000
Italy	37m	5.6m	460,000
U.S.A.	93m	4.3m	115,000

These approximate figures for population and numbers mobilized are taken from the *Encyclopaedia Britannica*[3] and the numbers of dead from Cruttwell[4]. The numbers of wounded were generally at least twice the number of dead. The figure of 460,000 Italian dead was given by the

Italian Comando Supremo soon after the end of the war[5] and by Tranfaglia in 1995.[6] Between these two dates the figure has varied considerably. In 1928 Mussolini[7] quoted 652,000 dead, in 1932 Villari[8] quoted 680,000, and in 1938 Maravigna[9] quoted 533,000. Pieropan[10] (1988) gives some discussion of these figures, but the only conclusion one can draw is that probably at least 460,000 Italians died in the war.

Arithmetical comparisons to determine the relative contributions of each of the Allies must of course be treated with care, both because of uncertainties in the statistics and because of the different circumstances in which each country found itself. For example, the number of Americans killed was relatively small, because they were only present in force during the last year of the war. Yet the arrival of fresh strong troops in great numbers was crucial for the Allied effort. Even so the casualty figures, rough as they may be, provide a sobering reminder of the enormous numbers mobilized by all the participants and of the enormous cost in dead, maimed and wounded.

The First World War began as a war of movement in France and Russia, but by the end of 1914 had become a war of attrition, fought in many countries and on the oceans. The naval blockade of Britain by the German submarine campaign in 1917 was one of the most critical campaigns of the war, and the British blockade of Germany produced significant effects on the supplies of food and materials both to civilians and the army. The war was fought on the home fronts where it was necessary to produce the prodigious amounts of guns,ammunitions and supplies demanded by the armies. The propaganda war for the minds of both civilians and soldiers became increasingly important as the war dragged on, particularly after Germany had given Lenin a free passage from Switzerland to Russia.

The war ended when one side was so exhausted that it could continue no further, and the exhaustion was not the result of any one battle but a steady process of attrition in which all the Allies had played a part, and in which Italy's contribution had been substantial.

2. The French and British Contribution in Italy

After the Austro-German breakthrough at Caporetto, French and British Expeditionary forces were rapidly transported according to previously prepared plans, and by the end of 1917 six French and five British divisions had arrived in Italy, perhaps in all 103,000 French and 113,000 British.[11] But this speedily provided support was soon accompanied by misunderstandings between the Allies. As described in Chapter 2, the Italian Comando Supremo had expected that as soon as these troops arrived they would take up positions in the front line to replace and reinforce Italian units now tired and overstretched. The Italians also appeared to have assumed that the disposition of these Allied units would be decided primarily by the Italian staff.

The French and British Governments, advised by Foch and Robertson, took a different view. Even on the Western Front neither was willing to extend control of their forces to the other, and both were doubtful of the ability of the Italian staff. Moreover, it was obvious to Foch and Robertson that there was no reserve force behind the front line should a further breakthrough occur. Hence they saw that the most immediate task was the formation of a reserve army behind the Piave, ready to deal with any further incursion of the enemy, across the Piave or from Monte Grappa or the Trentino, just as Cadorna had assembled a reserve army at the time of the Strafexpedition (Section 1.2).

The Italians continued to hold their line throughout November by their own efforts. During the month six French and four British divisions arrived in Italy and a further British division was on its way. These troops were now sufficient both to maintain a reserve force and for some Allied divisions to relieve Italian divisions in the front line. As events ensued, the enemy chose not to attack any of these French and British divisions, which therefore played virtually no part in the fighting which finally halted the Austro-German army, as is clearly set out in Edmonds and other British accounts.[12]

There was just one French or British engagement with the enemy in 1917, the short but very successful attack on Monte Tomba (Section 3.4) by a French division on 30 December. Nevertheless the French and British forces played a significant, and perhaps crucial, role in 1917. Without these troops the Italian Armies would have been left without any coherent reserves, and without any sign of support from their allies. Their presence undoubtedly had a considerable effect in maintaining the morale of the Italian Army and of the civilian population at a very difficult time. Moreover, the arrival of the Allied troops was also observed by the Germans, and was one of the considerations behind their decision at the end of November to close down their offensive.

After the Austro-German assault had been held on the Piave, French and British divisions remained in Italy until the end of the war and played a part at Asiago during the Austrian offensive in June 1918. Then during the final battle of Vittorio Veneto, the British XIV Corps played an outstanding and perhaps decisive role. One of the key moves of the whole battle was the proposal by the Corps Commander, General Babington, to occupy Papadopoli Island prior to the start of the main offensive. It was only because of this move that the 10th Army was able to cross the Piave so successfully on the first day of the main offensive, and thus play a part in the battle which is described by the IOH as *"di primissime piano"*[13] (of the greatest importance).

British accounts emphasize the part played by the pontieri, the Italian boatmen. The divisional history of the 23rd Division refers to the crossing as one of the finest feats by British troops in the First World War, but one that was only possible because of the magnificent services of the pontieri.[14] Crosse, who was with the 7th Division wrote that it was impossible to speak too highly of the boatmen. Their skill was perfectly uncanny, and quite apart from this skill, their unremitting toil and courage were equally conspicuous.[15]

The French and British expeditions were both effective and efficient, with relatively low casualties. The troops had been sent to perform a definite task with clear military objectives which they had achieved, and they had reason to be well satisfied with the way they had acquitted themselves. Nevertheless some regrettably erroneous accounts of these events have continued to appear in British publications.

Harington in his book on Plumer in 1935 found it necessary to write that "a certain number of letters have appeared in the Press from time to time detracting from the services of the Italian troops and representing that the retreat from Caporetto was only stopped by the British and French troops almost at the point of the bayonet. This is totally untrue".[16] More recently A Dictionary of Battles(1977) refers to five British and six French divisions and states that "After a four-day battle in the Brenta valley (11–15 December), these experienced divisions stopped the Austro-German advance".[17] This is pure fantasy. No French or British troops took part in any combat in November or December save for the small French action on Monte Tomba, let alone any "four-day battle in the Brenta valley". This remarkable entry was subsequently repeated in quite similar words in The Paladin Dictionary of Battles (1986) with a foreword which commends the book by saying that "all who are interested in military history will reach eagerly to the shelf on which it rests to check their facts".[18]

Babington in his book For the Sake of Example (1983) states that in 1917 "Six French and five British divisions had been rushed down from the Western Front and with their assistance the onslaught had been stemmed"[19]. It can hardly be denied that the presence of these divisions gave "assistance" to Italy, but any casual reader would also assume that these divisions actually took part in the fighting! The World War I Source Book (1992) states that at the battle of Vittorio Veneto "The Piave was finally crossed by French units of Twelfth Army and British units of Tenth Army (under the Earl of Cavan) who drove back the Austrian Fifth Army".[20] No mention is made of the very considerable number of Italians in the 12th, 8th and 10th Armies who also made the crossing!

Whatever their origin, these misstatements or myths have continued to run for a long time, perhaps due to chauvinism, but also because some authors appear ill-informed of the most basic facts of the situation. For example, Haythornthwaite in *The World War I Source Book* states that "from 24 October [1918] the Italian Eighth Army was stalled at Vittorio Veneto", that is at a point fifteen miles or so <u>beyond</u> the Piave![21] Falls in his book *The Battle of Caporetto* (1965) places Vittorio Veneto on the Asiago Plateau. He also states that the 4th Army offensive during the battle of Vittorio Veneto was launched on 24 October by a sudden decision taken on the initiative of General Giardino because weather conditions on the Piave were so bad.[22] In fact the 4th Army started at the time which the Comando Supremo had laid down on 21 October, and it was only on the evening of 24 October that Diaz decided to postpone the attack across the Piave. More recently, the *Oxford Dictionary of 20th Century History 1914 to 1990* stated in an entry for Caporetto that "Ludendorff bombarded the town on 24 October and crossed the river",[23] whereas Ludendorff took no part in the direction of the campaign, and Caporetto was never bombarded.

3. Italian Euphoria

General Diaz's communiqué on 4 November which announced the final defeat of Austria ended with the entirely accurate statement that "The remains of what was once one of the most powerful armies in the world are retreating, disordered and dejected, back up the valleys they descended with such proud assurance".[24] There was naturally great satisfaction in Italy that the war was over and that Austria had been totally defeated after the recovery from Caporetto, but satisfaction soon turned into euphoria. Even as early as 3 November an article in the journal *Popolo d'Italia* had said that "It is the great hour of divine joy, when the tumult of emotion suspends the beating of hearts and gives us a lump in the throat. The long passion, crowned at last by triumph, draws tears even from eyes which have seen much and wept much . . . Who is the Italian, worthy of the name, who does not grasp the immense historic significance of what has been accomplished in these days by our heroic armies?" The article was signed "Mussolini".[25]

This new mood was similarly encouraged by the Prime Minister, Signor Orlando. Addressing the Italian Parliament on 20 November he said that *"nostra vittoria, che per la sua ampiezza e le sue conseguenze pare che oscuri ogni altro, anche le piu grandiose, che la storia recordi"* (our victory by its extent and its consequences seems to cast a shadow over all others, even the greatest that history records).[26] Even allowing for the Italian generous partiality for superlatives, this was extreme exaggeration.

The Austrian Empire had been moving inexorably through a process of disintegration since Karl's declaration of 16 October. Nor did the military actions during the Battle of Vittorio Veneto merit such outstanding commendation. Indeed, General Faldella's book on Italy's war *La Grande Guerra* published in 1965 devotes less than one of 780 pages to describing the battle.[27] Nevertheless, the tone of Orlando's speech was in accord with public opinion and was applauded by the press and the public, and by politicians including Mussolini who saw opportunities for political advancement.

Orlando himself could hardly have been unaware of the extent of his exaggeration. On 9 November he had prevented the publication of a draft communiqué from Diaz describing the woeful state of the Austrian Army, including the disorders and horrors among the troops attempting to return home by the Brenner railway, for he feared that such information would tend "to lessen the importance of our victory against an army which we now describe in such a disastrous condition".[28]

However, it should be remembered that Orlando's remarks on Vittorio Veneto came as part of a lengthy speech not primarily concerned with making a military assessment of the campaign. Like all the Allies, Italy had suffered grievous losses during the war with a terrible toll of dead, wounded and mutilated. The finances were in a poor state with a massive national debt. There had been shortages of raw materials, particularly of coal which produced much hardship during the winters. As a result Italy was now faced by serious economic and social problems. Orlando had banned Diaz's proposed communiqué on 9 November as he thought it would encourage anti-war and anarchist movements. Socialists and communists were numerous and presented a serious threat to social order. An Italian cavalry division had been stationed in Piedmont and Lombardy during the summer of 1917 to ensure public order in the face of strikes and industrial unrest. On 14 November 1918 Lord Cavan wrote to London saying that British troops in Italy must not become involved in any way in keeping internal order.[29] Hence the principal aim of Orlando's speech was probably to reassure the country that all the suffering and hardship of the war had been worthwhile, and that the forebodings of the anti-war politicians in 1915 had been unfounded.

In addition, Orlando was also aware that Italy's standing and influence at the Peace Conference would depend on an adequate appreciation of her military effort by her Allies. It was therefore unfortunate that until 24 October 1918 no Italian offensive had been launched against Austria since Cadorna's decision to go on the defensive on 18 September 1917. The Italian intention had been to prepare for an offensive in early 1919, and Orlando was much concerned in October 1918 when it appeared that both Austria and Germany might obtain an armistice before any Italian action. Hence Orlando probably sought to exaggerate the success of Vittorio Veneto in order to strengthen Italy's bargaining position at the Peace Conference.

Unfortunately such exaggerations raised undue expectations regarding the outcome of the Peace Conference. It was particularly unfortunate that the Italian public was largely unaware of the political collapse of Austria which had preceded the armistice, and of the race against time to begin the Battle of Vittorio Veneto before the war with Germany and Austria was over. Nor was it generally recognized in Italy that Italy's war against Austria had become an integral part of the much wider struggle of the First World War from which it could not readily be separated. Nor did there appear to be much appreciation of the significant assistance received from France and Britain. Hence, immersed in a mood of euphoria engendered by the success of Vittorio Veneto, the Italian government approached the Peace Conference with too little consideration of the views of their allies, and insufficiently prepared to present the Italian case to the best advantage.

4 The Peace Conference

All the fighting had come to an end by 11 November on terms dictated by France, Britain, Italy and America, and accepted by Germany, Austria, Turkey and Bulgaria. The Central Alliance of Germany and her partners had been decisively beaten, and Italy looked forward to receiving those benefits of victory accorded to her by the Treaty of London.[30] Namely, (a) the essentially Italian region of the Trentino, and also Trieste, would be transferred to Italy; (b) a more defensible frontier which to the north would run along the watershed of the Brenner pass, and in the east on the far side of the Isonzo river, extending down to include Istria and Pola; (c) security and influence in the Adriatic by control of the Dalmatian coast and the Albanian port of Valona; (d) various colonial concessions. However, since the Treaty had been signed in 1915 the war had completely changed the face of Europe in ways quite unforeseen by any of the signatories.

Most of the gains promised in 1915 had then been viewed by all the signatories of the Treaty as transfers of various territories from a beaten Austro-Hungarian Empire to Italy. But by the end of the war the Empire had disintegrated and was in no position to arrange for any transfer of its territories. The different ethnic groups of the Empire had been encouraged by President Wilson's Fourteen Points and Four Principals, and by the Emperor Karl's Manifesto of 16 October, to set up their own governments. This was already being done and none of the groups involved had any intention of replacing Austrian by Italian control.

Although Italy was later to complain of her treatment at the Peace Conference, her principal objectives of gaining the Trentino and Trieste were obtained with little difficulty. In addition, the predominantly German-speaking province of South Tyrol immediately north of the

Trentino was also incorporated into Italy in order to take the frontier across the summit of the Brenner. This last transfer was clearly against the principle of self-determination but was justified by the possibility that Austria might one day be annexed by Germany.[31] (As indeed was foreseen by Colonel Hoffmann of the German General Staff in 1918,[32] and realized by Hitler in 1938.)

Other provisions of the Treaty, including those concerning the Dalmatian coast and the port of Valona in Albania, were to prove more difficult. The various Slav races along the far shore of the Adriatic, Slovenes, Croats, Bosnians and Serbs, had renounced the Empire and were coming together to form the new state of Jugoslavia with allegiance to a National Council at Zagreb. Initially the Italian Government appeared to take a fairly relaxed view of these events, for the Italian claims on the Dalmatian coast, Valona and the adjacent island of Saseno aroused none of the emotional overtones associated with the Trentino and Trieste. Nevertheless these areas with their bases had provided the Austrian Navy with at least the possibility of dominating the whole of the Italian coast from Venice to Campania. The Empire was now no more but there were soon signs that the new state might be a difficult neighbour.

On 30 October, as part of the general disintegration of the Austrian Empire, a mutiny broke out in ships of the Austrian Fleet at Pola, about 50 miles south of Trieste. The crews of the ships who came largely from the areas forming the new Jugoslavia declared allegiance to the new National Council at Zagreb, and this arrangement was recognized by the Emperor Karl on the following day. However, under the Armistice conditions then being negotiated, the Allies expected that various units of the Austrian Fleet would be surrendered to them, and it was hardly likely that they would agree to these enemy ships with their enemy crews going elsewhere. On the night of 31 October an Italian submarine sank a dreadnought in Pola harbour and, after a vain attempt by Jugoslavia to justify ownership, the Fleet at Pola surrendered to an Italian Naval Force on 5 November. The episode was now over but had given notice that the new state might not be a friendly neighbour.[33]

More serious difficulties arose over the Croatian port of Fiume further down the Dalmatian Coast beyond Pola. The town had for many years been under the jurisdiction of Hungary, to which it was connected by a good rail link. According to the 1910 Census the population of the town itself was predominantly Italian: 22,488 Italians, 13,351 Slavs, and some Hungarians, Germans and others.[34] However, if the largely Slav suburbs across the river were included the numbers of Italians and Slavs were about equal. The city was apparently run by a coalition of Hungarian officials and Italian businessmen. Of the seven secondary schools in

Fiume, six taught in Hungarian and one in Italian. The Croats had no schools in their own language.[35]

At the time of the negotiations over the Treaty of London in 1915 the status of Fiume was not an issue and the city was part of the territory assigned to Croatia.[36] It was only on 18 October 1918 that Italians in Fiume claimed the right of self-determination. Events came to a crisis on 28 October when the Hungarian governor of Fiume informed the mayor that the ministers in Budapest had decided to abandon Fiume both militarily and politically. Whereupon on 30 October the municipal council reconstituted itself as the Italian National Council of Fiume. Later that day substantial numbers of Croat troops arrived and each successive day brought more Serb and Croat units into the town, so the National Council sought to obtain the support of the Italian Army to defend its interests.

On 4 November the Italian Navy arrived at Fiume to act as an observer, and the next day a French warship arrived to support her traditional ally Serbia. For the next two weeks the Italian troops remained on the ship while other troops under French command poured into the city to protect Jugoslav interests.[37] Thus within days of the Austrian armistice the two Allies found themselves at odds over a matter which, even at the beginning of October, had not been thought of as an issue.[38]

Allied troops, predominantly Italian, took over Fiume on 17 November, but by then these events had produced an unfavourable reaction in Italy. During the war Slovene, Croat and Bosnian troops in the Austrian Army had fought hard against Italy, and in his book on Caporetto General Krafft refers more than once to his "trusty Bosnians". Yet now the Italians had to face the fact that these soldiers, still in the same uniforms, were claiming to be on the side of the Allies and demanding to be treated as allies.[39]

Unfortunately, Italian opinion was all too readily inflamed by episodes such as those at Pola and Fiume. The Nationalists produced a violent campaign against Jugoslavia in an attempt to ensure that Italy gained all the territories on the far side of the Adriatic promised by the Treaty of London, and in addition the town of Fiume. All the nationalistic rhetoric of May 1915 was brought out again, and as in 1915, both the liberal press and liberal opinion were incapable or unwilling to make an effective counter-attack. Therefore, as in 1915, the Government was forced by the tide of populist opinion to take an increasingly uncompromising stance in the negotiations prior to the Peace Conference. However, the country did not realize that Italy no longer held the bargaining power it had in 1915 when the Allies had hoped that the entry of Italy would bring the whole war to an early conclusion,[40] and were therefore ready to endorse all her claims (which at that time were all at the expense of the Central Powers).

Furthermore Italy's position at the Peace Conference was not much helped by the Allies' impression that Italy had regarded her fight against Austria as something rather distinct from the First World War except when it was to her advantage. There had been unfavourable comment by the Allies that, despite her obligations under the Treaty of London, Italy did not declare war on Germany until August 1916.[41] (In fact Italy was somewhat constrained by the presence of between 300,000 and 500,000 Italian emigrant workers living in Germany.[42]) In addition the reluctance of the Italians to launch their offensive in the second half of 1918 had not gone unnoticed by the Allies who had been engaged in very severe fighting all this time. (Churchill gives the British casualties on the Western front from July to November as about 400,000, and the French casualties as over 500,000,[43] while during the same period the Italian casualties are stated to have been about 35,000 in Italy, and about 15,000 in France.[44]) Finally the exaggerated claims for Vittorio Veneto did little to increase Italy's standing.

Because of the above background the boundaries of the new Jugoslavia proved to be one of the most difficult problems discussed both before and during the Peace Conference. The extensive Italian claims, set out in some detail by Albrecht-Carrié,[45] were confronted by Wilson's determination to hold to the principle of self-determination, at least as far as possible. The discussions became increasingly protracted, to the irritation of the Allies and to Wilson in particular. Finally, in desperation, while Orlando and the Italian Peace Commission were still negotiating in Paris behind closed doors, Wilson issued a statement to the press on 23 April evidently designed as an appeal to the Italian people over the heads of their negotiators in Paris.[46] Orlando felt that he had no option but to break off the negotiations and return to Rome, and there received a hero's welcome. According to the American Ambassador the Allies had produced a more united Italy than even the Central Powers had been able to achieve during the war.[47]

Before all the implications of Wilson's Fourteen Points and Four Principals had become apparent, Wilson had been extremely popular in Italy. This was not entirely due to his promise of some American military assistance. Although Diaz had asked Pershing for twenty-five divisions (page 118) the first American contingent, a single infantry regiment, arrived at the front only a day or so before the armistice. In fact Wilson's popularity was primarily due to the very large and generous effort made by the American Red Cross in Italy which took the form of medical aid and canteens for the Italian Army and food and medical aid to the civilian population.[48] American Red Cross workers dressed in army style uniforms had become a very visible and popular sight in towns and villages over the whole of Italy. Indeed on 25 November in a letter to the War Office Lord Cavan commented that references to the

Americans in public speeches produced much greater enthusiasm than the mention of either the French or British, who had provided virtually all the Allied military assistance.[49]

Orlando's return to Rome produced an abrupt end to American popularity and Wilson was said to be the most unpopular man in Italy. Freya Stark, then living in Italy, has described how in towns and villages throughout the country, paint and whitewash were brought out to obliterate the name "Wilson" on the name boards of a multitude of only recently rechristened streets and piazzas.[50]

The Italian people were firmly behind Orlando but he had overplayed his hand. The negotiations continued in Paris and Orlando was informed that the Treaty with Germany would be signed on 6 May with or without Italian participation. He was also informed that if Italy did not return, then the Treaty of London would be null and void, and on 5 May he hurried back to Paris. Nothing had been achieved by his return to Rome except to still further encourage Italian expectations. Hence, when Orlando finally came back from Paris with these expectations unfulfilled his position was gravely damaged, and the government fell on 19 June.

In Paris the negotiations over Jugoslavia continued to drag on, without Italy obtaining much satisfaction, until the Treaty of Rapallo was signed in 1920. The Dalmatian coast and Valona remained with Jugoslavia. Fiume, which had been taken over by D'Annunzio in 1919, was declared a Free City and finally became part of Italy under Mussolini in 1924. Discussions over spheres of influence and colonial possessions in Asia Minor and Africa produced only minor gains, probably because Italy had not mounted any colonial campaigns during the war. Italy also complained on being excluded from the secret Sykes-Picot agreement between France, Britain and Russia in 1916 allocating spheres of influence in Syria and other adjacent parts of the Turkish Empire. On the other hand, at the time of this agreement Italy had not yet declared war on Germany.

As a result of the war Italy had gained her essential requirements of the Trentino and Trieste, *Italia Irredenta*. She had gained the South Tyrol and thus a more defensible northern frontier. Her eastern frontier had been advanced to the high ground on the far side of the Isonzo River, and now included Istria and the port of Pola. These were substantial gains, but Italy was left in a dissatisfied mood. The extravagant expectations following Vittorio Veneto had not been achieved and politicians of all shades began working on these dissatisfactions, a process that was to have unhappy consequences.

5.   History and Myth

In his speech to the Italian Parliament on 20 November 1918 Signor Orlando, the Italian Prime Minister, warmly acknowledged the efforts of the French and British in Italy. General Gathorne-Hardy, the Chief of Staff of the 10th Army, has recorded that before leaving Italy Lord Cavan was told by the Duke of Aosta "Goodbye, General, I am indeed sorry that you are leaving Italy, without the presence of your troops there would have been no victory at Vittorio Veneto".[51] However, there were soon arguments and disagreements. Although Italy was to gain the Trentino and Trieste there were significant disappointments at the Peace Conference over hoped-for acquisitions on the further shore of the Adriatic.

It is probably relevant to recall that relations between France and Italy have always been somewhat ambivalent, certainly since Napoleon had occupied the whole peninsula. Even in 1945 President Truman was obliged to inform General de Gaulle that unless he withdrew his troops from north-west Italy the United Sates would withhold all supplies except rations from the French forces.[52] Hence, it is not too surprising that one of the most notable of the ensuing controversies centred on the part played by General Foch during his stay in Italy from 30 October to 23 November 1917.

A detailed account of the Foch debate is given by Gatti in his book *La Parte dell'Italia* (1926) dedicated "To Italy, glorious with knowledge and with justice". According to Gatti's account, particular exception was taken to an article entitled "Foch and Pétain" in *Le Petit Parisien* of 21 November 1919. This was written by M.Painlevé, the French Prime Minister and War Minister at the time of Caporetto, and was a typical celebratory article on the two Marshals of France printed just after the ceremony at which Pétain received his baton. In the middle of a lengthy article dealing mainly with the war on the Western Front it was said that Foch "*était aux côtés du General Diaz en ces jours de novembre 1917, où se renouvela sur le Piave le miracle de l'Yzer*". This remark might seem a courteous reference of no particular significance, but Gatti chose to read the article as making the rather different claim that Foch "was the inspiration of the Italian defence of the Piave".[53]

An Italian reply appeared at the end of 1919 in a book *Il Proccesso di Cadorna* by the Italian historian Ezio Gray. This author claimed not only that the decision to stand on the Piave had been due to Cadorna alone, but that Foch had advised against it, and had preferred a defence line further back behind the Mincio or the Po. However, there appears to be no evidence at all that Foch was ever against making a stand on the Piave, and his Memoirs state that on 2 November he emphasized to Orlando that "It is on the Piave that we must resist".[54]

186

Gray's comments were followed by a French riposte in the *Revue de Deux Mondes* of 15 July 1920. A long anonymous article took exception to what it termed the "Italian legend". Namely the suggestion that Foch had advised against standing on the Piave, that he had played no part in its defence, and that the honour of its defence was due exclusively to General Cadorna. The French article then continued to give a detailed account of Foch's contribution not unlike that described in Chapters 2 and 3, and then completely rejected the "Italian legend". The controversies continued, fuelled further by an article by General Tasker Bliss, the former Chief of Staff of the American Army in France, which appeared in the journal *Foreign Affairs* in December 1922. This article was concerned primarily with the evolution of a unified command in France, but *inter alia* included the comment that General Foch had "visited the Italian General Headquarters and arranged for a complete rehabilitation of that army".[55]

In 1923 Cadorna published a book[56] and an article[57] setting out his account of events, and giving a general defence of his conduct of the war. We note here only his account of his first meeting with Foch on 30 October, when they talked together without anyone else being present. Cadorna says he was taken aback both by Foch's questions and his insistence that the Italians should stand on the Piave. For, as he told Foch, this had already been arranged. After this exchange, again according to Cadorna, they were soon on better terms, and from then on Foch "ceased giving me his unsolicted advice".[58]

There seems little reason to doubt Cadorna's intention to stand on the Piave, for it was in fact an obvious decision. The Official History comments that, although Cadorna was in the habit of issuing advance warning of future moves, no documentation had been found relating to any move beyond the Piave.[59] On the other hand it would have been surprising if there had not been some discussion of defence positions behind the Piave. Indeed on 11 and 12 November, after Cadorna had been replaced by Diaz, Gatti refers in his diary to the advantages of retiring behind the Mincio,[60] and on 12 and 17 November Diaz issued precautionary directives on the conduct of such a retirement.[61] It seems probable that at some time Foch would have remarked that a stand should be made on the Piave but this is hardly sufficient for him to be claimed the saviour of Italy. Yet it is not out of place to ask how Foch spent his time during the three weeks he passed in Italy as Commander of the French troops and the senior French or British officer in close contact with the Comando Supremo.

Foch's own account in his Memoirs, published posthumously in 1931, said only that "General Foch had aided and supported the Comando Supremo; had helped it to take the energetic decisions which the gravity of the situation exacted. Here, as in the Battle of Flanders three years

187

earlier, he was listened to by reason of the clearness of his vision, his buoyancy, his promptness to act and his unreserved devotion to the common cause of all the Allies".[62] This account gives a very different picture from the Italian claim quoted in the *Revue de Deux Mondes* that the honour of the battle was due exclusively to General Cadorna. It is therefore not surprising that when Foch was asked to repudiate the French article his secretary replied that he declined to do so.[63]

The controversy did little to help relations between France and Italy, already strained by Italy having been forced to accept French assistance in 1917. Nor were matters helped by Professor Arnould's claim in 1923 that the French had been the first to reach the far bank of the Piave at the Battle of Vittorio Veneto.[64] This may well be true but was of little consequence, as the Italians on their right were across very soon after, and in any case the battle had been opened two days previously on Monte Grappa by the Italians.

There were no such comparable polemics between Britain and Italy, but even good friends of Italy felt that the Italian press gave too little attention to the part played by the British forces in Italy, see for example Page (the wartime American Ambassador to Italy),[65] Goldsmid (the British liaison officer with the Italian 3rd Army),[66] and Cavan.[67] Some reluctance to give a full acknowledgement of the Allied help was no doubt understandable to some extent as the result of the embarrassing circumstances of 1917. Winston Churchill has described his meeting in Paris on 18 November 1917 with the Italian Minister of Armaments, General Ballolio. "It was a most cheerless experience . . . defeat was not leniently viewed by overstrained allies. We all went through it in our turn – the politeness which veiled depreciation, the sympathy which scarcely surmounted resentment, and here I must pay tribute to the quiet courage of the Italian minister."[68]

With the rise of Mussolini and the fascist era the phrase *da solo* appears. Rocca quotes the journal *L'Idea Nazionale* as writing in 1923 that "*L'Italia arresto da solo l'invasione straniera*"[69] (Italy alone stopped the foreign invasion). The phrase *da solo* was still in use in 1933 when Caviglia in the preface to his book *Caporetto* stated that "in the autumn of 1918 Italy, alone [*da solo*], definitely overcame, and eliminated the Austro-Hungarian Empire from the face of the earth". To claim that the fall of Austria was brought about solely by Italy ignores the fearful Austrian losses inflicted by Russia, and the political collapse of the Austrian Empire.

The French and British made a significant contribution in stemming the Austro-German offensive in 1917. The Italian request for assistance in October 1917 included, *inter alia*, a telegram from the British Military Mission in Italy on 27 October to the British Government stating that the Italian General Staff were "very anxious that there should be announced even small contingents of French and British troops as on their way in order to encourage country and army".[70] The British and French provided a large military force to act as a reserve and to signify to Italy that they were not alone. Yet the index of Caviglia's book *Caporetto* (1933) makes no mention of Foch, Lloyd George, France, French, Britain or British.

General Caviglia's use of the term *da solo* was particularly unfortunate when refering to the collapse of Austria, for the French and British contributions to the battles of June and October 1918 are clearly set out in his own book *Le Tre Battaglie*. Perhaps the most crucial decision leading to the success of Vittorio Veneto was that of General Babington commanding the British XIV Corps when he proposed that the Corps should occupy Papadopoli Island prior to the main attack. This point is generally ignored in Italian accounts. On the other hand Caviglia's decision to pass the Italian XVIII Corps across the Piave over the only available bridges, those in the British sector, is often described in glowing terms. According to Villari "General Caviglia now conceived one of those master strokes which so often decide the fate of battles".[71] Even the Official History refers to "the brilliant manoeuvre",[72] and gives a sketch map[73] which shows the Italian XVIII Corps on 27 October advancing far beyond the Italian and British bridgeheads, almost to Conegliano, although it was only at nightfall on the 27th that the Corps began to cross the river.

In addition there were claims that not only did the Italians defeat Austria *da solo*, but that their victory at Vittorio Veneto also brought about the capitulation of Germany eight days after the signing of the Austrian Armistice. A very clear expression of this point of view was given by Caviglia in *Le Tre Battaglie*, where he remarks that at the end of October the Allies on the Western Front had not obtained a decisive victory, and that "*La battaglia decisiva, invece, era stata vinta in Italia dagli Italiani. Esse pose fine anche alla battaglia di Francia ed alla guerra*".[74] (In contrast, the decisive battle had been won in Italy by the Italians. It put an end also to the battle of France and to the war.) This conclusion is much at odds with events elsewhere.

Between July and September the Allies on the Western Front had driven the Germans up to 40 miles back from the line between Ypres and Château-Thierry which they had reached in their July offensives. As early as 8 August Ludendorff, who was then the virtual ruler of Germany, had come to believe that Germany could no longer win the war, and wished to end it on as best terms as possible. Then on 29 September his already uncertain nerves failed completely and he personally insisted that an armistice be sought immediately.[75] A new and more parliamentary government was formed on 2 October and the next day a note was sent to President Wilson asking for an armistice and negotiations for peace.[76]

The resulting discussions both in Germany, and between the Allies, are described in the book by Rudin. They continued throughout October and do not concern us here except to show that Germany's position was steadily deteriorating. Germany's ally Bulgaria had signed an armistice on 29 September and Turkey was to do so on 30 October.[77] On 26 October the German Ambassador in Vienna telegraphed that "the [Austrian] monarchy is done for; if it fails to conclude peace immediately, there is no escape from revolution in Hungary, Croatia, Bohemia and even in Vienna".[78] Also on 26 October Ludendorff who by now had changed his mind, and wished to fight on for better conditions, was dismissed by the government. On 30 October there was a full-scale mutiny of the German High Seas Fleet following a plan for a last desperate sortie against the British Fleet. Ludendorff had set in motion processes which by the end of October were leading inexorably to the surrender of Germany.

The Italian offensive of Vittorio Veneto opened on 24 October on Monte Grappa, but the crossing of the Piave began only on 27 October, and the advance from the bridgeheads one or two days later. No doubt the news of this success and of the subsequent armistice with Austria, and the threat of an Allied advance into Bavaria, was further confirmation of the need for Germany to conclude an armistice. But Germany's negotiations were now so far advanced and the state of the country now so fragile that an armistice had become inevitable.

Several Italian accounts[79] have continued to refer to a letter said to have been written by Ludendorff to Count Lerchenfeld on 7 November 1919, in which he claimed that but for Vittorio Veneto both Germany and Austria would have been able to continue the war, at least through the winter, and obtain better terms. In fact the condition of both countries in October 1918 made any continuation of the war virtually impossible. Hence it is difficult to take Ludendorff's remark as anything more than an attempt by the then dismissed First Quartermaster-General to rewrite history for his own rehabilitation.

During the fascist era after 1922 relations between Italy and her former allies continued to deteriorate. In 1917 the French and British had made a rapid response to Italy's appeals, and in 1918 Orlando had paid generous tributes to these forces, but when writing to Caviglia in 1930 he refers to the allied contingents as an influx of foreigners.[80] Accounts on the lines of *da solo* became increasingly widespread, as for example in several accounts of the crossing of the Piave on 27 and 28 October, 1918. Gario[81] in a thirty-eight-page account of the war published in English says only that "the Italians, surmounting great difficulties, were crossing the River Piave at various points. In spite of strong enemy opposition, by October 28 the whole of the Italian and Allied forces in the lower Piave were across the river." Mussolini in his autobiography (1928) summarizes the crossing by saying no more than that "the enemy's front was pierced at Sernaglia; our army rushed through the break"[82] (Sernaglia being the Italian bridgehead).

In view of the predominantly partisan tone of the Italian accounts during the Mussolini era, it is hardly surprising that the British Official History commented that "Italian accounts have not rendered justice to the moral support and sound advice given to the Comando Supremo by Marshal Foch, or to the vital assistance given by the French and British troops both in the mountains and on the plains . . . if a true account were given it could not be overlooked that the British were first across the Piave, and that they received the surrender of the Austrian forces in Trent before the Italian troops arrived there".[83]

The British Official History generally presents a fair account of the events in Italy, but the authors were no doubt stung by the Italian accounts and went too far in saying that British troops received the Austrian surrender of Trent. It is clear that on 3 November various units of the Italian Armies were converging on the Trentino, and that by 15.15 Italian troops had occupied Trent. At the start of this day the British 48th Division had continued its march up Val d'Assa (Map 12) with orders to occupy Caldonazzo and Levico, two villages about 10 miles from Trent, and thus block the road through Val Sugana.

The Division arrived at Passo Vezzena early in the morning and obtained the surrrender of a large number of Austrians, and the advance guard reached Caldonazzo by 12.30. Edmonds states that until 15.00 Major General Walker, in command of the Division had lost communication with both Corps and Army, and was out of touch with the Italian Divisions on his right and left. Nevertheless, after his meeting with an Austrian general at his HQ he drew up terms of surrender to present to the Austrian Army Commander in Trent. These terms stated, *inter alia*, that "in accordance with orders, he [Walker] has given orders for his troops to occupy Levico, Pergine and Trent. He demands the unconditional surrender of hostile troops in the above area".[84]

General Walker's terms were carried forward by his Chief of Staff (Lieut.-Colonel Howard) and an Intelligence Officer. They had no dificulty in reaching Trent by 13.30, for as Edmonds states they "were cheered the whole way as they drove through the retreating Austrian troops".[85] According to the British account the terms "were accepted" but the significance of this is unclear. The Austrians were actively engaged in withdrawing from Trent before the Italian troops arrived, and they were not likely to be deterred by the lone presence of two British officers.

It is also not clear on what authority General Walker claimed that he had orders to occupy Trent in addition to Levico and Pergine, for the Divisional orders for the next day, issued on the evening of 3 November, directed the Brigades to areas north of Lake Caldonazzo.[86] It appears likely that General Walker, carried away by over excitement and enthusiasm, had been exceeding his orders. In any case the claim by Edmonds that the British "received the surrender of the Austrian forces in the Trentino before Italian troops arrived" is entirely misleading. The Austrians were already evacuating the city and there is no evidence that any document of significance was signed. Nor is there any mention of the incident in General Walker's report of 8 November.[87]

Following the end of the Second World War in 1945 there was a marked lack of interest in the previous conflict, and it was not until 1965 that books by Seth and Faldella revived the old controversies. General Faldella who had fought as a young officer in 1915 published his two-volume account of the war against Austria. Although this gave a detailed military history of the war up to and including Caporetto, subsequent events were dealt with more briefly. Half of the extremely short account of Vittorio Veneto is given over to a complaint that the 12th and 10th Armies were created without any military justification, merely to find positions for French and British generals.[88] Seth in his book *Caporetto* (1965) returned to the Foch – Cadorna controversy with the novel suggestion that Foch was uncooperative because he was jealous of Cadorna's generalship during the retreat from the Isonzo to the Tagliamento, which "would make Cadorna's name ring not only through his own country but throughout the world, and Italian arms would bask in the reflected glory of their commander".[89]

At this time any writer dealing with the last year of the war from Caporetto to Vittorio Veneto was faced with the difficulty that many of the previous accounts were polemical rather than factual, and had to make do with the available material. Substantial new information came only in 1967 with the publication of the volume of the Italian Official History dealing with the Battle of Caporetto, which set out events in much detail but only to the end of 1917. Melograni's book *Storia Politica della Grande Guerra*, published in 1972, gave a critical review of social and economic aspects of the war, of military discipline, and their influence on the military actions, with an extensive set of references not otherwise readily available. Since then various books have been published, some of which are listed in the bibliography. (Of these the book by Pieropan *1914–1918 Storia della Grande Guerra* (1988), making use of official sources, gives the most extensive detailed summary of the fighting on the Italian front.)

The outstanding contribution in this period has been the much-delayed appearance of the final sections of the Italian Official History. These sections published in 1967, 1982 and 1988 amount in all to about 2800 pages of text, over 2500 pages of documents, and some excellent maps and photographs of the ground, particularly in the 1967 volume.

192

This Official History provides a detailed and ordered account of all the military actions, accompanied by analyses and critical assessments of the strength and failings of the Italian Army. Produced many years after the war, the authors have felt able to express themselves freely and have arrived at a more realistic view of the achievement of the Italian Army, and of its contribution to the fall of Austria and the Central Powers. A contribution which stands out more clearly when stripped of the rhetoric produced immediately after the war and in the fascist era.

References

The full details of the books referred to in the references are given in the Bibliography, pp. 211 et seq.

Chapter 1 (pp. 5–18)
1   *Encyclopaedia Britannica (1947)* Vol 9, 815d
2   Ibid Vol 6, 279d; Fiala (1990), 36
3   Mack Smith, 210
4   Page, 210
5   Page, 211, Rodd, 251
6   Falls, 17
7   CGOCG *Asiago*, 57
8   Krafft, 49
9   Trevelyan, 176
10   Ibid,
11   IOH (IV,3), 46,72
12   IOH (IV,3,Doc), 52
13   IOH (IV,3,Doc) 54
14   IOH (IV,3) 157
15   Trevelyan, 169ff
16   Ibid, 178
17   Stark, 212ff
18   Dalton, 97
19   Hemingway, Chaps 27–30
20   IOH (IV,3) 521

Chapter 2 (pp. 19–35)
1   Robertson, 129
2   LLoyd George, 838
3   Robertson, 135
4   Ibid, 136
5   Lloyd George, 838
6   Edmonds, 25
7   Ibid, 26

8   Lloyd George, 854
9   Edmonds, 27
10 Edmonds,28
11 Ibid, 28
12 Ibid, 31
13 Foch, 254
14 Edmonds, 29
15 Ibid, 29
16 Ibid, 40
17 Ibid, 42
18 Ibid, 43
19 FOA (VI,1), Annexe 22
20 Edmonds, 58
21 Robertson, 239
22 Ibid, 240
23 FOA (VI,1), Annexe 26
24 Edmonds, 59
25 Ibid, 59
26 IOH (IV,3), 617
27 FOA (VI,1), 95/96, Annexe 33
28 IOH (IV,3,Doc), 443
29 FOA (VI,1), Annexe 37
30 Callwell Vol 2, 25
31 *Army Quarterly* Vol 7, (1924), 235
32 FOA (VI,1) 96, Annexe 38
33 FOA (VI,1) 97
34 IOH (IV,3), 422
35 Ibid, 619
36 FOA (VI,1), 97
37 *Army Quarterly* Vol 45, (1942), 46
38 Edmonds, 90
39 *Army Quarterly* Vol 9, (1925), 375
40 Edmonds, 88, 97
41 e.g. Stacke, 385
42 Wright, 93
43 Barnett,10
44 Edmonds 91
45 Edmonds, 91, 98, 102, 112
46 Lloyd George, 1396; Callwell Vol 2, 22
47 IOH (IV,3,Doc), 500, 501
48 FOA (VI,1), 101
49 Gatti, (1965), 148
50 Villari, 165
51 Gatti, (1965), 275

52 Foch, 262
53 Seth, 176
54 Rocca, 301; Cervone (1992), 88
55 Edmonds, 73
56 Orlando, 240
57 Seth, 182
58 Callwell Vol 2, 24
59 FOA (VI,1), Annexe 68
60 PRO WO 79/67
61 Edmonds, 92; FOA (VI,1), 103
62 Edmonds 92; Baldini 32
63 IOH (IV,3), 521
64 Edmonds, 143
65 Villari, 188
66 IOH (V,1), 90 footnote
67 Ibid, 75; FOA (V1,1), 122; Edmonds, 134
68 Edmonds, 119
69 Bachi, 98, 123
70 Edmonds, 120
71 Ibid, 23

Chapter 3 (pp. 36–54)
1   Edmonds, 90; PRO WO 79/67
2   Hardie and Allen, 14
3   Barnett, 5
4   IOH (V,1), 51, 58
5   CI Vol 1, 374
6   *The Times* 5 Nov. 1917, 7f
7   *The Times* 9 Nov. 1917, 8c
8   PRO FO 371 2948, p.216
9   *The Times* 8 Nov. 1917, 9f
10 Hardie and Allen, 14
11 Melograni, Chap. 7
12 Gatti (1965), 110
13 Ibid, 317
14 IOH (IV,3), 544
15 Caviglia (1934), 49
16 Melograni, 421
17 Gatti (1965), 403
18 IOH (V,1,Doc), 60
19 Ibid. 103
20 Baldini, 54ff
21 Ibid, 55
22 *The Times*, 20 Dec. 1917, 6c

23 Melograni, 501
24 IOH (V,1,Doc), 67
25 Gatti (1965), 147
26 CI Vol 2, 326
27 Baldini, 51
28 CI Vol 2, 326
29 IOH (IV,3), 578; Pieropan, 535
30 Ibid, 577
31 IOH (IV,3,Carta), No 25
32 Ibid, No 24
33 IOH (IV,3), 581
34 Ibid, 546
35 Ibid, 547
36 Pieropan, 576
37 Riassunto, 429; IOH (IV,3), 593; Schiarini, 82
38 IOH (V,1 Doc), 92
39 IOH (IV,3,Doc), 298
40 Fadini, 271
41 Krafft, 329
42 Rommel, 323
43 FOA (VI,1),118
44 Riassunto, 445; CGOCG *Monte Grappa*, 8,68,70;
45 Fadini, 269
46 Krafft, 309
47 Ibid, 329
48 Fadini, 273
49 Fadini, 275; Krafft, 340
50 Fadini, 276
51 Krafft, 340
52 Ibid, 342
53 Fadini, 278
54 Krafft, 342
55 Fadini, 278
56 Krafft, 344
57 Edmonds, 424
58 Ibid, 95
59 Robertson, 257
60 PRO WO 79/67
61 Edmonds, 98
62 PRO WO 79/67
63 Foch, 266
64 FOA (VI,1), 116, Annexe 158
65 Ibid, Annexe 170; Edmonds, 110
66 Wingfield, PRO CAB 45/84

67 PRO CAB 45/84; Edmonds, 111
68 Edmonds, 117
69 Delmé-Radcliffe, HL, F/44/3/29 No 503
70 e.g. Atkinson, 437

Chapter 4 (pp. 55–78)
1   Barnett, 29; Cruttwell (1922), 136; Hardie and Allen, 31; Wright, 98
2   Gladden, 35
3   Pickford, 37
4   Rolleston, 146
5   Edmonds, 115
6   Ibid, 138
7   Ibid, 132
8   Gladden, 48ff
9   Edmonds, 131
10 Ibid, 140
11 FOA (VI,1) 124, Annexe 314
12 Edmonds, 159
13 Ibid, 160
14 Ibid, 146
15 Pershing, Vol.1, 268
16 PRO WO 79/67
17 Robertson, 257
18 Baldini, 98
19 Edmonds, 148
20 Ibid, 150
21 Ibid, 151
22 Ibid, 152
23 Ibid, 159
24 Ibid, 156
25 Ibid, 161
26 Ibid, 166
27 Ibid, 157; IOH (V,1), 35
28 CGOCG, *All'Estero* 38; Cruttwell (1936), 535,543
29 *Army Quarterly* Vol 7 (1926), 237
30 Gatti (1965), 286
31 Robertson, 251
32 Herbillon Vol 2, 156
33 Pershing Vol 1, 261
34 FOA (VI 1), 23
35 Edmonds, 99
36 Herbillon Vol 2, 172
37 Faldella Vol 2, 286
38 IOH (V,1,Doc), 140

39 National Portrait Gallery, London
40 *IWM Review* No.6, 49
41 Cruttwell (1936), 437
42 *IWM Review* No.6, 39
43 Cruttwell (1936), 436
44 Liddell Hart (1931), 417
45 Harington, 82
46 Ibid, 80
47 Barnett, 31
48 Gladden, 71
49 Powell, 240
50 Melograni, 485
51 Powell, 241
52 Longmore, PRO CAB 45/84
53 Wingfield, PRO CAB 45/84
54 PRO WO 106/805
55 PRO WO 106/810
56 FOA (VI,1), Annexe 253; Edmonds, 128, 134
57 Hardie and Allen, 123
58 Edmonds, 145
59 Cavan PRO CAB 45/84
60 Cervone (1992), 95
61 Gladden, 77
62 Wright, 99
63 Edmonds, 169; Rolleston, 146
64 Dopson, 114
65 Hody, 104
66 Barnett, 45ff
67 Sandilands, 246
68 Edmonds, 165, 181
69 Edmonds, 175
70 Cruttwell (1936), 518
71 Edmonds, 175
72 Ibid, 176
73 Ibid, 176
74 PRO CAB 45/84
75 Edmonds, 168
76 Atkinson, 446
77 Barnett, 42
78 Cavan, *Army Quarterly* (1920), 14
79 IOH (V,1,Doc), 159
80 Edmonds, 177
81 Ibid, 177
82 FOA (VI,2), Annexe 122

83 IOH (V,1,Doc) 165
84 Edmonds, 178
85 Ibid, 178
86 Ibid, 181
87 FOA (VI,2), Annexe 644
88 Edmonds, 183
89 Ibid, 184
90 Ibid, 185
91 FOA (VI,2), Annexe 1484
92 Jones, 273
93 IOH (V,1), 97
94 Jones, 285

Chapter 5 (pp. 79–91)
1   Pieropan, 637 ff
2   Fiala (1982), 24 ff
3   Edmonds, 187
4   Ibid, 190; IOH (V,1,Carta) No.29
5   Ludendorff Vol 2, 609
6   Viazzi, 151 ff
7   IOH (V,1), 262; Viazzi, 375
8   IOH (V,1), 348
9   Ibid, 349
10 Riassunto, 483
11 IOH (V,1), 346; Viazzi, 404
12 Viazzi, 413
13 IOH (V,1), 327; Carta 32
14 Pieropan, 660
15 IOH (V,1), 356–399
16 IOH (V,1), 428
17 IOH (V,1), 392
18 IOH (V,1,Doc), 306
19 Pieropan, 669
20 Giardino, Vol 2, 105–145
21 Ibid, 401 (Map)
22 IOH (V,1), 471
23 Ibid, 481
24 Ibid, 489
25 Pieropan, 684
26 Ibid, 686
27 IOH (V,1), 706
28 Ibid, 334
29 Fiala (1982), 254
30 Pieropan, 696

31 IOH (V,1), 558
32 Pieropan, 715
33 IOH (V,1), 336
34 IOH (V,1, Carta), No.35
35 Ibid, No.35
36 Jones, 285
37 Fiala, (1982), 349
38 IOH (V,1), 641
39 Riassunto, 506
40 IOH (V,2), 90
41 Ibid, 91
42 Ibid,91
43 IOH (V,1), 497
44 Ibid, 497 footnote
45 Ibid, 525
46 Ibid, 526
47 IOH (V,1,Doc), 337
48 IOH (V,1), 526
49 Ibid, 555
50 IOH (V,1,Doc), 318
51 Pieropan, 703
52 IOH (V,1), 543
53 IOH (V,1,Doc), 404, 406
54 IOH (V,2), 94
55 Ibid, 90

Chapter 6 (pp. 92–116)
1   FOA (VI,2), 355
2   Ibid, 360
3   FOA (VI,2) Annexe No.1609
4   Sandilands, PRO CAB 45/84
5   Edmonds,202
6   Ibid, 199
7   Ibid, 200
8   Gladden, 121
9   Edmonds, 204
10 Sandilands, 260
11 Berry and Bostridge, 128
12 Sandilands, 267
13 Wyrall, 337
14 PRO WO 95/4244
15 Edmonds, 201
16 *Army Quarterly* Vol 14 (1927), 306
17 Gladden, 141

18 Sandilands, 257
19 Edmonds, 211
20 Ibid, 212
21 Ibid, 212
22 Wright, 112
23 Barnett, 89; Wyrall, 342
24 Edmonds, 201
25 Pickford, 86
26 Ibid, 85
27 PRO CAB 45/84
28 Edmonds, 252
29 PRO CAB 45/84
30 Ibid
31 Ibid
32 Ibid
33 Barnett, 70
34 Edmonds, 217; Morshead, PRO CAB 45/84
35 Edmonds, 195
36 Prior, PRO CAB 45/84
37 Barnett, 61
38 Edmonds, 217
39 Waller, PRO CAB 45/84
40 Barnett, 91
41 Ibid, 95
42 Edmonds, 216
43 Pieropan, 669
44 Sandilands, 240
45 Edmonds, 218
46 PRO WO 95/4194
47 PRO CAB 45/84
48 Edmonds, 200
49 PRO WO 95/4245
50 PRO WO 95/4199
51 PRO WO 95/4244
52 Greenwell, 225
53 PRO CAB 45 84
54 Ibid
55 Ibid
56 Pickford, 20
57 PRO CAB 45/84; Greenwell, 211
58 *The Times*, 17 June 1918, 9f
59 Caviglia (1934), 74
60 IOH (V,1), 430
61 Pieropan, 662

62   Cervone (1992), 95
63   Edmonds, 128
64   Ibid, 175

Chapter 7 (pp. 117–128)
1   Cavan, PRO WO 79/70; Edmonds, 215
2   IOH (V,2), 966
3   Pershing, Vol 2, 256; IOH (V,2,Doc), 297
4   Foch, 292; Travers, 68
5   FOA (VI,2) Annexe No.1699
6   Ibid, Annexe No.1821
7   Ibid, Annexe No.1949
8   Ibid, Annexe No.2280
9   Edmonds, 244
10   FOA (VI,2), Annexe No.2338
11   Ibid, Annexe No.2340
12   Ibid, Annexe No.2343
13   IOH (V,2 Doc), 208
14   Ibid, 252
15   Ibid, 608
16   Ibid, 280
17   IOH (V,2), 115ff
18   Edmonds, 247
19   Ibid, 248
20   Ibid, 260
21   IOH (V,2,Doc), 325
22   Caviglia (1934), 103
23   Edmonds, 248
24   IOH (V,2,Doc), 316
25   Ibid, 320
26   Edmonds, 255
27   Ibid, 262
28   IOH (V,2,Doc) 322
29   Edmonds, 249; IOH (V,2), 889,893
30   Atkinson, 449
31   Sandilands, 276
32   Ibid, 273
33   Edmonds, 255
34   Ibid, 258
35   Barnett, 102, 107
36   Wright, 153
37   Edmonds, 259
38   Ibid, 263
39   Barnett, 112

40 Edmonds, 263
41 PRO WO 106/835
42 Edmonds, 263
43 Rudin, 400
44 Snow and Kral, 11,182
45 Albrecht-Carrié, 347
46 Melograni, 524
47 Rudin, 19
48 Ibid, 27
49 Ibid, 50ff
50 Primicerj, 41
51 Rudin, 131
52 Cruttwell, (1936) 578
53 Wilson, 56
54 Primicerj, 323; Edmonds, 361
55 Zivojinovic, 172

Chapter 8 (pp. 129–173)
1   IOH (V,2,Doc), 692
2   IOH (V,2), 362 (Schizzo 20)
3   Edmonds, 270
4   IOH (V,2), 372
5   IOH (V,2,Doc), 820
6   Ibid, 822
7   IOH (V,2), 329
8   Ibid, 166
9   Bragg et al., 12; Rolleston, 146; Dalton, 239
10 Jones, 290
11 IOH (V,2), 358 (Schizzo 19)
12 IOH (V,2,Doc), 706
13 Ibid, 707
14 Ibid, 707; Foch, 316
15 IOH (V,2,Doc), 708
16 Ibid, 710
17 Ibid, 711
18 Ibid, 712
19 IOH (V,2), 293
20 IOH (V,2,Doc), 714
21 Ibid, 719
22 Caviglia (1934), 299
23 IOH (V,2), 317
24 Edmonds, 265
25 Pieropan, 773,776
26 Edmonds, 274

27 IOH (V,2), 460; IOH (V,2,Doc), 912,913
28 Edmonds, 284
29 Crosse, 34
30 Ibid, 48
31 Ibid, 51
32 Ibid, 49
33 Gladden, 160ff
34 Gladden, 163
35 Caviglia (1934), 128
36 IOH (V,2), 517
37 Ibid, 518
38 Caviglia (1934), 175
39 Edmonds, 285
40 Ibid, 286; Crosse, 54
41 Edmonds, 288
42 IOH (V,2,Carta), No.27
43 Sandilands, 309
44 Gladden, 169
45 Atkinson, 473
46 Edmonds, 292; Sandilands, 311
47 Atkinson, 474
48 Sandilands, 312
49 Atkinson, 476
50 IOH (V,2), 535
51 Edmonds, 294; IOH (V,2, Carta), No.31
52 IOH (V,2), 536,537
53 Sandilands, 314
54 Jones, 291
55 Edmonds, 294
56 IOH (V,2), 537
57 Riassunto, 534
58 Ibid, 533
59 Primicerj, 47
60 Ibid, 49
61 Ibid, 78
62 Ibid, 85
63 Riassunto, 547; IOH (V,2), 284
64 Primicerj, 89
65 Riassunto, 547
66 Edmonds, 363; Primicerj, 112
67 Edmonds, 363
68 Ibid, 364
69 Ibid, 296; Riassunto, 543
70 Edmonds, 364

71 Ibid, 303
72 Pieropan, 804; Villari, 264
73 IOH (V,2,Doc), 823
74 Edmonds, 292
75 Sandilands, 315,
76 Edmonds, 299
77 Sandilands, 317
78 Atkinson, 477
79 Edmonds, 299
80 IOH (V,2), 559
81 Edmonds, 302
82 Edmonds, 315,; Riassunto, 549
83 IOH (V,2), 592, 622
84 Ibid, 586ff
85 Edmonds, 317; PRO CAB 45/84
86 Sandilands, 321
87 Ibid, 322
88 Edmonds, 309
89 Sandilands, 324
90 Atkinson, 480
91 Edmonds, 305, 315
92 IOH (V,2), 592; Edmonds, 312
93 IOH (V,2,Doc), 602
94 Ibid, 692
95 Ibid, 757
96 Ibid, 714
97 IOH (V,2,Carta), No.19
98 IOH (V,2), 341
99 Giardino Vol 3, 102
100 IOH (V,2), 500
101 IOH (V,2,Doc), 761
102 IOH (V,2), 340
103 Ibid, 343
104 Ibid, 409
105 Ibid, 316
106 Ibid, 438, 650
107 Ibid, 940
108 IOH (V,2,Doc), 926
109 IOH (V,2), 490
110 IOH (V,2,Doc), 931
111 Ibid, 951
112 IOH (V,2), 610
113 IOH (V,2,Doc), 975
114 IOH (V,2), 612; Primicerj, 181

115 IOH (V,2), 611
116 CGOCG *Monta Grappa*, 62
117 IOH (V,2), 613
118 Pieropan, 816
119 IOH (V,2), 624
120 Atkinson, 483; Sandilands, 325
121 IOH (V,2,Doc), 985
122 IOH (V,2), 639
123 Pieropan, 824
124 Edmonds, 322; Sandilands, 326
125 IOH (V,2), 963
126 Edmonds,324
127 Ibid, 324
128 Riassunto, 553
129 Jones, 292
130 IOH (V,2,Doc), 998
131 Edmonds, 367
132 Ibid, 374
133 Edmonds, 374; Primicerj, 256
134 Edmonds, 375; Primicerj, 257
135 Atkinson, 484; Crosse, 91
136 Edmonds, 351; Primicerj, 272
137 Atkinson, 485; Edmonds, 352
138 Edmonds, 307, 354
139 IOH (V,2,Doc), 1042
140 IOH (V,2), 745
141 Barnett, 116; Edmonds, 329
142 Barnett, 121
143 Ibid, 128
144 IOH (V,2), 753
145 Edmonds, 341
146 IOH (V,2), 770; Pieropan, 838
147 Villari, 273
148 Edmonds, 338
149 Melograni, 552; Primicerj, 289
150 IOH (V,2), 957
151 Primicerj, 289
152 Pieropan, 848
153 Edmonds, 355
154 IOH (V,2), 948
155 Edmonds, 345
156 PRO WO 79/68
157 Primicerj, 290
158 IOH (V,2), 1020

Chapter 9 (pp. 174–193)
1   Cruttwell (1936), 53, 92; Liddell Hart (1970), 159
2   Stone, 254, 261
3   *Encyclopaedia Britannica (1947)* Vol 23, 775
4   Cruttwell (1936), 630
5   Trevelyan, 235
6   Tranfaglia, 131
7   Mussolini, 63
8   Villari, 294
9   Maravigna, 695
10   Pieropan, 850
11   PRO FO 371 2948, p.74; Edmonds, 355
12   e.g. *Encyclopaedia Britannica (1947)* Vol 4, 814; Buchan, 213;
     Cruttwell (1936), 464; Liddell Hart, 455
13   IOH (VI,2), 970
14   Sandilands, 332
15   Crosse, 48
16   Harington, 137
17   Young, 349
18   Bruce, 59
19   Babington, 149
20   Haythornthwaite, 45
21   Ibid, 45
22   Falls, 169, 171
23   Teed, 79
24   IOH (VI,2), 958
25   Villari, 274
26   Orlando (1965), 1431
27   Faldella Vol 2, 375
28   Melograni, 553
29   PRO WO 79/68
30   Edmonds, 410
31   Albrecht-Carrié, 90
32   Hoffmann Vol 1, 245
33   Albrecht-Carrié, 52
34   *Encyclopaedia Britannica (1947)* Vol 9, 339a
35   Ledeen, 22
36   Albrecht-Carrié, 336
37   Ledeen, 29
38   Nitti, 71
39   Page, 389
40   Asquith, 501,540
41   Albrecht-Carrié, 34, 236
42   ASQ, 126, Hankey 6 April 1916

43   Churchill, Vol 2, 1427
44   Pieropan, 848; CGOCG *All'Estero*, 38
45   Albrecht-Carrié, 90ff
46   Ibid, 141
47   Page, 401
48   Bakewell, 72ff
49   PRO WO 79/68
50   Stark, 232
51   PRO CAB 45/84
52   Harris, 320
53   Gatti (1926), 162
54   Foch, 262
55   Bliss, 4
56   Cadorna (1923,1934)
57   Cadorna, *Army Quarterly* Vol 7 (1924), 235 (translated from *Rassegna Italia*, 1923)
58   Ibid, 237
59   IOH (IV,3), 433
60   Gatti (1965), 369, 378
61   IOH (IV,3 Doc), 433, 437
62   Foch, 266
63   Cadorna (1934), 585
64   Gatti (1926), 226
65   Page, 317
66   Goldsmid, 171
67   PRO WO 79/68
68   Churchill Vol 2, 1215
69   Rocca, 334
70   HL F44/3/27, No.503
71   Villari, 263
72   IOH (V,2), 590
73   Ibid, 527
74   Caviglia (1934), 197
75   Rudin, 50
76   Ibid, 80
77   Ibid, 54, 217
78   Ibid, 214
79   e.g. Gario, 31; Faldella Vol 2, 376; Meregalli, 231
80   Cervone (1992), 190
81   Gario, 30
82   Mussolini, 62
83   Edmonds, 358
84   Ibid, 339
85   Ibid, 338

86   Ibid, 343
87   PRO WO 95/4224
88   Faldella Vol 2, 374
89   Seth, 186

BIBLIOGRAPHY

Official Histories

Edmonds The Official British History: *Military Operations Italy 1915–1919* Edmonds,J.E. and Davies, H.R. London, 1949

FOA The Official French Account: *Les Armées Françaises dans la Grande Guerre*, Ministre de la défense, Paris
Tome VI: Vol.1 (1931), Vol.2 (1935)
Each volume is accompanied by one or more volumes of Annexes.

IOH The Official Italian History: *L"esercito italiano nella grande guerra*, Stato Maggiore dell'Esercito, Ufficio Storico, Rome
Vol.IV Tome 3 *Gli avvenimenti dall Ottobre a Decembre (1917)*, 1967
Vol.V Tomo 1 *Gli avvenimenti dal Gennnaio al Giugno (1918)*, 1980
Vol.V Tomo 2 *La conclusione del conflitto*, 1988

A particular tome of the narration is indicated by its volume and tome number, e.g. IOH (IV,3).
The accompanying document and map (carta) sections are denoted by IOH (IV,3,Doc) and IOH (IV,3,Carta).

C.I. *Relazione della Commissione d'Inchiesta, Dall'Isonzo al Piave*, Rome, 1919

CGOCG Commissariato Generale Onaranze Caduti in Guerra (The Italian War Graves Commission)
Sacrari e Cimiteri Militari Italiani, Rome, 1979–1980)

Riassunto *Riassunto della relazione ufficiale sulla guerra 1914–1918*. A six hundred page résumé of the official Austrian history, edited by A.Bollati, Stato Maggiore dell'Esercito, Ufficio Storico, Rome, 1946

Abbreviations
HL   House of Lords Library

211

IWM   *Imperial War Museum Library*
PRO   *Public Record Office*
ASQ   *Asquith Papers, Bodleian Library, Oxford*

Divisional, Regimental and Battalion Accounts

Atkinson,C.T. *The 7th Division,* London, 1927

Barnett,G.H. *With the 48th Division in Italy,* Edinburgh and London, 1923

Carrington,E.C. *The War Record of the 1/5th Battalion, the Warwickshire Regiment,* Birmingham, 1922

Crosse,E.C. *The Defeat of Austria as seen by the 7th Division* London, 1919

Cruttwell,C.R.M.F. *The War Service of the 1/4 Royal Berkshire Regiment,* Oxford, 1922

Dopson,F.W., *The 48th Divisional Signal Company in the Great War,* Bristol (privately printed),1938

Pickford, P., *War Record of the 1/4th Oxfordshire and Buckinghamshire Light Infantry,* Banbury, 1919

Sandilands,H.R., *The 23rd Division 1914–1919,* Edinburgh, 1925

Stacke,H.FitzM., *The Worcestershire Regiment in the Great War,* Kidderminster, 1929

Wright,P.L., *The 1st Buckinghamshire Battalion 1914–1919,* London, 1920

Wyrall,R.E., *The Gloucestershire Regiment in the War 1914–1918,* London, 1931

List of other Books

Alberti,A., *Testimoniaze Straniere sulla Guerra Italiana 1915–1918,* Rome, 1936

Albrecht-Carrié,R., *Italy at the Peace Conference,* New York, 1938

Asquith,H.H., *Letters to Venetia Stanley,* editors M.& E.Brock, Oxford,1985

Babington,A.P., *For the Sake of Example,* London, 1983

Bachi,R., *L'Alimentazione e la Politica Annonaria in Italia* in serie Storia Economia e Sociale della Guerra Mondiale, Bari, 1926

Bakewell, C.M., *The Story of the American Red Cross in Italy,* New York, 1920

Baldini, A., *Diaz* (translated W.J.Manson), London, 1935

Berry, P. and Bostridge, M., *Vera Brittain,* 1995

Bliss, T.H., *Foreign Affairs,* Vol 1, December 15 1922, New York

Bragg,L., Dowson, A.H. and Hemming, H.H., *Artillery Survey in the First World War,* London, 1971

Britannica, *Encyclopaedia Britannica,* Chicago, 1947

Brittain,V., *Testament of Youth,* London, 1933

Bruce, G., *The Paladin Dictionary of Battles*, London, 1986

Buchan,J. (editor), *Italy*, New York, 1923

Cadorna,L., *La Guerra alla Fronte Italiana*, Milan, 1923 (2 Vol); 1934 (1 Vol)

Callwell,C.E., *Field-Marshal Sir Henry Wilson*, Vol 2, London, 1927

Caracciolo, M., *L'Italia e i suoi Alleati nella Grande Guerra*, Milan, 1932

Caviglia,E., *La Dodicesima Battaglia (Caporetto)*, Verona, 1933

Caviglia,E., *Le tre battaglie del Piave*, Milan, 1934

Cervone,P.P., *Enrico Caviglia,l'anti Badoglio*, Milan, 1992

Cervone, P.P., *Vittorio Veneto L'ultima Battaglia*, Milan, 1994

Churchill,W.S., *The World Crisis 1911–1918*, 2 volumes,London, 1938

Cruttwell, C.R.M.F., *The War Service of the 1/4 Royal Berkshire Regiment*, Oxford, 1922.

Cruttwell,C.R.M.F., *A History of the Great War*, 2nd Ed.,1936

Dalton,E.H.J.H., *With British Guns in Italy*, London, 1919

De Simone,C., *L'Isonzo Marmorava*, Milan, 1995

Fadini,F., *Caporetto dalla parte del Vincitore*, Milan, 1992

Faldella,E., *La Grande Guerra*, 2 volumes, Milan, 1965

Falls,C., *Caporetto*, British edition, London, 1966

Fiala,P., *Il Piave*, Milan 1982, translated by G.Primicerj from Die letzte Offensive Altösterreichs

Fiala,P., *Il FeldMareschiallo Franz Conrad von Hotzendorf*, Vicenza 1990, translated from the German by G.Pieropan

Foch,F., *The Memoirs of Marshal Foch*, translated by T.B. Mott, London, 1931

Gario,G., *Italy 1914–1918*, London, 1937

Gatti, A., *Le Parte dell'Italia*, Rome, 1926

Gatti,A., *Caporetto, Diario*, 4th Edn., Bologna, 1965

Giardino,G., *Rievocazioni e Riflessioni di Guerra*, 3 volumes, Milan, 1929–1935

Gladden,N., *Across the Piave*, London, 1971

Goldsmid,C.J.H., *Diary of a Liaison Officer in Italy*, London, 1920

Greenwell,G.H., *An Infant in Arms*, London, 1935

Hardie,M. and Allen,W., *Our Italian Front*, London,1920

Harington,C.H., *Plumer of Messines*, London, 1935

Harris,C.R.S., *Allied Military Administration of Italy 1943–1945*, London, 1957

Haythornthwaite,P.J., *The World War I Source Book*, London, 1992

Hemingway,E., *A Farewell to Arms*, London, 1929

Herbillon,E.E., *Du Général en chef au Gouvernement*, 2 volumes, Paris,1930

Hody,E.H., *With "The Mad 17th" to Italy*, London, 1920

Hoffman,C.A.M., *War Diaries*, Vol 1, translated by E.Sutton,London, 1929

Jones, H.A., *War in the Air, Vol 6, Italy*, London, 1937

Krafft von Dellmensingen,K., *Lo Sfondamento dell'Isonzo*, Milan, 1981, translated by G.Pieropan from *Der Durchbruch am Isonzo*, Berlin, 1926,1928

Ledeen,M.A., *The First Duce, D'Annunzio at Fiume*, Baltimore and London,1977

Liddell Hart,B.H., *Foch: Man of Orleans*, London, 1931

Liddell Hart, B.H., *History of the First World War*, London, 1970

Lloyd George,D., *War Memoirs*, 2 volumes, London, 1938

Ludendorff,E., *My War Memories*, London, 1919

Mack Smith,D., *Italy and its Monarchy*, London, 1989

Macmillan, N., *Offensive Patrol*, London, 1973

Maravigna,P., *Guerra e Vittoria*, Turin, 1935

Melograni, P., *Storia Politica delle Grande Guerra*, Bari, 1972

Meregalli, C., *Grande Guerra 15–18 dal crollo alla gloria*, Bassano, 1994

Mussolini,B., *My Autobiography*, London, 1928

Nitti,F., *The Wreck of Europe*, Indianapolis, 1922, (translation of *L'Europa senza Pace*)

Orlando,V.E., *Memorie 1915–1919*, Milan, 1960

Orlando,V.E., *Discorsi Parlamentari*, Vol 4, Rome 1965

Page,T.N., *Italy in the World War*, London, 1921

Pershing,J.J., *My Experiences in the World War*, Vol 2, New York, 1931

Pieri,P., *L'Italia nella Prima Guerra Mondiale (1915–1918)*, Turin, 1965

Pieri,P. and Rochat,G., *Pietro Badoglio*, Turin, 1974

Pieropan,G., *1914–1918 Storia della Grande Guerra*, Milan, 1988

Powell,G., *Plumer*, London, 1990

Primacerj,G., *1918 Cronaca di una Disfatta*, Milan, 1983

Robertson,W.R., *The Military Correspondence of Field-Marshal Sir William Robertson*, editor D.R.Woodward, Army Records Soc. London, 1989

Rocca, G., *Cadorna*, Milan, 1985

Rochat,G., *L'Italia nella Prima Guerra Mondiale*, Milan, 1976

Rochat,G., *Gli Arditi della Grande Guerra*, Milan, 1981

Rochat,G. & Massobrio,G., *Breve Storia dell'Esercito Italiano dal 1861 al 1943*, Turin, 1978

Rodd,J.R., *Social and Diplomatic Memories*, Vol 3, London, 1925

Rolleston, A.G., *J. Royal Artillery*, Vol 48 (1921–1922), 146, London

Rommel,E., *Attacks*, Vienna (Virginia, USA), 1979, translated by J.R.Driscoll from *Infanterie Greifft An*, Potsdam, 1937

Rudin,H.R., *Armistice 1918*, New Haven, 1944

Schiarini *La Battaglia d'Arresto, Asiago*, Stato Maggiore dell' Esercito, Ufficio Storico, Rome, 1934

Seth,R., *Caporetto*, London, 1965

Snow,C.D. and Kral,J.J., *German Trade and the War*, U.S.Department of Commerce, Washington, 1918

Stark, Freya, *Traveller's Prelude*, London, 1950

Stone,N., *The Eastern Front 1914–1917*, 1975

Teed,P., *A Dictionary of Twentieth Century History*, Oxford, 1992

Travers,T., *How the War was Won*, London, 1992

Trevelyan,G.M., *Scenes from Italy's War*, London, 1919

Tranfaglia,N., *Storia d'Italia*, editor G.Galasso, Volume 22, *La Prima Guerra Mondiale e il Fascimo*, Turin, 1995

Viazzi,L., *I Diavoli dell'Adamello*, Milan, 1981

Villari,L., *The War on the Italian Front*, London, 1932

Young, P., *A Dictionary of Battles 1816–1976*, London, 1977

Ward, A., *The Participation of British troops in the War in Italy during 1918*, in *La Prima Guerra Mondiale e il Trentino*, Convegno Internazionale 1978, (editor Benvenuti, S.) Rovereto, 1980

Wilson,H.H., *The Military Correspondence of Field-Marshal Sir Henry Wilson*, editor, Jeffrey,K., Army Records Soc. London, 1985

Zivojinovic,D.R., *The United States and the Vatican Policies 1914–1918*, Boulder,Colorado, 1978

Index

218

character and methods, 64ff
tact, 64, 66
assessments of military
   situation, 65–6
return to France, 61, 67
see also, 48, 50, 56, 58, 61
Porro, Gen., 29, 30, 38

Rawlinson, Gen. Sir Henry, 62
Reynolds, Lieut.-Col. L.L.C., 100,
   107, 112
Robertson, Gen. Sir William,
   British CIGS to 18 Feb 1918
   visits Italy, 22, 32
   see also 19–21, 24, 29, 31–2, 48,
      60, 63–4, 118, 177
Rommel, Lieut. E., 16
Ross, Lieut.-Col. H.A., 148
Ruggera, Captain, 165

Salandra, A., 11
Sandilands, Lieut.-Col. H.R., 93
Schoerner, Lieut., 16
Segre, Gen., 82, 92, 115
Shoubridge, Major-Gen. T.H., 62,
   120, 139
Sladen, Br.-Gen. G.C., 100, 101,
   105
Smuts, J.C., 61
Sonnino, Baron, 11, 29, 61
Stark, Freya, 17
St. Hill, Lieut.-Col, A.A., 98, 147
Steele, Br.-Gen. J.McC., 139
Stirling, Captain, 98, 141, 147
Sundermann, Gen., 166

Thullier, Major-Gen. H.F., 120
Tomkinson, Lieut.-Col. F.M., 101,
   107, 109
Townley, Sergt.-Major R., 105,
   109
Trevelyan, G.M., 17

Vacari, Gen., 153
Victor Emmanuel III, King of
   Italy, 24, 30

Waldstatten, Gen., 166
Wales, H.R.H. Prince of, 24
Walker, Major-Gen. Sir H.B., 110,
   120, 123, 191
Waller, Major N.H., 112
Wardrop, Br.-Gen. A.E., 96, 102,
   114
Weber, Gen., 165–7
Weygand, Gen., 20, 31–2, 49
Wilhelm, Kaiser, German
   Emperor, 126–7
Wilson, Gen. Sir Henry, British
   CIGS from 18 Feb. 1918, 19,
   29, 31–2, 49, 61–2, 73, 128
Wilson, W., President U.S.A.,
   Fourteen Points, Four
      Principles, 125ff, 181
   see also, 120, 127–8, 184
Wood, Private W., VC, 154

Youll, 2nd Lieut. J.S., VC, 106,
   147